DR. BERGER'S IMMUNE POWER COOKBOOK

OTHER BOOKS BY
Stuart M. Berger, M.D.

Divorce Without Victims

The Southampton Diet

Dr. Berger's Immune Power Diet

DR. BERGER'S IMMUNE POWER COOKBOOK

by

Stuart M. Berger, M.D.

With recipes by Rosemary E. McCoy

NAL BOOKS

NEW AMERICAN LIBRARY

NEW YORK AND SCARBOROUGH, ONTARIO

Note to the Reader

The menus, charts, recipes, and guidelines contained
in this work embody a practical application of the principles
underlying the Immune Power Diet Plan. As with any other diet
plan, you are urged to consult with your physician before
beginning this diet program.

Published simultaneously in Canada by
The New American Library of Canada Limited

 NAL BOOKS TRADEMARK REG. U.S. PAT. OFF. AND FOREIGN COUNTRIES
REGISTERED TRADEMARK—MARCA REGISTRADA
HECHO EN HARRISONBURG, VA., U.S.A.

SIGNET, SIGNET CLASSIC, MENTOR, ONYX, PLUME,
MERIDIAN and NAL BOOKS are published *in the United States* by
New American Library, 1633 Broadway, New York, New York 10019,
in Canada by The New American Library of Canada Limited,
81 Mack Avenue, Scarborough, Ontario M1L 1M8

Library of Congress Cataloging-in-Publication Data

Berger, Stuart.
  Dr. Berger's immune power cookbook.

Includes index.
  1. Immunity—Nutritional aspects. 2. Cookery.
I. McCoy, Rosemary E. II. Title. III. Title: Immune
power cookbook. IV. Title: Immune power diet.
RM222.2.B4523 1985 Suppl.   613.2′5   86-23640
ISBN 0-453-00520-9

Designed by Julian Hamer

First Printing, January, 1987

 2 3 4 5 6 7 8 9

PRINTED IN THE UNITED STATES OF AMERICA

To my father,
my earliest and
most important teacher

ACKNOWLEDGMENTS

This book would not have been possible without Lorna Darmour, Oscar Dystel, Walter Anderson, Rosemary McCoy, and Kathleen Moloney.

I would like to acknowledge my special friends Roger Wood, Pat Miller, Harriett Johnson, Scott Meredith, Lee Wurlitzer, and Danny Klein.

For their help in creating and testing the Immune Power recipes, special thanks to Janet Lindemann, Pat Morrison, Robin Gavin Billotto, Marisa Panecki, and Michelle St. Louis. For their assistance in typing, analyzing, and proofreading recipes and coordinating charts and tables, thanks to the test kitchen editorial staff: Nina Marcos, Modane Marshbanks, Mary Ann O'Leary, Kathy Gorman, Pam Fontana, Maureen Yasso, and Angela Viglietta.

Most of all, I am eternally grateful to my parents for their love and support.

Contents

Introduction:
The Immune Power
Journey

WELCOME! For those of you who are old friends, I'm glad we're together again. And if we're meeting for the first time, I'm thrilled to be joining you on your journey of renewal.

For that's exactly where we'll all heading—toward renewed health, renewed vitality, and a renewed sense of self. All this is possible when we start to rethink and change something we've been doing all our lives—eating.

Today, physicians and researchers in many branches of medicine are confirming what our grandmothers have been saying for generations: eating right improves health, increases resistance, boosts energy, and even extends life. But thanks to modern medical advances, we (unlike our grandmothers) now have a much more detailed understanding of just *how* this takes place.

Long-term studies have now confirmed earlier suspicions that many major diseases, including cancer, heart disease, high blood pressure, and diabetes, have important nutritional causes and that their incidence can be radically altered by diet. But we're now much more aware of the *positive* aspects of nutrition, too. Using recently acquired knowledge, we can now bypass some of the biochemical obstacles that made obesity and overweight such frustrating, refractory problems in the past. Making use of recently discovered aspects of nervous system chemistry in its relation to nutrition, we can design a diet that not only avoids the depression, irritability, fatigue, and annoyance traditionally associated with weight-loss programs but also increases our energy, calms our nerves, helps us to withstand stress, and enhances our mood.

In particular, we are now realizing we can manipulate the good and ill effects of nutrition on the immune system—the body's natural defense against illness, which supports the ability of all other systems xii • Introduction: The Immune Power Journey

to function. We have discovered that you can actually enlist your immune cells to work more efficiently just by feeding them right—and that you may have been damaging them for years with a kind of nutrition that is not right for you.

The key to dramatically enhanced protection against disease, and in turn a radically transformed sense of vitality and well-being, lies to a remarkable extent in simply choosing and cooking those foods most consistent with optimum nutritional principles and, furthermore, selecting those most compatible with your individual immune system profile. I'm here to show you that changing your current diet and food and cooking habits can only help the way you look and feel. Just listen to what it did for me.

Confessions of a Former Blimp

Not too long ago, I weighed 420 pounds—about as much as three average-sized women. Even at 6 feet 6½ inches tall, I was grossly, unbelievably fat—so fat that I became sick. I suffered from ulcers, depression, joint problems, and severe headaches.

In an effort to shed those extra pounds, I did what millions of overweight people do every day—I went on a diet. The summer before I started medical school, I put myself on a 300-calorie-a-day regimen. In five weeks I dropped 40 pounds.

Unfortunately, I also came close to dying. I became so weak, I could barely get through the day. Dizziness, nausea, and extreme fatigue were added to my list of problems. On the first day of medical school, I dragged myself into a doctor's office, begging for help. After examining me, the doctor told me the horrifying news: I was in a state of life-threatening starvation.

She put me on a typical weight-reduction diet that was well balanced and low in calories and carbohydrates. I was no longer facing starvation, but the pounds came off very, very slowly. And I wasn't feeling any healthier.

Then my health took a severe turn for the worse. During my second year of med school, I was plagued by severe stomach pains, bleeding ulcers, tremendous mood swings, and excruciating migraine headaches. Traditional medical tests did not uncover the cause, so I decided to do some intensive detective work of my own.

To unravel this mystery, I began looking for clues that might forge a food–health connection. My goal was to find out everything I could about the physiological, biochemical, immunological, and psychological aspects of nutrition and weight loss. The more information I uncovered, the more excited I became. It seemed that all my problems—mood swings, obesity, stomach and nerve disorders, headaches—could be directly related to what I ate.

That's when I started experimenting on myself. First I varied specific elements of my diet to see how I was affected. I tried different combinations of foods, vitamins, minerals, carbohydrates, proteins, fiber, and amino acids, and I kept track of the results. I noticed some surprising changes. Eating specific types of protein helped to stabilize my mood and energy levels, but when I ate a large amount of sugar, the mood swings returned. Wheat and dairy products often caused irritability and fatigue, and certain B complex vitamins and amino acids calmed me down and encouraged a good night's sleep. When I followed a steady regimen of vitamins A, C, and E, I was sick less often. It did not take me long to conclude that my immune system was the key to my health and well being.

The links I observed between nutrition and illness were similar to those reported by prominent medical experts. One of them, Dr. Robert Good, one of the country's foremost immunologists and the former director of New York's Memorial Sloan-Kettering Cancer Center, proved that diets high in fat would speed up the shrinking of the thymus gland—the organ responsible for processing some crucial disease-fighting immune cells. In work done at the U.S. Army Medical Research Institute of Infectious Diseases, a connection was established between specific nutrients and the functioning of the immune system. For instance, a lack of vitamin B_6 could bring on a serious deficiency in the body's immune cells, and low vitamin C intake could impair the body's ability to keep itself well.

Meanwhile, at MIT, Dr. R. K. Chandra reported that certain minerals, such as zinc, helped strengthen our immunities. And a discovery was made that vitamins A and E could increase our ability to fight infection.

The Incredible Shrinking Man

When I completed medical school, I weighed a trim, fit 210 pounds and felt better than I had in years. With a specialty in psychiatry in hand, I continued my research into bariatrics, the science of weight control. As a student at the Harvard School of Public Health, I began unearthing the brand-new findings that were emerging in the fields of immunology, nutrition, and weight-control psychology. Many of these findings were on the leading edge of science—some not yet known outside the laboratory.

I learned from my own experience that weight loss and health depend on a delicate balance of diet, exercise, and attitude. And new research developments reveal that you can actually help your body lose weight and promote health by fine-tuning your immune system—I'll show you how in the chapters that follow. Immunology is still an infant science, and some of the most exciting research is being reported in this book for the first time.

On a Trip to Good Health

As you read this book, you will be revisiting some of the spots we visited in *Dr. Berger's Immune Power Diet*, but we'll also be exploring some fascinating new terrain, made possible through the most up-to-the-minute nutrition research findings. Together, we are going to unravel more of the mystery surrounding nutritional enhancement and optimum support for your immune system and discover how immune power can work for you right in your own kitchen.

Here's how *Dr. Berger's Immune Power Cookbook* will help:

- By offering you a refresher course in the immune power theory—a theory that can help you lose weight and achieve optimum health.
- By teaching you the most up-to-date nutritional concepts and discoveries, which will help you eat well and feel healthier.
- By providing you with more than 200 recipes featuring simple-to-cook, delicious foods.
- By providing you with a variety of day-by-day menus and menu-planning tips to make the Immune Power Diet mistake-proof.
- By providing hints about shopping and cooking the Immune Power way.
- By offering you personalized guidelines for a life full of healthful, happy eating.

Even if you're already slim and trim, you can greatly enhance your health and well-being by following the Immune Power Diet—by cutting down on salt, fat, alcohol, sugar, and caffeine, upping your intake of complex carbohydrates and fiber, and tailoring your diet to your personal lifestyle, stress level, eating style, and immune system. I'll be teaching you how to design an individualized health/nutrition plan geared precisely to your needs. This plan will put *you* in control—of your diet, your body, and your life. Therein lies the secret to the success behind immune power.

PART I

The Immune Power Diet

CHAPTER 1

The Food–Health Connection

IF YOU'RE LIKE most Americans, you eat an average of 5.3 times a day, counting snacks and meals. That means that about 2000 times a year you give your body the raw materials it needs to rebuild itself and keep you going.

Whether your idea of a perfect lunch is a charbroiled burger and fries or a tofu salad with bean sprouts, each mouthful you take gives your body a little nudge—toward fitness or fat, health or disease. Because you are "dosing" yourself with food day after day, year after year, what you eat adds up to the largest single influence on your body's well-being and functioning. It is no exaggeration, then, to say that true fitness is found at the end of your fork.

The New Findings

In 1977, when the Senate Select Committee on Nutrition and Human Needs proposed its Dietary Goals for the United States, they recommended a diet with less cholesterol, less refined and processed sugars, less salt, less alcohol, fewer calories, and more complex carbohydrates and roughage. Now, hardly a week goes by without some new data being reported on the connection between diet and health. A sampling of this research reads like a Who's Who of medical science:

- Studies sponsored by the American Heart Association have shown a clear link between the fats we eat at the dinner table and our likelihood of suffering from heart attack, stroke, and other cardiovascular problems—diseases that afflict more than 42 million Americans and kill more than all other causes of death combined. In 1984, results of a ten-year Heart Association study demonstrated a clear reduction in heart attack and heart disease rates (up to 50 percent) in individuals who reduced their cholesterol levels.

• In February 1985, the National Institutes of Health held a conference on the health implications of obesity. Among the presentations: in a large group of patients that have been followed for over thirty years (The Framingham Study), the degree of obesity was clearly correlated with increased risk of coronary artery disease and a shorter life span.

At the same conference, the American Cancer Society Study of more than a million men and women showed that obese men had a higher death rate from cancer of the colon, rectum, and prostate. Obese women had higher death rates from cancer of the gall bladder, biliary passages, breast, uterus, and ovaries. The NIH panel issued a statement calling obesity "a killer disease" and warned that Americans who are "even five pounds" overweight should be concerned about the health risks involved.

• An important study in the *Journal of the National Cancer Institute* looked at avoidable risks of cancer and found that dietary factors comprise the *largest single category* of modifiable risks. About 35 percent of all cancer deaths, the investigators suggested, might be related to dietary factors. That figure was alluded to in March 1985, when the Department of Health and Human Services, in cooperation with the NIH, launched a long-range Cancer Prevention Awareness Campaign intended to reduce deaths from cancer. They stressed a decrease in fats and increase in fiber in the diet.

• Similar indications resulted from a 1985 study done by a group at the National Cancer Institute. The investigators reported in the journal *Cancer Research* that women who consumed three or more servings of fruits or vegetables a day had only *half* the risk of developing cancers of the mouth and throat as women who ate less than one and a half servings daily, even when cancer-promoting habits such as smoking or alcohol consumption were taken into account. Their results supported earlier findings that frequent consumption of foods rich in vitamins A and C can protect against cancer and diets high in fat could increase cancer risk.

• Beta carotene in the body turns into vitamin A, and is found in many green and yellow fruits and vegetables. Researchers from Harvard Medical School, reporting in the 1985 *American Jour-*

nal of Clinical Nutrition, cited earlier studies showing that beta carotene may act as an inhibitor of carcinogenesis and that an inverse relationship exists between the incidence of certain cancers and the amount of green and yellow vegetables in the diet. They found that increased green and yellow vegetable intake lowered cancer deaths in an elderly population—indicating that the protective effect of the nutrient may act even in later stages of carcinogenesis.

• A conference of experts convened by the National Institutes of Health in April 1984 issued a statement listing calcium, along with estrogen, as the "mainstays of prevention and management of osteoporosis" the debilitating bone disease that afflicts up to 20 million Americans, mostly women over forty-five, and leads to 1.3 million fractures each year.

• The colon cancer that struck President Reagan is the second most common cancer in men and third most common in women, with about 138,000 new cases and 60,000 related deaths in 1985 alone. Specific dietary factors such as the benefit of high fiber and low-fat diets are increasingly recognized. In 1985 a research team presented evidence in the medical journal *Lancet* that the risk of colon and rectal cancer significantly decreased in proportion to dietary vitamin D and calcium. In the same year, investigators from Memorial Sloan-Kettering Cancer Center, reporting in the *New England Journal of Medicine*, found that malignant processes in the bowel could be inhibited by supplementary calcium.

• Also in 1985, a study published in *Annals of Internal Medicine* documented that supplemental calcium was a safe, effective means of lowering blood pressure in some patients with hypertension, itself a major risk factor for heart disease.

• Diabetics have long been known to be affected by diet, and for years, they have been put on strict high-protein regimens. But a number of studies in the United States and at England's Oxford University have shown that a diet high in *complex carbohydrates* (found in fruits and vegetables, pasta, dried beans, and potatoes) may actually be far more beneficial to diabetics, stabilizing the need for insulin and, in some cases, making insulin unnecessary. The benefits of the high-carbohydrate diet were most evident when combined with high levels of soluble fiber, especially from oats.

• In the 1970s, scientists at MIT, Harvard Medical School, and other centers were doing preliminary work on the revolutionary discovery that the consumption of amino acids—the building blocks of the proteins we eat—directly affects the levels of certain crucial brain and nervous system chemicals—including serotonin (deficiency of which has been indicted as a major cause of depression), norepinephrine (a chemical related in structure and effect to adrenaline), and acetylcholine (deficiency of which has been associated with disorders of memory, such as senile dementia and Alzheimer's disease). Amino acids are made from precursor molecules obtained from the diet—tryptophan, tyrosine, and choline. Contrary to previous belief, the concentration of the important chemicals known as neurotransmitters in the brain fluctuates in response to dietary consumption of the revelant precursors. Most important, it is possible to design a diet that ensures an adequate supply of these precursors to the brain, or even to enhance their absorption and effect. A diet high in carbohydrates, for example, was found to increase brain absorption to tryptophan, the scarcest and possibly most important dietary amino acid.

• Dr. Norman Rosenthal, a psychiatrist at the National Institute of Mental Health, has suggested that supplemental tryptophan may be promising in the treatment of some forms of depression. In 1985, Dr. Harris Lieberman and coworkers at MIT, Harvard University, and Massachusetts General Hospital demonstrated the significant sedative-like properties of tryptophan and its effectiveness in promoting sleep without the side effects of sedative or hypnotic drugs. Dr. Samuel Seltzer and coworkers at Temple University in Philadelphia found that 3 gm of tryptophan in conjunction with a high-carbohydrate, low-fat, low-protein diet significantly reduced pain in patients with chronic facial pain syndromes.

• Other precursors of important neurotransmitters are also being studied. Since norepinephrine appears to be reduced in some forms of depression, Dr. Alan J. Gelenberg and coworkers at Harvard Medical School, Massachusetts General Hospital, the University of Ontario, and MIT have been studying the use of its chemical precursor, tyrosine, in depressed patients. They have had positive results in preliminary studies and are now comparing the effects of tyrosine with those of standard antidepressant drugs and a placebo.

• Choline, the precursor of acetylcholine, may also be therapeutically important. Neurologist John Growden at Massachusetts

General Hospital has investigated the effects of choline, given in the form of lecithin, on patients with memory disorders, including senile dementia and Alzheimer's disease. Dr. Raymond Levy at Maudsley Hospital in London has already shown improvement in some patients with Alzheimer's disease treated with lecithin in a long-term controlled study.

• Many obese individuals, especially those who crave carbohydrates, may actually be using their meals as mood-altering drugs, researchers now say—finding real relief from anxiety and depression, perhaps as a result of the tryptophan-serotonin connection. Dr. Bonnie Springer and coworkers at Harvard University have investigated this question, looking at the effects of protein and carbohydrate meals on mood and performance in a variety of settings. Their results so far indicate that protein meals promote alertness or tension, and carbohydrate meals promote calmness or sleepiness.

• Drs. Richard and Judith Wurtman at MIT have also suggested that the tryptophan-carbohydrate relationship may be an important factor in appetite regulation. Their studies suggest that the brain's appetite for carbohydrates diminishes when serotonin levels reach a certain point, so that serotonin levels serve to monitor and regulate the relative proportions of proteins and carbohydrates consumed. They have found that the tendency of carbohydrate cravers to snack on sweets and starches is suppressed by low doses of the drug fenfluramine, which increases serotonin levels. Individuals who binge on sweets or carbohydrates may actually be seeking the mood-altering effects of increased serotonin.

• An equally fascinating topic of recent research is the role of endogenous opiates, the body's natural, narcotic-like painkillers, in regulating appetite. Increasing evidence suggests that these opiates may be stimulated by the ingestion of certain kinds of food in relationships that may be unique to each individual, and that part of the incentive to overeating is indeed the addictive "high" of these substances stimulated by the diet. In separate studies, Dr. Daniel Porte, Jr., of the University of Washington and Dr. Martin Cohen of the National Institute of Mental Health have been looking at the effect of such endogenous substances. In one NIMH study, subjects were given naloxone (a chemical that blocks the effect of opiate drugs) before meals consisting of an unlimited quantity of their favorite foods. When naloxone was given, the subjects consumed 28 percent less than when naloxone was not given—suggesting that the opiate effect was a significant factor in their overeating.

The Immune Connection

We have made astounding progress in understanding the nutritional connection between diet and health. Medicine's most advanced current research is currently focusing specifically on the nutritional aspects of the immune system, which is ultimately responsible for our fitness and well-being. The immune system is our means of defense against invading bacteria, viruses, and toxic substances. It also acts as an internal monitor to control cells undergoing precancerous changes. (That is one reason why the most promising new cancer treatments take advantage of natural defenses by stimulating the immune system with substances such as interleukin-2.) When the immune system is not functioning properly, we become susceptible to a wide variety of chronic, debilitating infections that we may not even recognize as such, but simply experience as a chronic condition of lingering, nagging poor health and feeling "under par." This, in turn, contributes to a sedentary lifestyle conducive to obesity, depression, and further immune problems. In addition, a disordered immune system can cause a variety of serious ailments by attacking or otherwise irritating the body's own tissues, failing to distinguish them from invading foreign substances. This is the source of autoimmune diseases such as rheumatoid arthritis and lupus erythematosus, and diseases with a strong autoimmune component, such as Crohn's disease. The immune system is also responsible for allergic or hypersensitivity reactions, in which the response of immune cells to various foreign substances actually ends up irritating or harming the body in several ways and at several sites.

We are becoming increasing aware of outside factors that can influence the immune system for good or ill in surprising ways. That psychological factors can influence the course of allergic conditions has long been recognized, and other aspects of the immune system are now seen to be responsive to psychological factors as well. For example, investigators from the University of Colorado, writing in the journal *Science*, showed that chronic, inescapable stress in animals brought about measurable immune system suppression—evidenced by reduced numbers of lymphocytes, the disease-fighting white blood cells. Humans placed under similar circumstances through stress or depression may undergo similar changes, the investigators speculated, accounting for the association of such states with an increased risk of cancer and increased incidence of disorders suggesting impaired immunity.

Research over the past ten years has made it increasingly clear that proper nutrition is also directly essential to proper immune function, increasing the number of immune cells, stimulating them to maximum activity, and regulating the processing of some of these cells in the crucial thymus gland. We are also becoming increasingly aware of the role of hidden food allergies in a variety of immune disturbances. And there is strong evidence that maintaining a strong immune system is more important—and more difficult—in our modern world than it may have been before.

In fact, looking at our statistics for cancer, autoimmune conditions, and allergies, we can't help but conclude that we're surrounded by signs of immune-system vulnerability—an impression that intensifies as researchers uncover immunologic bases for many diseases of previously unclear origin. The causes of this state of affairs are difficult to pinpoint exactly, but some obvious areas of concern stare us in the face:

Chemicals. One clear source is the presence of environmental toxins in our chemical-ridden society; we already know their association with cancer, and the involvement of the immune system in this type of carcinogenesis is only now being unraveled.

Food Additives. Another source is the presence of harmful food additives, such as MSG, BHT, polysorbate, disodium inosinate, and sodium benzoate, which may have immunologic effects even apart from direct organ toxicity. The effect of these additives is matched by a corresponding lack of adequate nutrients in our overly processed and refined foods.

Drugs. Recreational drugs, including alcohol and tobacco, are almost taken for granted in contemporary life, and they exert a constant deleterious effect on the immune system itself and on the levels of nutrients needed to support it. Medicinal drugs are also a problem. We are still just beginning to understand the alterations in internal ecology brought about by the advent of the antibiotic era; we do know that antibiotics radically affect our normal microbial flora.

Stress. An apparently ubiquitous accompaniment of life in fast-paced modern industrial societies, stress places physical burdens on our bodies—in part, we now know, through interferences in immune function—and also depletes the nutrients necessary for immune-system maintenance.

All these are compelling reasons for adopting a nutritional approach that is aimed specifically at bolstering immune functions. But some of the most significant revelations of current immunologic research also concern ways in which "normal" nutritional habits may inflict chronic damage on the immune system. Most important, we are only now becoming aware of the pervasive effect of hidden food sensitivities on certain components of the immune system. This, too, may be largely a modern phenomenon; modern distribution and industrial food production permit year-round exposure to all kinds of foods, whereas in former times, seasonal availability ensured a diversified diet that may have inhibited the development of sensitivities.

Using blood tests such as the IgG RAST, the IgE RAST, and others, we can measure a patient's food sensitivities by isolating a drop of blood with a wide range of food extracts. In doing so, we find dramatic immune reactions manifested by direct destruction of hundreds of thousands of immunologically crucial white blood cells on exposure to the allergenic foods. In testing thousands of patients for more than 150 such hypersensitivities, I have rarely discovered a patient without some significant, unrecognized immune damage created by regularly eaten foods. Most Americans have hidden intolerance to foods that make up a significant part of their diets and are, in effect, exposing their immune systems to quiet, chronic sabotage.

Equally important is the other side of the coin—the extent to which vitamins and minerals necessary to the maintenance of healthy immune defense are lacking in the typical modern diet. As in the case of food allergies, the majority of patients with vitamin and mineral deficiencies severe enough to impair immune function may be unaware of any specific symptoms—and if they are, the nutritional connection is too often overlooked by physicians. Our processed foods are already low in nutritional value; we now understand that Food and Drug Administration recommendations for the essential vitamins and minerals—though sufficient to protect against deficiency diseases such as scurvy or rickets—are inadequate to meet the needs of an optimally functioning immune system.

These, then, are the main pieces of the nutritional puzzle that the Immune Power Diet has set out to solve. In the next chapter we'll look at the immune system more closely, and explore the effects of food sensitivities. And I'll show how a well-considered nutritional program can get all these forces working—for you.

CHAPTER 2

How Immune Power Works

ARE YOU A LITTLE CONFUSED about how your body fights its immunities, and why food can help build your immune health? Before we go any further, let me answer some of the questions about immune power that I'm most often asked:

Q. Exactly what is the immune system?
A. It's our body's defense mechanism. It guards us against invaders that damage our tissues. These invaders can be bacteria, a virus, or a cancer cell. They can cause infection, colds, flu, even cancer.

Q. What makes up our immune systems?
A. There are four basic components common to everyone's immune system—the thymus gland; the T-cells; antibodies; and macrophages.

Q. How do these components work together?
A. The first line of defense is a special kind of lymphocyte (a type of white blood cell) called a T-cell. Your body contains literally millions of lymphocytes. Some of these pass through the thymus gland, a small organ at the base of your neck, where a special hormone changes them into aggressive fighting cells that can distinguish anything that is "foreign" to your body (germs, etc.). Whenever a foreign substance enters your body, it is attacked by troops of these T-cells, (*T* is for thymus). T-cells can reproduce to outnumber the invader and make their attack as effective as possible.

Whenever a T-cell meets an enemy, it slots into it like a key into a lock, holds on tight, and alerts your entire immune system to wage a battle. Then the other immune fighters—antibodies and macrophages—spring into action. At the first call of the T-cell alert, thousands of antibodies pour into the bloodstream and surround and inactivate the enemy. Then the macrophases ("big eaters"), another type of white blood cell, engulf or eat up any foreign invader covered with antibodies.

Q. Do these immune fighters join forces only when a germ or virus invades?
A. No. Our immune systems are engaged in a continuous battle throughout our lives. Our bodies contain trillions of microorganisms and foreign substances that must be eradicated.

Q. How can our immune systems help fight cancer?
A. Research conducted by Dr. Lewis Thomas, former director of Memorial Sloan-Kettering Cancer Center in New York, showed that the lymphocytes keep a constant patrol to locate and destroy cells that have changed from their normal form. If the immune system is not functioning at its best, these mutated cells might turn cancerous.

Q. What does nutrition have to do with our immune systems?
A. In order to create the 200,000 new immune cells and thousands of antibody molecules you need every second of your life, you must provide the vital nutrients your system requires —vitamins, minerals, and the amino acids in protein.

Q. What role do vitamins play in all this?
A. Different vitamins play different roles at every stage of the immune battle. Vitamin A is needed to help produce an adequate number of T-cells. The B-vitamins—especially B_6 and B_{12}—assist in the manufacture of those crucial antibodies. Vitamin C plays a vital role in helping the macrophages. And vitamin E helps protect the cells from toxic elements in the body.

Q. Are minerals as important as vitamins?
A. Yes—particularly zinc. In a study conducted by Eby, Halcomb, and Davis and analyzed by the Clayton Foundation Biochemical Institute at the University of Texas at Austin, subjects with viral colds were given either zinc supplements or an inert look-alike tablet, without knowing which was which. After being instructed to suck on the tablets, many of the subjects taking zinc-treated tablets became well within twenty-four hours, but none of those taking the inert tablets became well within this time. Zinc shortened the duration of colds by an average of seven days.

Zinc's role in treating viral colds has greater implications for the treatment of other illnesses. Zinc is crucial to the smooth operation of the thymus and other lymph glands, and it affects the formation of the T-cells. Low zinc means fewer T-cells and less effective macrophages.

Q. What about other minerals?
A. Calcium is critical to your overall health. Recent findings show that calcium may play a major role in protecting against osteoporosis, colon cancer, and hypertension.

Q. How can protein strengthen the immune system?
A. Amino acids, the chief components of protein, are essential for the growth, maintenance, and repair of our cells—including the T-cells. And four of the amino acids—tryptophan, phenylalanine, lysine, and methionine—are necessary for the manufacture of antibodies.

Q. How many nutrients affect our immune power?
A. There are over fifty crucial nutrients that must be carefully balanced in order for the immune cells to defend you efficiently. Nourishing your immune cells properly will maintain this balance.

Q. You talked about how nutrients can strengthen our immune systems. Can food weaken our immune power too?
A. Yes. Certain foods we eat can actually cause thousands of our vital lymphocytes to explode. These foods are not naturally destructive. They are nutritious, healthy foods, but in a person with hidden sensitivities, they can cause white blood cell destruction, diminishing our immune defenses and often triggering various physical and psychological problems (see Chapter 3).

Q. Can exercise help our immune function?
A. Yes. Regular exercise greatly improves the body's metabolic rate, which, in turn, helps enhance the immune system function.

Q. How can I keep my immune system performing at its peak?
A. By eating properly and exercising regularly. It's critical that you give your immune cells what they need for maintenance and renewal if you want them to protect and defend you against illness. The best way to do this is through a diet that will help you overcome your sensitivities and maximize your immune power. The Immune Power Diet does just that.

The Immune Power Diet

The Immune Power Diet is designed to strengthen and revitalize your body's immune system, and as thousands of people well know, the diet works. But *why* does it work?

It's simple. The condition of your immune system influences your ability to fight disease, your energy level, and your weight. When your immune balance is upset, you can become vulnerable to a whole range of problems, including obesity, headaches, nausea, hives, anxiety, heart palpitations, and stomach cramps. And one of the most common causes of this imbalance is the food you eat.

That's exactly what writer-actress Renée Taylor found out when she came to me for her weight and circulatory problems. I tested her for allergies to see if the foods she ate most were causing her distress and I found she was allergic to about forty-five things, one of which was a food she loved—bread. The new diet I designed for this talented lady eliminated the foods she was sensitive to, including wheat, yeast, chocolate, and coffee. The result was a drop in weight of over forty pounds.

The foods that were staples of Renée Taylor's diet were poisoning her system. Why? Because food is essentially a foreign substance. A well-balanced immune system can handle foreign substances— it's fine-tuned to remove toxins and build up cellular components. But a hypersensitivity to certain foods can damage your immune cells, throwing the immune system into a state of imbalance. This shock inhibits the work of the immune cells.

The immune cells—actually the white blood cells—are essential in warding off illness. When your immune system cannot fight hard enough because of insufficient, weakened cells, you become susceptible to physical, sometimes emotional, ailments. To make matters worse, an immune imbalance sometimes causes the immune cells to attack the healthy parts of the body. This is called an autoimmune response and is related to such conditions as rheumatoid arthritis, diabetes, colitis, and dermatitis. Even more severe diseases such as cancer, kidney disease, diabetes, and lung disease can also be attributed to a weakened immune system.

Your Personal Immune Blueprint

Each individual has a distinct set of immune reactions to various foods. One person might get headaches from eating oranges, and another may experience chronic fatigue because of a sensitivity to wheat. Your particular pattern of immunosensitivities is as unique as your fingerprints. That's why in my practice, I tailor a diet to meet a patient's own needs, symptoms, and lifestyle. Whether you're young or old, rich or poor, active or lazy, immune power can work for you.

I have rarely tested a patient who didn't show some immune damage from foods eaten regularly. But once these sensitive foods are brought to light through testing, they can be removed from the diet, and the damage can be repaired.

Incredibly, the change is almost immediate. Leslie Browne saw this happen to her after years of suffering. Since she was a small child, this ballerina-actress had been constantly sneezing and blowing her nose. The continuous sniffling became so exhausting in her adult life that she found herself too tired to move her career onward and upward.

I tested Leslie for the "major food culprits" that were dragging her down. They turned out to be tunafish, melon, and celery—mainstays of her diet. Once these foods were removed from her meals, she stopped sniffling and began dancing with greater vigor than before.

In the next chapter I'll show *you* how to figure out which foods are best for you and how to identify and remove those that can wreak havoc on your immune cells.

CHAPTER 3

Food Sensitivities

So FAR, we've uncovered a number of clues that seem to cement the link between food and health. Now it's time to figure out which foods are most beneficial to *your* personal well-being, and which may be threatening it.

Maybe you've been eating the same, familiar foods for as long as you can remember, occasionally venturing off to sample something new. You feel okay, but not up to par. Or perhaps you try every new diet that comes along in a last-ditch effort to lose those extra pounds, and you're always feeling tired and irritable. You might even be experiencing more severe problems—headaches, congestion, wheezing, muscle and joint pains, palpitations, and stomach cramps. In any case, you may be eating yourself into serious immune weakness without realizing it.

The reason for your ailments may well be masked or hidden food sensitivities or food allergies. Dr. Theron Randolph, the Chicago physician who is recognized as the founder of our modern science of food allergies, discovered that many of us may acquire or lose sensitivities according to how often we're exposed to a given food. In the past, Mother Nature regulated what and how we ate—most foods were only available "in season." That forced us to rotate and vary our diets, making it almost impossible to overdose on a small set of foods.

Today, however, most foods are available year-round, which means that we have more opportunity to get used to, and overdose on, a variety of foods. So more people than ever are experiencing allergic reactions or food sensitivity symptoms to what they eat.

Because the immune system is so far-reaching, every bodily function can be affected by the immune imbalances food sensitivities cause. Table 1 lists some of the most common problems such immune imbalances can lead to.

As you see, an allergic reaction doesn't have to show up in what most people think of as the usual symptoms—hives, skin rash, and vomiting; it can be much more mysterious and covert.

Table 1: Symptoms Food Sensitivities Can Produce

Head and Upper Respiratory Tract
Headaches, dizziness, feeling faint, runny nose, blocked nasal passages and sinuses, watering eyes, earache, trouble hearing, throbbing or ringing in the ear, sore throat, bleeding gums, itchy eyes and ears, canker sores, chronic ear, eye, or throat infections.

Chest and Stomach
Feeling of fullness in the chest, asthma, congestion or fluid in the lungs, persistent cough, hoarseness, palpitations, rapid heart rate, nausea, vomiting, cramps, gas and flatulence, diarrhea, constipation, stomach that feels heavy and bloated after meals.

Skin
Red spots, rashes, dermatitis, eczema, hives, itching.

Extremities
Weakness in limbs, sore muscles, miscellaneous aches and pains, joint pains, swelling (edema) of feet, ankles, and hands.

Miscellaneous
Chronic fatigue, urgency of urination, excessive hunger, rapid or significant changes in weight.

Psychological
Confusion, lethargy, fatigue, aggression, irritability, hyperactivity, anxiety, depression, crying easily, inability to concentrate, trouble sleeping, sudden sleepiness soon after meals.

Janice

When Janice, a nurse in her thirties, came to me as a patient, she was suffering from rheumatoid arthritis that necessitated the use of a hand brace. She was unable to care for her children and was taking 4000–5000 milligrams of pain medication a day. Desperate to avoid the steroids and antiinflammatory agents she had been taking and eager to avoid the surgery that had been recommended for her to relieve the excruciating joint pain, she made the trip to New York as her last hope.

We did some immune function tests and planned a good nutrition program for her, and she returned to the midwest and started her diet. She went through a withdrawal period, similar to the withdrawal you would see in a heroin addict, for several days. She was angry and in pain, but she decided to give the diet every chance to work. One morning at the start of the second week, her husband looked at her when she woke up, and asked, "Are you okay?" She responded, "Yes, I'm fine." What was especially significant about that morning was that it was raining; on rainy days in the past her arthritis had always been immobilizing. At that moment she was pain-free and totally mobile—exclusively as a function of food, vitamins, and minerals.

Mary

Mary had recently graduated from a small college. Through friends, she got a job as a copy editor at one of the nation's most prestigious weekly magazines. She looked forward to this chance to prove herself in New York, the publishing capital of the world. But this dream almost fizzled when she became afflicted with constant, excruciating migraine headaches which sometimes lasted for days. It became torture for her to maintain the concentration and attention to detail needed for her work, and she was terrified that a major mistake would slip by her. She seriously considered giving it all up and returning to her hometown.

Finally she came to my office. Because of my own experience and the reports I had read describing food allergies as a major—perhaps *the* major—cause of migraine headaches, I had a strong suspicion of the cause of her trouble.

After testing and questioning Mary about her eating habits, I explained why I suspected food sensitivity as the source of her headaches. At first she was skeptical, claiming that the headaches had no obvious pattern of relationship with what she ate. But I explained that migraines, like other food allergies, often arise as a delayed response to the foods that trigger them, sometimes occurring days after ingestion.

My studies suggested that Mary was hypersensitive to milk, eggs, chocolate, and cinnamon, among other foods, some of which she particularly liked. Desperate for relief, she agreed to go on a strict elimination diet.

The second day into the diet she telephoned me from home, saying that her headaches were now so bad that she'd had to miss work. I explained that food sensitivities often induce a severe withdrawal phase when the offending foods are removed, and this was probably a good sign that we were on the right track.

We were. After a week, Mary's headache problem had cleared up, and she reported that she'd never felt as clear-headed in her life. Over the ensuing months, as she followed a specially designed version of the Immune Power Diet, supplemented by vitamins, nutrients, and amino acids, she felt a great deal stronger and more able to meet the challenges of her life. Gradually we were able to reintroduce some of the foods that had brought about hypersensitivity reactions in the laboratory, narrowing her migraine-causing allergens down to milk and chocolate.

Walter

When he came to see me, Walter was seventy-six years old, lethargic and depressed. Here was a man who had devoted his life and career to the great outdoors. As a member of the American Geographical Society, he had mapped mountainous terrain and established a geographical research lab in the Yukon. He had always been a healthy, rugged individual. But now he was concerned that his advancing age and declining physical fitness would force him to give up his time in the mountains. And he thought that getting old was the cause of his depression.

I found another cause: certain food sensitivities were affecting his physical and emotional well-being. Walter was actually suffering from wheat and yeast intolerance. We had to eliminate both these things from his diet, including baked goods, pickled and fermented foods, and other products containing baker's yeast. Since sugar promotes yeast growth, that had to go too.

I also prescribed nutritional supplements for him. Research shows that certain vitamins and minerals—such as vitamin C, zinc, and copper—can improve the immune response compromised by yeast growth. And a well-supervised exercise program will also speed the immune system's recovery.

Three weeks after his first visit, Walter returned to my office looking and acting like the healthy, robust man he had always been. "I didn't cheat once," he said, "and it worked. I feel like a totally different person. My depression has lifted, and I'm full of energy. I feel fabulous."

Food Sensitivities and the Binge Eater

Although the exact mechanism is not completely understood, we have observed clinically in obese patients a repeated pattern of food-binge behavior. The binge eater will consume food uncontrollably until he or she reaches a state of physical discomfort, even pain. Until recently this has been regarded as a purely psychological problem, but it is now believed that there is a physiological component as well. People tend to binge on exactly the foods to which they have immune sensitivities. Under this constant assault the immune system gives up its battle with the sensitive food and begins to adapt, even develop a need for or addiction to the offending food. This constant stress severely weakens the immune system, compromising its ability to function properly.

Damage to the immune system can leave you feeling depleted both emotionally and physically. The depression, lethargy, and torment food toxins can cause often plunge you into even more destructive, compulsive eating. That is one reason food-sensitive people are often obese.

Solving Your Own Immune Mystery

For Renée Taylor, it was bread. For Leslie Browne, it was tunafish. For other patients of mine, foods as diverse as beets, barley, pickles, and potatoes have weakened their immune systems. How can you discover what enemies lurk within your refrigerator and cupboards.

Accurate testing is the most reliable way to uncover hidden food sensitivities. There are six major testing methods for food sensitivities:

1. Traditional allergists often use the *scratch test*, which involves introducing food extract into the skin in tiny scratches on the back or arm and measuring the reaction. The test is time-consuming and often fails to point up hidden food sensitivities. One reaction can hide another, or the test may fail to pick up a powerful allergy to a certain food.

2. In the *sublingual test*, potent extracts of food products are put under the tongue, where they are absorbed quickly, and the patient is observed for signs of sensitivity. This test can also be time-consuming, and although it is symptom-specific, it fails to indicate some hidden food intolerances.

3. The cytotoxic is an experimental blood test not yet approved by the FDA. Clinically, we have found it very helpful in diagnosing complicated cases of food sensitivities. The test can be done quickly in the laboratory, using only a blood sample, so there is no unnecessary evoking of possible allergic reactions. A drop of blood is exposed to various food extracts and observed for white blood cell

destruction. The test can provide information about hidden food sensitivities, and many foods can be tested quickly.

4. The *IgG RAST (radioimmunoassay) test* is also done with a sample of the patient's blood. The blood serum sample is incubated with a food allergen, and levels of specific antibody are enumerated. The IgG RAST is used to identify delayed hypersensitivity reactions. It is more specific than the other food tests and is reproducible, which means that the test can be repeated with virtually the same results.

5. The *IgE RAST* is also a blood test. It is used most often when a patient's symptoms develop immediately after exposure to specific allergens. The intensity of an allergy can be measured, and a serum can be developed to treat the allergy.

6. The most reliable test is the *isolation test*. The patient is put into a hospital environment—controlled and absolutely nonallergenic. One by one, foods are introduced, and the physician observes the reactions. Because of the complete control, this is the best and most accurate way to test for sensitivities, but the complexity of this kind of testing makes it prohibitively expensive and time-consuming for all but the most severe sufferers.

In the absence of the above resources, you can get an idea of your own sensitivities by embarking on the Elimination menu plans outlined in Part III of this book.

The Sinister Seven

Yeast, milk, wheat—the same danger foods were showing up again and again when I tested my patients for allergic reactions. And scientific research backed up my findings. The overwhelming majority of food problems are caused by a select group of seven major food culprits. Because of the damage these foods can do, I dubbed them the "Sinister Seven." In order of frequency they are: cow's milk products, wheat, brewer's and baker's yeast, eggs, corn, soy products, and cane sugar. Following close behind are citrus fruits, red meats, coffee, chocolate, and certain spices.

These substances are responsible for about 85 percent of the food reactions I've detected in thousands of my patients—stiffened joints, headaches, stuffiness, fatigue, depression, and all those other aches that keep you from living life to the fullest.

Have you noticed any of these trouble signs in your own body?

The Immune Power Eating Plan, Menus, and Recipes detailed in the following chapters act to remove all of the Sinister Seven from your diet. Other common "perils" are removed as well, including additives, preservatives, and chemicals, which are eliminated because processed foods are prohibited on the diet. (Many of these substances not only have their own toxic effect on immune health, but also magnify toxic responses caused by other foods.)

In Part III of this book I outline the three diet plans—Elimination, Reintroduction, and Maintenance—that will banish the Sinister Seven and desensitize your immune system against these enemy foods. Once you remove those foods that could potentially damage your immune fitness, you then carefully and methodically reintroduce them, one by one, into your diet. It's up to you to play detective and closely observe the clues. As you reintroduce each target food, you can see if the danger signs return. For example, when you stopped eating cheese, were you symptom-free, but when you started eating it again your stomach cramps returned?

But before we get into the specifics of the diet plans, it would be helpful to have a solid foundation of general knowledge about nutrition and healthful food preparation. Be sure to read the next few chapters carefully.

CHAPTER 4

Nutrition Know-How

AS WE HAVE SEEN, proper nutrition is essential to proper immune function. Before embarking upon the Immune Power Eating Plan, we need to look at the basic elements of proper nutrition.

All living things need nourishment. Plants do just fine on a simple diet of water, carbon dioxide, and small amounts of minerals, but people are more demanding—they need a greater number and variety of substances in order to survive and thrive. Those essentials can be divided into seven categories.

1. *A source of energy to fuel the body*. This is provided primarily by carbohydrates but also by protein and fat.
2. *Eight different amino acids*. These synthesize the proteins that are a major part of each and every one of our cells.
3. *One unsaturated fatty acid*. This is a source of energy and is also needed for healthy skin and hair.
4. *Fiber*. This is necessary for the proper functioning of the intestinal tract.
5. *Vitamins* (some of which we probably have not yet identified). These assist in the processing of other nutrients and aid in the function of our organs.
6. *Minerals*. These help regulate body processes and provide structural material for body parts.
7. *Water*. This is essential for all body processes and structure.

Nutritionists have grouped these crucial ingredients under more general headings.

1. *Macronutrients*. These provide fuel in the form of calories. They include carbohydrates, fats, and proteins.
2. *Micronutrients*. These help the body function. They include vitamins and minerals.
3. *Water*.
4. *Fiber*. This is really a type of carbohydrate.

The chart below shows how all these ingredients interact to nourish your body.

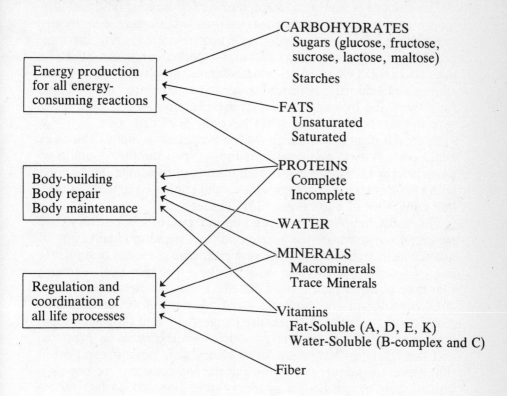

The Macronutrients

Carbohydrates, fats, and proteins—the energy-supplying macronutrients—might be thought of as your body's fuel. Like gasoline in a car, they supply the energy needed to make your body go. But the analogy is not perfect. An automobile or any other mechanical machine requires no fuel when it's in the "off" position. That's not so with the human body. Even when the body appears to be completely at rest, fuel is still needed so the heart can beat, the intestines may churn, the nerve cells may fire impulses, and so on.

Calories

The amount of energy contained in carbohydrates, fats, and proteins is expressed in those familiar units called *calories*. Scientifically speaking, a calorie is the amount of heat needed to raise the temperature of about one quart of water by one degree. An ounce of pure fat has 252 calories; an ounce of pure carbohydrate or protein contains 112 calories; fiber and water have no calories at all. Thus, foods with the highest fat content are the most caloric, and those with the most fiber and/or water have the least calories.

Believe it or not, some high-fat foods contain as many calories as explosives. A two-inch square of fudge, for example, contains as much energy (185 calories) as a small stick of dynamite, and a cone with two scoops of ice cream releases the energy equivalent to one-half cubic foot of natural gas (334 calories)!

The body, happily, does not go up in a puff of smoke every time we eat. Energy consumed is released slowly and gradually, not all at once as in an explosion. The slow, stepwise reactions that release energy from food, together with all the other chemical reactions that take place in the body's cells, are known as *metabolism*.

Obviously, our bodies need a lot of calories to function optimally (this is why "starvation" diets are dangerous), and they need them from each of the three energy sources—carbohydrates, proteins, and fats. But just because a lot of calories are good doesn't mean that more are better. All of the calories we consume are not used immediately by our bodies as energy (metabolized). Instead, some are stored in the body tissues for future use. The calories in fats are used for stored energy. Fats are also needed to insulate and cushion our body organs, but too much fat in the tissues produces unnecessary weight gain. Carbohydrates contain only half as many calories as fats. Those of you who are weight conscious or have dieted have probably heard how "fattening" carbohydrates are, but in fact most of the calories in carbohydrates are burned up as a direct energy source, supplying about two-thirds of the body's fuel; some are also converted to fat for storage. Proteins, which are essential for building and maintaining body tissues, contain as many calories as carbohydrates but the trouble is, the foods that contain the best (most complete) proteins also contain a lot of unwanted fat and cholesterol.

When too few carbohydrates are eaten, your body will need to borrow essential body fats and proteins to supply its energy demands. Therefore, most leading nutritionists today agree that the bulk of the calories we eat—about 60 percent—should come from carbohydrate foods.

Carbohydrates

Of all the macronutrients, carbohydrates—starches, sugars, and fiber—have the worst reputation in the weight-gain department, but it's largely undeserved. As we have seen, carbohydrates play a key role in fueling our bodies, and also supply essential bulk.

Starches are probably the most misunderstood carbohydrate. But if you look closely at our food supply, it's easier to see why starches are so important in the diet. Plants like rice, wheat, and other cereal grains, potatoes and legumes store their energy in the form of starch. In addition to providing energy, these plants also contain a wealth of key vitamins, minerals, and fiber. For that reason, starchy foods are often referred to as *complex carbohydrates*. Starches are contained in bread, pasta, and oatmeal, as well as potatoes, cereals, dried beans, and fresh fruits and vegetables.

On the other hand, sugary foods usually do not provide any nutrients besides carbohydrate, which is why nutritionists refer to them as *simple carbohydrates* or *empty calories*. They fuel the body with energy—calories—but little else. Sugars are contained naturally in fruit, corn, and young vegetables.

In my Immune Power Eating Plan, 60 percent of the daily intake is *complex carbohydrates*. This recommendation comes out of solid scientific evidence that has evolved over the past few years and is in agreement with dietary recommendations made by leaders in the field of nutrition.

Hidden Sugar

About half of the carbohydrate calories consumed in the United States come from refined sugars—the sugars that are *added* to foods—in other words, are not there naturally. Since about 50 percent of the average American's total calories come from carbohydrates, this means that one-quarter of his or her daily diet is made up of refined sugars. And most of this sugar has been added by processors of food.

It has been suggested in many studies that refined sugar may be related to heart disease, diabetes, obesity, and dental caries. In fact, two sugars often added to foods, sucrose and fructose, have been shown to cause tooth decay. Health professionals almost universally agree that a reduction in refined sugar intake would definitely make room in our diets for other more health-promoting sources of nutrients.

Following the Immune Power Eating Plan, you'll automatically increase your complex carbohydrate intake while decreasing your refined sugar consumption. But sugar is sneaky—it can appear where you least expect it. So it's up to you to take out your magnifying glass; read food labels carefully for signs of added sweeteners.

It's no surprise that brown sugar and confectioner's sugar, as well as plain, ordinary white table sugars are refined sugars. But there's also a lot of other "sweet talk" in ingredient lists. A product can be high in sweeteners even if the word *sugar* doesn't appear on the label. Molasses, honey, fructose, sucrose, and corn syrup are simply sugar by another name. (For a list of "hidden sugars," see page 104).

If a sweetener is given as a first or second ingredient on a food-product label (or if two or more appear anywhere in the ingredient listing), assume the food contains a considerable quantity of sugar. There is a surprising amount of sugar added to processed foods— even those we don't usually regard as "sweet," such as ketchup and cornflakes.

Those of you who find out that corn is one of your danger foods must also be alert to sweeteners on food labels. Corn syrup often appears, and high fructose corn syrup (HFCS) is gradually becoming a major sweetener in commercial food products. A mixture of different sugars, HFCS has a greater sweetening power than regular corn syrup. You will need to avoid foods containing these sweeteners.

GRAINS AND LEGUMES

Grains are an excellent source of the complex carbohydrates you need for the Immune Power Diet. They are filled with starch and other essential nutrients and are naturally low in calories because they're high in water and belly-filling, calorie-free fiber. There's no need to feel restricted in sources of complex carbohydrates if common grains such as wheat are identified as your personal danger foods. Now's the time to broaden your culinary horizons. Experiment with rice, oats, barley, rye, millet, and buckwheat—grains that lend themselves to an almost infinite variety of delicious health-promoting fare.

Legumes are also excellent starch and fiber storehouses. Some of the most commonly used legumes are peas, kidney beans, lima beans, lentils, chick-peas, black-eyed peas, peanuts, mung beans, broad beans, pinto beans, and navy beans.

Grains and legumes are available year-round. Recipes for each appear in Part IV.

FRUITS AND VEGETABLES

The other major source of complex carbohydrates—and of dietary fiber—is fruits and vegetables. All fruits are healthful and are part of the Immune Power Diet, but some fruits are more nutritious than others, especially apples, blackberries, grapefruit, lemons, oranges, papaya, pineapple, and strawberries. Whenever possible, eat fresh rather than canned fruits (if you do have canned fruit, be sure that it's canned in its own juice) and eat the edible skin as well, for it contains valuable minerals and fiber.

All fresh vegetables, particularly if they are unpeeled and served steamed, are a good source of essential nutrients. Some of the most highly recommended vegetables are cabbage, carrots, celery, cucumber, lettuce, onions, potatoes, spinach, and watercress. Frozen vegetables are acceptable if fresh are unavailable, but canned vegetables should not be used for they contain too much salt.

Use Table 2 as a guide when planning fresh fruits and vegetables for your daily meals. Take advantage of best buys during peak seasons to stretch your food budget. Buy extras when they're most plentiful and can or freeze them for off-season enjoyment.

Fiber

Dietary fiber is the substance in the plants we eat that is nondigestible or only partly digestible. It is essential for our digestive systems because it helps move wastes and undigested food quickly through the intestines and out of the body, thus promoting a healthy intestinal tract.

Since the mid-1970s, fiber has been getting more and more attention as a "must" for everyone. Although the evidence underlying

Table 2: Fruits and Vegetables in Season*

Fruits	Plentiful or Near Peak	Vegetables	Plentiful or Near Peak
Apples	October through December	Beets	June through September
Apricots	June and July	Broccoli	November through March
Cantaloupe	June through September	Cauliflower	October and November
Cherries	June and July	Celery	October through June
Cranberries	October through December	Corn	June through September
Grapefruit	January through April	Cucumbers	May through August
Grapes	August through November	Green beans	May through August
Lemons	June and July	Mushrooms	November through January
Oranges	December through May	Peppers, green	June through August
Peaches	June through September	Potatoes, sweet	October through December
Pears	August through November	Radishes	March through May
Rhubarb	February through June	Rutabagas, Turnips	November through January
Strawberries	April through June	Spinach	March and April
Tangerines	November through January	Squash, summer	June through August
Watermelons	May through August	Squash, winter	September through November
Bananas, cabbage, carrots, onions, lettuce, and potatoes usually are in good supply year-round.		Tomatoes	May through August

* Sources: U.S. Department of Agriculture; United Fresh Fruit and Vegetable Association.

these claims varies, fiber *has* been shown to have beneficial protective powers. According to a number of studies, it can:

- Alleviate problems associated with constipation.
- Act as a deterrent to the development of hemorrhoids, diver-
  ticulosis, and cancer of the colon.
- Displace calories from the diet, thereby aiding people who are
  trying to reduce their weight.
- Increase glucose tolerance in diabetics.
- Reduce serum cholesterol levels.

Vegetables, fruits, and whole grain foods contain several different
types of fiber, each of which differs in its protective abilities.

How much fiber should be included in the diet? Americans now
eat an average of 10 to 20 grams daily, but the American Cancer
Society suggests that we double that amount, consuming 25 to 40
grams of fiber a day. The best way to achieve this level of fiber
intake is to substitute high-fiber complex carbohydrates—whole grains,
beans, fruits, and vegetables—for some of the refined sugars and
animal fats currently in your diet.

Table 3 will give you an idea of foods that are rich in fiber. Eat
several servings of these foods each day. *A health tip*: leave on the
skins of fruits and vegetables whenever possible to increase your
fiber intake even more.

Protein

For years, Americans have built their meals around a hunk of
meat, often red meat. Meat is a good source of protein, and the
thinking was that "you can never get enough protein." Unfortunately, we began getting too much and protein began to elbow those
vital carbohydrates out of our diets.

Today, most nutritionists feel that carbohydrates should comprise
the major part of your meals, but you still need your protein—to
the tune of about 30 percent of your total calories. Meat and other
animal protein sources are important in the diet, but they're far
from perfect.

Protein does play many different essential roles in the body's cells.
Enzymes, hormones, antibodies, and the cells themselves are all
made up of proteins. The structural components of muscle, skin,
and hair are proteins. Proteins regulate fluid balance, and they provide energy at the rate of 112 calories per ounce—the same as
carbohydrates.

Table 3: Dietary Fiber Content of Selected Foods

Food	Amount	Fiber (grams)*
BREADS		
Rye krisp, sesame	2 triple crackers	1.7
Rye krisp	2 triple crackers	1.6
CEREALS		
Rice Chex	1⅛ cup	0.2
Oats, cooked	¾ cup	1.6
Puffed rice	1 cup	0.1
Rice Krispies	1 cup	0.1
FRESH FRUITS		
Blackberries	1 cup	6.6
Raspberries	1 cup	5.8
Blueberries	1 cup	4.4
Pear	1 medium	4.1
Apple	1 small	2.8
Strawberries	1 cup	2.8
Grapes	1 cup	2.6
Plums	2 medium	2.3
Mango	1 medium	2.2
Tangerine	1 medium	1.8
Banana	1 medium	1.6
Apricots	3 medium	1.4
Grapefruit	½	1.3
Cherries	10	0.9
Pineapple	½ cup	0.8
Peach	1 medium	0.5
GRAINS		
Buckwheat, cooked	1 cup	9.6
Millet, cooked	1 cup	6.4
Brown rice, cooked	1 cup	2.6
Barley, cooked	1 cup	1.0
Bulgur, cooked	1 cup	0.2
LEGUMES		
Kidney beans, cooked	½ cup	5.0
Chick-peas, cooked	½ cup	6.0
Pinto beans, cooked	½ cup	4.5
Lima beans, cooked	½ cup	5.8
Lentils, cooked	⅔ cup	5.5
NUTS & SEEDS		
Almonds	1 cup	3.7
Cashews	1 cup	2.0
Peanuts, raw	1 cup	2.8
Peanuts, roasted	1 cup	0.8
Pecans	1 cup	2.5
Sunflower seeds	½ cup	3.3
Pumpkin seeds	½ cup	1.5

Food	Amount	Fiber (grams)*
COOKED VEGETABLES		
Peas	½ cup	9.1
Parsnips	½ cup	4.4
Potatoes, baked	1 medium	4.2
Broccoli	4 spears	4.0
Zucchini	½ cup	3.0
Squash, summer	½ cup	2.3
Carrots	½ cup	2.2
Tomatoes	½ cup	2.0
Brussels sprouts	½ cup	1.8
Beans, string	½ cup	1.7
Onions	½ cup	1.6
Rutabagas	½ cup	1.6
Beets	½ cup	1.5
Kale	½ cup	1.4
Turnips	½ cup	1.3
Asparagus	½ cup	1.2
Eggplant	½ cup	1.2
Cauliflower	½ cup	0.9
Beans, sprouted	½ cup	0.9
RAW VEGETABLES		
Radishes	½ cup	1.2
Cucumber	½ cup	0.8
Lettuce	½ cup	0.5

* Fiber figures will vary somewhat from source to source because the method for analyzing dietary fiber has not been standardized.

AMINO ACIDS

Amino acids are the building blocks of protein. Think of the twenty-six letters in the alphabet. From those twenty-six letters, you can make any word. There are twenty-two different amino acids, and from them our bodies can synthesize any protein. Eight of the amino acids are known as *essential* because we *must* get them from our diet. The remaining amino acids are called *nonessential* because *we do not have to* rely on our food supply to get adequate amounts; our bodies can manufacture these from the eight essentials.

Protein derived from animals contains all of the eight essential amino acids, so we refer to animal protein as "complete protein" or "high biological value protein." On the other hand, protein from plant sources is usually deficient in one or more of the essential amino acids, so we refer to it as "incomplete protein" or "low biological value protein."

PROTEIN SOURCES

There are several ways we can be sure of supplying the body with all the essential amino acids needed for protein synthesis:

1. Eat animal products. Red meat, eggs, poultry, fish, and goat milk and goat milk cheese are all complete protein foods. People who are not sensitive to eggs and cow's milk may also include those products.

2. Eat two or more *different* proteinaceous plant products—particularly grains and legumes—at the same meal. (By different, I mean those that have different essential amino acid deficiencies.) This is known as combining proteins that are *complementary*. Examples of complementary combinations are rice and black-eyed peas (Hopping John), rice and beans (Arroz con Gondules), baked beans and brown bread, and peanut butter on rice cakes or rye wafers. Those not sensitive to wheat and corn may also try such combos as corn and lima beans (succotash) or peanut butter on whole wheat bread.

3. Eat proteinaceous plant foods supplemented with a small amount of animal foods. Since all the essentials are in animal-derived foods, adding a small amount of animal products to a large amount of plant products is a good bet for getting all your amino acids. Supplementary protein combinations include Turkey with Wild Rice casserole (see p. 193), feta cheese with rice cakes, and cereal and milk. Those who are not sensitive to eggs and cow's milk might also include American cheese on rye wafers or rice pudding made with eggs and milk.

According to food consumption surveys, protein intake in the United States is far too high. We're eating too much animal protein—steaks, burgers, eggs, and the like. Since these foods are high in fat and cholesterol, we'd obviously be better off eating less. No need to worry about protein deficiency as long as you supplement and complement to get all the essential amino acids you need. The Immune Power Menus and Recipes do all the work for you—mixing and matching amino acids for maximum nutrition. You'll note that the Immune Power Diet includes veal and lamb but no beef. Veal and lamb are relatively high in cholesterol, but they are lower in saturated fat than beef.

Fats

Fats are the most concentrated source of energy, so a food that is high in fat content is *always* high in calories. Almost half the calories eaten by most people in this country right now come from fats. There's no doubt about it—high-fat diets are fattening. What's more, fattening foods can be addictive. The more of them you eat, the more you want to eat.

The scientific evidence also implicates fat as a causative factor in heart disease. Additionally, high-fat diets have been linked with increased risk of developing cancers of the breast, colon, ovaries, uterus, and prostate, as well as other serious diseases such as toxemia during pregnancy and multiple sclerosis.

Therefore, the American Heart Association, the American Cancer Society, and other medical groups recommend that you reduce the risk of these diseases and other diet-related problems by:

1. Reducing fat intake to only one-third of your calories, with the ratio of polyunsaturated to saturated fatty acids at 1:1.
2. Decreasing cholesterol intake from the national average of 600 mg a day to 300 mg.

In order to meet these recommendations, you need to eat fewer fats altogether, choose fats with a higher percentage of polyunsaturated fatty acids, and reduce your cholesterol intake. All of these health-promoting goals are easily attainable on the Immune Power Diet. My Eating Plan brings fat intake down to 10 percent and stresses the consumption of foods low in cholesterol and fatty acids.

TYPES OF FATS

Before we go any further, let's investigate some of the terms we've been tossing around. Exactly what are cholesterol and polyunsaturated fat?

The general term for fats and oils is lipids. Of all the fats and oils that occur in our food supply, two have nutritional significance— the *triglycerides* (which make up 95 percent of the lipid content of our food), and the other 5 percent are *sterols*.

It's important to understand what triglycerides are from a chemical point of view, because then you can understand the difference between saturated and unsaturated fats. Triglycerides are composed of fatty acids that are *saturated, monosaturated*, or *polyunsaturated*.

Saturated means that the fatty acid is holding as many atoms of hydrogen as it possibly can—it's literally "saturated" with hydrogen atoms, *Monosaturated* means that hydrogen is missing from one site on the fatty acid. And *polyunsaturated* means that many hydrogen atoms are missing. In general, the more saturated a fat is, the more solid it is at room temperature. And the more unsaturated a fat is, the less solid it is at room temperature (Coconut and palm oil are exceptions—both are highly saturated.) Fats that are not very solid at room temperature but are actually liquid, are referred to as oils.

Sterols, the other nutritionally significant type of lipid, include Vitamin D and cholesterol. High levels of cholesterol in the blood can lead to clogged arteries and heart disease. Saturated fats tend to raise the level of cholesterol in the blood. Therefore, for the most part, nutritionists and health experts today advocate a reduction in foods containing saturated fats and cholesterol.

Tables 4, 5, and 6 will help you make wise "fat" choices. Table 4 lists the basic general dietary guidelines offered by the U.S. Department of Agriculture and the U.S. Department of Health, Ed-

Table 4: Guidelines for Avoiding Fat and Cholesterol

Government	Immune Power Diet
1. Choose lean meat, fish, poultry, dry beans, and peas as protein sources.	1. Same.
2. Use low-fat or skim milk and milk products as calcium sources.	2. Eliminate cow's milk. Use sheep and goat's milk and milk products and take a calcium supplement as directed by your physician.
3. Moderate the use of eggs and organ meats.	3. Eliminate eggs. Moderate the use of organ meats.
4. Limit use of butter, cream, saturated fats, shortenings, and foods containing palm and coconut oils.	4. Eliminate all of these.
5. Trim excess fat from meats.	5. Same.
6. Broil, bake, steam, or boil. Do not fry foods.	6. Same.
7. Read labels carefully to determine amount and type of fat present in foods.	7. Same.

ucation, and Welfare for limiting fats and cholesterol, and compares them to the Immune Power Diet guidelines. Table 5 shows you that foods with the highest polyunsaturated to saturated fat ratios are

Table 5: P/S Fat Ratios* of Foods

High (more than 2½ times as much polyunsaturated as saturated fat)	Almonds Corn oil Cottonseed oil Linseed oil Soft margarine Mayonnaise (made with any of the oils in this group) Safflower oil Sesame oil Soybean oil Sunflower oil Walnuts
Medium-high (about twice as much polyunsaturated as saturated fat)	Chicken breast, skin, or thigh Freshwater fish Peanut oil Semisolid margarine
Medium (about equal amounts of polyunsaturated and saturated fat)	Beef heart and liver Chicken heart Hydrogenated or hardened vegetable oils Peanut butter Pecans Saltwater fish Solid margarines
Low (a tenth to a half as much polyunsaturated as saturated fat)	Chicken liver Lard Olive oil Palm oil Pork
Very low (less than a tenth as much polyunsaturated as saturated fat)	Beef, lean and fatty Butter Coconut oil Egg yolk Milk and milk products Mutton, lean and fatty

* Polyunsaturated to saturated fats

Table 6: Cholesterol Content of Nonplant Foods

Food	Cholesterol per Portion (mg.)
Beef	
Cooked, trimmed, 4 oz.	102
Cooked, untrimmed, 4 oz.	106
Brains: cooked, no fat added, 3 oz.	2674
Butter: 1 pat	18
Cheese	
Cheddar and processed, 1 oz.	28
Cottage, creamed, (4% fat), 1 cup	48
Cream, 1 oz.	32
Spreads and cheese foods, 1 oz.	19
Chicken, turkey: cooked, 4 oz.	102
Cream	
Light (20% fat), 1 tbsp.	11
Half and half (12% fat), 1 tbsp.	6
Egg	
Whole, 1 med.	252
White, 1 med.	0
Yolk, 1 med.	252
Fish	
Lean and medium fat, cooked—sole, flounder, swordfish, tuna, salmon, 4 oz.	70
Very fat, cooked—mackerel and herring, 4 oz.	110
Gefilte fish: 3 oz.	54
Heart (Beef): cooked, 3 oz.	233
Ham	
Cooked, trimmed, 4 oz.	99
Cooked, untrimmed, 4 oz.	101
Ice Cream	
Rich, (16% fat), 1 scoop	40
Regular (10% fat), 1 scoop	28

Food	Cholesterol per Portion (mg.)
Ice milk: 1 scoop	14
Kidney: cooked, no fat added, 3 oz.	683
Lamb	
Cooked, trimmed, 4 oz.	113
Cooked, untrimmed, 4 oz.	113
Lard (and other animal fat): 1 tbsp.	14–17
Liver	
Cooked, no fat added—	
beef, 3 oz.	372
Chicken liver, 3 oz.	634
Margarine (all vegetable fat): 1 pat	0
Mayonnaise (and mayonnaise-type salad dressing):	
1 tbsp.	8
Milk	
Fluid, whole, 1 cup	34
Fluid, skim, 1 cup	5
Fluid, 1% fat, 1 cup	14
Pork	
Cooked, trimmed, 4 oz.	99
Cooked, untrimmed, 4 oz.	101
Shellfish	
Clams, 4 oz.	71
Lobster, 4 oz.	96
Shrimp, cooked, 4 oz.	170
Crabs, 4 oz.	113
Sweetbreads: cooked, 3 oz.	396
Tongue	
Cooked fresh, 3 oz.	119
Cooked smoked, 3 oz.	179
Veal	
Cooked, trimmed, 4 oz.	112
Cooked, untrimmed, 4 oz.	114

the ones to emphasize for a healthier diet. And Table 6 gives you an approximation of how much cholesterol is contained in certain common foods from animal sources. (Note: Cholesterol is not present in foods of plant origin, such as fruits, vegetables, cereal grains, legumes, nuts, or oils.)

One further word about fat—it does have some redeeming qualities. Besides providing stored energy, it protects the body from heat loss and cushions our organs, and it aids in the absorption of the fat-soluble vitamins—A, D, E, and K. And remember that *one* essential fatty acid we mentioned at the beginning of the chapter? Its name is *linoleic acid*, and it is essential for maintaining the health of our skin and hair.

The Micronutrients

Although you only need minute amounts of the micronutrients—vitamins and minerals—in your daily diet, those tiny quantities play a tremendous part in promoting and maintaining well-being. A lack of just one micronutrient can cause your immune system to go "atilt," wreaking havoc on your health.

Vitamins

Vita means life, and vitamins are the lifeguards of your body. They are organic substances which are essential factors in metabolism, the chemical reactions that promote growth and maintain health. Although vitamins do not serve as a source of energy, some facilitate the release of energy from protein, fat, and carbohydrate. All vitamins are essential nutrients—and they must be obtained from the food you eat. For those who cannot get their total daily vitamin quota from their meals, vitamin supplements help fill in the gaps.

Until recently, nobody knew too much about vitamins. It wasn't until the twentieth century that scientists discovered that without very small daily doses of these organic substances, a person could not be totally healthy. These days, new discoveries are rapidly unfolding about the health-enhancing effects of vitamins.

I myself have made some of these discoveries as I've tried to unlock the immune mysteries of my patients. I've had tremendous success in stimulating the body's immune system and improving its defenses through the proper use of vitamins and minerals. For example, I've found that:

- Vitamin C can help destroy pathogenic bacteria, can neutralize toxins, and can increase the body's production of interferon—a powerful anticancer substance.
- Vitamin A can help cure chronic infections by increasing the number of T-cells and increasing the body's tolerance against poisons.
- Vitamin B-complex and vitamin B_{12} can help the body produce antibodies, assist in our metabolic and enzymatic processes, and promote the regeneration of the red blood cells.
- Vitamin E can inhibit the damaging effects of toxins.

Vitamins exist in two forms—fat-soluble and water-soluble. The fat-soluble vitamins—A, D, E, and K—are found in animal and plant fats and oils. Humans store these vitamins in their body tissues. The water-soluble vitamins include all the B vitamins and vitamin C.

Table 7 will help you sort out the functions of food sources of the vitamins you need daily. Of course, the Immune Power Menus have been carefully planned and varied to maintain a proper vitamin balance. The roles of many of the vitamins are interrelated—they work together to help each other function—so it's crucial to maintain that delicate balance. When it's not possible to obtain all your vitamins from what you eat, I recommend taking a multiple vitamin supplement.

Table 7: The Major Functions and Food Sources of Vitamins

Vitamin	Recommended Daily Allowance for Adults	Functions	Sources
A	5000 I.U.	Helps form and maintain healthy skin, hair, and mucous membranes; aids in night vision; assists in bone and tooth growth and reproduction	Carrots, green and yellow vegetables, whole cow's milk, goat's milk and goat cheese, fish liver oil, margarine, yellow fruits, eggs, liver
D	400 I.U.	Helps form and maintain bones and teeth by assisting in the absorption and use of calcium and phosphorus	Fish liver oil, sardines, herring, salmon, tuna, vitamin-D-fortified cow's milk, goat's and sheep's milk cheeses and other products.
E	30 I.U.	Helps form red blood cells, muscles, and other tissues; aids in the function of vitamin A and fatty acids	Wheat germ, soybeans, vegetable oils, leafy greens (spinach, bok choy, etc.), broccoli, Brussels sprouts, whole-grain cereals
K	none (300 mcg. is generally recommended)	Acts with other substances to help blood clot; maintains normal bone metabolism	Alfalfa, safflower and soybean oils, leafy green vegetables, kelp, fish liver oil
B_1 (thiamine)	1.5 mg.	Helps release energy from carbohydrates; aids in the function of the nervous system	Rice, whole wheat, oatmeal, peanuts, pork, most vegetables, bran, goat's and sheep's milk products, lima beans, pasta

Vitamin	Recommended Daily Allowance for Adults	Functions	Sources
B_2 (riboflavin)	1.7 mg.	Helps release energy from carbohydrates, proteins, and fats; maintains mucous membranes	Fish, leafy green vegetables, whole-grain cereals, cow's milk, goat's and sheep's milk products, dried peas and beans, mushrooms, pasta, eggs, liver
B_3 (niacin)	20 mg.	Works with thiamine and riboflavin to release energy	Poultry, tuna, beef, nuts, whole-grain cereals and breads, dried beans and peas
B_5 Pantothenic Acid	10 mg.	Aids in the metabolism of carbohydrates, protein, and fat; helps form hormones	Whole-grain cereals and breads, nuts, dark green vegetables, eggs, liver
B_6 (pyridoxine)	2mg.	Helps the body absorb and metabolize proteins and use fats; aids in the formation of red blood cells	Whole grain cereals and breads, cantaloupe, cabbage, beef, potatoes, fish, green beans, bananas, nuts
B_{12} (cyano-cobalamin)	3 mcg.	Helps form red blood cells and build genetic material; aids in nervous system function	Beef, pork, cow's milk, goat's and sheep's milk products, fish, oysters

Table 7: The Major Functions and Food Sources of Vitamins (cont.)

Vitamin	Recommended Daily Allowance for Adults	Functions	Sources
Folacin (folic acid)	400 mcg.	Works with B_{12} to build genetic material and form red blood cells	Dark green leafy vegetables, carrots, cantaloupe, apricots, pumpkins, whole wheat and rye flour, beef, liver
Biotin	150–300 mcg.	Helps form fatty acids and release energy from carbohydrates	Liver, dark green vegetables, green beans, rice, nuts, many fruits
C	60 mg.	Helps form collagen and build body tissue; maintains capillaries, bones, and teeth; protects other vitamins from oxidation	Citrus fruits, tomatoes, green and leafy green vegetables, peppers, cauliflower, potatoes, sweet potatoes, berries, melon

Minerals

Minerals are inorganic chemicals that are essential components in various body structures and also participate in various metabolic reactions of the body. For example, calcium is an important component of our bones and teeth, and iron is a constituent of hemoglobin in red blood cells.

Seven mineral elements—calcium, phosphorous, potassium, sulphur, sodium, chlorine, and magnesium—are required in larger amounts than the others. They're referred to as *macrominerals*. The remaining minerals, required in smaller quantities, are known as the *trace minerals*. Included in this group are iron, iodine, zinc, fluorine, chromium, and copper.

Like vitamins, minerals perform a number of functions that are interrelated in the body, and piece by piece, we are trying to put together the puzzle that will show us exactly how they work together.

In the past year alone, the trace minerals—especially zinc and iron— have been recognized as having a great significance to our health. And the interaction of minerals and vitamins is just beginning to be explored.

Table 8 will help you maximize the mineral content of your meals.

Table 8: The Major Functions and Food Sources of Minerals

Mineral	Recommended Daily Allowance for Adults	Functions	Sources
Calcium	800–1200 mg.	Builds bones and teeth; maintains bone strength and cell membranes; helps in blood clotting and muscle contraction; aids in absorption of B_{12} and in activation of enzymes	Sheep's and goat's milk products, soybeans, sardines, salmon, peanuts, walnuts, sunflower seeds, dried beans, dark green leafy vegetables
Phosphorus	800–1200 mg.	Helps build bones and teeth; aids in releasing energy from carbohydrates, proteins, and fats; assists in formation of genetic material and cell membranes	Fish, poultry, beef, whole grains, nuts, and seeds
Magnesium	300–450 mg.	Helps build bones and manufacture proteins; aids in releasing energy from muscle glycogen; essential for generation of nerve impulses	Raw leafy green vegetables, apples, figs, lemons, grapefruit, corn, almonds, seeds

Table 8: The Major Functions and Food Sources of Minerals (cont.)

Mineral	Recommended Daily Allowance for Adults	Functions	Sources
Sodium	none (1000–3000 mg. suggested)	Helps maintain balance of water and dissolved substances in body, as well as acid-base balance in body fluids and cells. (*Too much sodium can cause hypertension.*)	The Immune Power Diet contains enough naturally occurring sodium to carry out the function of the mineral.
Potassium	none (2000–5000 mg. suggested)	Helps maintain balance of water and dissolved substances in cells; needed for transmission of nerve impulses and in release of energy from carbohydrates, proteins, and fats	Citrus fruits, leafy green vegetables, bananas, potatoes, mint leaves, sunflower seeds
Sulfur	none	Aids in production and function of amino acids in cells; helps create protein in nails, skin, hair	Beef, wheat germ, dried beans, cabbage, peanuts, clams
Chlorine	none	Helps regulate balance of body fluids and acid/base balance; aids in digestion	Table salt, kelp, olives
Iron	10–18 mg.	Essential in formation of hemoglobin in red blood cells and myoglobin in muscles—both supply oxygen to cells; helps form enzymes and proteins	Liver, red meat, leafy green vegetables, dried fruits, dried beans and peas, whole-grain cereals, oysters, clams. (*Should be eaten with vitamin-C rich food for proper absorption.*)

Mineral	Recommended Daily Allowance for Adults	Functions	Sources
Copper	none (2–3 mg. suggested)	Helps in formation of red blood cells; production of respiratory enzymes	Seafood, dried beans and peas, prunes, whole wheat, cocoa powder
Zinc	15 mg.	Helps form about 100 enzymes	Red meat, chicken, seafood, wheat germ, pumpkin seeds
Iodine	150 mcg.	Helps form thyroid hormones; necessary for reproduction	Seafood, kelp, onions
Fluorine	none (1.5–4 mg. suggested)	Helps maintain strong bones and teeth	Seafood, tea, gelatin
Chromium	none (50–200 mcg. is average)	Helps metabolize glucose	Red meat, shellfish, chicken, clams
Selenium	none (50–200 mcg. suggested)	Helps prevent breakdown of fats and body chemicals; works with vitamin E	Wheat germ, bran, tuna, onions, tomatoes, broccoli
Manganese	none (2.5–5 mg. suggested)	Helps in the operation of the central nervous system; regulates bone structure and reproductive system; helps form enzymes	Nuts, leafy green vegetables, peas, beets, whole-grain cereals and breads, cocoa powder
Molybdenum	none (150–500 mcg. suggested)	Helps form enzyme xanthine oxidase	Dried peas and beans, whole grain cereals, dark leafy green vegetables

Water

Water, which makes up about half of the body's weight, is the only nutrient that comprises its own group. It is essential for the maintenance of cellular structure and for the regulation of all body processes. We can go for weeks, months, and even years without other nutrients—not in the best of health, of course—but a human deprived of water can live for only a few days. Besides the water you drink, there are many sources of this nutrient. It's a component of almost all foods—at least 80 percent of most fruits and vegetables, 50 percent of a piece of meat, and about a third of a slice of bread.

Water must be continuously replenished, and scientific evidence suggests that drinking approximately 64 ounces of water a day will contribute to your overall health.

Balancing Your Nutrients

Now that we've shown which foods contain which nutrients, it will be a cinch to put together meals with the perfect nutritional balance, right? Wrong! One of the trickiest things about eating is juggling your food to create a diet that supplies all the vitamins, minerals, protein, carbohydrate, fat, fiber, and water you need in just the right amounts.

Nutritionists have been trying to do this for ages, and the most widely accepted plan they've yet come up with is the Four Food Group Plan, shown in Table 9. Devised several decades ago, this eating guide has its shortcomings, but it does provide a framework for eating that can be adapted to the Immune Power Diet. Since the Four Food Group Plan was created, more nutrients have been discovered and studied. Table 10 shows the Four Food Group Plan updated to reflect the most recent changes in the thinking about nutrition, especially the increased needs for vitamin B_6, magnesium, zinc, and vitamin E. Finally, Table 11 shows the Plan as modified for the Immune Power Diet.

Table 9: The Original Four Food Group Plan

Food Group	Sample Foods	Main Nutrient Contributions	Servings (Adult)	Serving Size
Milk and milk products	Milk, buttermilk, yogurt, cheese, cottage cheese, soy milk, ice cream	Calcium, protein, riboflavin, zinc, vitamin B_{12}, thiamine	2	8 oz. milk; 1 cup yogurt; 1½ cup cottage cheese; 2 cups ice cream; 5 tbsp. milk pudding; 2 oz. cheese
Meat and meat substitutes	Beef, pork, lamb, fish, poultry, eggs, nuts, legumes	Protein, iron, riboflavin, niacin, zinc, vitamin B_{12}, thiamine	2	2–3 oz. cooked meat, fish, or chicken; ¼ cup tuna; 2 eggs; 4 tbsp. peanut butter; 1 cup cooked legumes; ½ cup nuts
Fruits and vegetables	All fruits and vegetables	Vitamin A, vitamin C, thiamine, additional iron and riboflavin, fiber, folacin	4	½ cup fruit, vegetable, or juice; 1 medium apple, orange, banana, peach, etc.
Grains (bread and cereal products)	All whole-grain and enriched flours and-products, buckwheat	Additional niacin, iron, thiamine; zinc in whole grains; fiber	4	1 slice bread; ½ cup cooked cereal or 1 cup ready-to-eat cereal; ½ hamburger or hot dog bun or English muffin; ½ cup cooked rice, grits, macaroni, or spaghetti; 2 tbsp. flour; 6 saltines; 1 6-inch tortilla

Table 10: The Four Food Groups Updated

Food Group	Servings/Size
Milk and milk products	Same as original
Meat, fish, poultry, eggs	Portion size 3 oz. (*not* 2–3 oz.)
Legumes and/or nuts	Portion size ¾ cup
Fruits and vegetables	Same as original
Grains (*whole* grains, *not* enriched grains)	Same as original
Fat or oil, for vitamin E and essential fatty acids	1 serving (1 tbsp.)

A Note to Vegetarians

Those who do not eat animal products have fewer food choices available. For vegetarians who will eat only plant foods, or those who include some eggs and/or dairy products besides, the Four Food Group Plan has to be modified to fit their needs. Here are some of the modifications to keep in mind:

- For milk products, drink soy milk fortified with vitamin B_{12}.
- For protein, women should include two cups legumes daily to help meet iron requirements; men and women should count 4 tablespoons peanut butter as 1 serving.
- For fruits and vegetables, women should include 1 cup dark greens to help meet iron requirements.

Putting It All Together

The key to your health is what you eat. We still don't know enough about nutrition to identify the "ideal" diet for each individual, but the Immune Power Diet comes very, very close. It takes into account all those variables that influence our well-being—heredity, lifestyle,

Table 11: The Four Food Groups Modified
for the Immune Power Diet

Food Group	Servings/Size
Milk and milk products	2 servings sheep's or goat's milk and/or sheep or goat milk products. One serving (3 oz.) canned sardines or salmon with bones can be used instead of one serving of milk. Use calcium supplements recommended by your physician.
Meat, fish, poultry, eggs	Same as the updated plan except: omit eggs and limit red meat intake.
Legumes and/or nuts	Same as the updated plan except exclude soybeans
Fruits and vegetables	Same as the updated plan.
Grains	Same as the updated plan except exclude wheat and corn
Fat or oil	Same as the updated plan except limit to polyunsaturated oil (never use palm or coconut oils)

personality, mental health, age, sex, and body size. And it also considers those chronic conditions where diet can mean the difference between life and death—heart disease, cancer, hypertension, and diabetes.

To recapitulate, here are the Immune Power Diet guidelines for healthier eating:

1. Eliminate the Sinister Seven: cow's milk, wheat, cane sugar, eggs, yeast, corn, and soy.
2. Avoid caffeine. No tea or coffee is allowed on the Immune Power Diet.
3. Do not eat the same food more than once every four days.
4. Experiment with a wide variety of foods. Explore health food stores and other specialty markets.

5. Beware of packaged and canned foods. They are usually high in salt, sugar, and other harmful additives.
6. Read labels carefully.
7. No more than 30 percent of your diet should be composed of protein. Restrict your intake of red meat (no beef is allowed on the Immune Power Diet). For protein, choose fish or poultry whenever possible. And don't forget that combining grains and legumes with meat can meet your dietary needs for protein.
8. At least 50 percent and as much as 60 percent of your diet should be made up of high-fiber complex carbohydrates—grains, legumes, cereals, and fresh fruits and vegetables.
9. Drink plenty of water—at least six glasses a day.
10. Avoid saturated fats. Use vegetable oil in cooking—and don't forget that while palm and coconut oils are vegetable oils, they are highly saturated. Don't use them.
11. Get out of the salt habit. Experiment with other seasonings.
12. Avoid all refined sugars. For sweetening use only pure honey, pure maple syrup, and juice concentrate or the natural sweetness of fresh fruit.

In Part I I've talked about the Immune Power way of eating for optimum health, and suggested nutritional guidelines, but guidelines alone can't guarantee health and well-being. It's up to you to put together all the knowledge you've gained so far and use it every day.

In the chapters that follow, we will take the Immune Power Diet into the supermarket and the kitchen and show you how to plan, shop for, and prepare meals that will boost you into radiant, robust health.

PART II

Immune Power Cooking

CHAPTER 5

Tips for Getting Started

I DON'T PROFESS to be an accomplished chef. In fact, my stove and I are not the best of friends, since I have very little time to cook. Many of you have been whipping up delicious meals for years and can probably teach me a thing or two. But in my practice, I have discovered (with the help of my staff of dieticians and food experts) that certain ways of cooking are more nutritious than others, and certain hints can make cooking a lot more enjoyable and successful.

So I will pass this information on to you. What follows immediately are general tips on cooking, shopping, substitutions, and equipment for the Immune Power cook. Then in the next chapter you will find specific information about selecting, cooking, and storing the most common ingredients.

Immune Power Cooking

The Immune Power Recipes use the most nutritious, low-fat cooking techniques—steaming, baking, cooking in parchment paper, stir-frying, poaching, and boiling in as little water as possible to preserve nutrients. Avoid cooking methods that might be hazardous to your health. These include:

- Charcoal broiling. The high heat used for this method can interact with the food being cooked—especially meat—and form carcinogens (cancer-causing agents).
- Deep-frying. Cooking in several inches of hot fat is a definite no-no. The food absorbs a lot of grease and gives you a wallop of cholesterol and/or extra fat.
- Shallow-frying. Using a hunk of butter, margarine, or shortening, or a few spoonfuls of oil adds a lot of unnecessary calories (100 per tablespoon!) and fat to your diet.

Microwave Cooking

The microwave oven can be a real boon for the Immune Power cook. Microwave cooking can help cut down on fat and conserve nutrients while it turns out food that's moist and flavorful.

Microwave-cooked food requires very little or no added fat or oil. Vegetables, fish, chicken, and meat are simply cooked in a little liquid in a covered, microwave-safe dish. Because the food cooks in its own juices, it is very natural-tasting and succulent.

As a bonus, cooking in the microwave can reduce vitamin loss—especially vitamin C. In a study conducted by Dr. Gertrude Armbruster at the New York State College of Human Ecology, Cornell University, it was found that up to 50 percent more vitamin C was preserved during microwave cooking, because a much shorter cooking time and less water were required. (Vitamin C, a water-soluble and heat-sensitive vitamin, can easily leach out into the cooking water or be damaged by heat when foods are cooked for longer times in a conventional oven or on top of the stove.) The shorter time involved in microwave cooking also means less protein damage than in traditional methods.

If you have a microwave oven, feel free to use it to cook—not just defrost or reheat—the foods recommended on the Immune Power Diet.

Measuring

Measuring correctly is one of the keys to good cooking. Here's a short lesson:

- Measure liquids in clear plastic or glass calibrated measuring cups. For accuracy, the top of the liquid in the cup should be at eye level. Remember: These cups have head space to prevent liquid from spilling over, so don't fill to the brim.
- Measure dry ingredients in nested measuring cups. Level off at the brim with a metal spatula or knife. Smaller amounts can be measured in graduated measuring spoons. The ingredients are scooped up, then leveled off with a spatula.
- To measure honey or other sticky substances, lightly oil the cup or spoon first. Otherwise, the measurement will be inaccurate because some of the honey will stick to the utensil.
- To measure ⅛ teaspoon of a dry ingredient, first measure a level ¼ teaspoon, then remove half of the measured amount.

A Few General Tips

- Use nonstick cookware or wipe just a tissue-thin layer of oil or margarine on the pan before cooking.
- Sauté in vegetable broth or vegetable juice instead of fat. A little liquid is all you need to sauté vegetables, fish, or chicken breasts in a skillet.
- Steam vegetables and fish. If you don't have a steamer, improvise by placing a colander or wire cake rack over boiling water and covering.
- Trim all visible fat from meat and fish before cooking. Remove the skin from poultry and whole fish.
- When a recipe yields three to four servings and you need only one, freeze the leftovers in an airtight container or freezer wrap. When the ingredients in that recipe come up again in your four-day rotation (see Part III), simply thaw and reheat the meal.
- Plan garnishes to fit in with the foods allowed on your four-day rotation plan. (For example, you can't sprinkle grated Parmesan cheese on a vegetable casserole if you're off dairy products for the day.)
- If you're sensitive to wheat or corn, use arrowroot for thickening instead of flour or cornstarch. Less is needed, it becomes very clear upon thickening, and it doesn't mask the natural flavors of the food. Health food stores and spice shops carry arrowroot.
- Prepare a large batch of herbal tea ahead of time and refrigerate. If it turns cloudy, simply add a small amount of boiling water.

Immune Power Shopping

Shopping for food means expanding your horizons. You probably won't be able to fill your shopping cart with just one stop at the supermarket or local deli. The Immune Power Diet will turn you into an explorer, stalking out health food stores, ethnic groceries (especially Oriental, Greek, and Italian), and specialty food shops. And the imported and health food aisles of your supermarket will become familiar ground. None of the foods required is terribly exotic or hard to find, but you may have to formulate a slightly different shopping game plan.

Your nearest health food store is handy for finding a large selection of grains, broths without MSG or yeast, yeast-free breads, pure wheat or rice cereal, dairy-free margarine, and products sweetened with honey or pure maple syrup.

Specialty food stores usually carry a selection of oils, cheeses, special pastas, and other ingredients that can be used with success in the Immune Power Recipes. Ethnic markets are treasure troves of health-promoting foods. Try Italian and Greek stores for sheep and goat cheeses; Korean markets for a terrific selection of fresh produce, rice products, and buckwheat noodles; and Spanish markets for exotic fruits and vegetables.

A Few General Tips

- Keep your menu fresh and seasonal whenever possible. Avoid frozen, canned, processed, or bottled products if you can.
- Buy food in small quantities. This helps protect the vitamin and mineral value of your foods by reducing storage time. If you find it more convenient to purchase in larger quantities, divide the food into single-serving portions, wrap it well, and freeze it. Thaw packages overnight in the refrigerator—not at room temperature—before preparation.
- Remember that when you buy raw fish, meat, or poultry, the raw weight will always be greater than the cooked weight since you lose a bit when these foods are trimmed and boned. So always buy a little extra.
- Be flexible in your food shopping. If you're going out expressly to buy bok choy for a recipe but you notice that spinach is fresher or on sale, you *can* substitute. Just pick a food that's similar in nutrient composition (see Chapter 6).

The Importance of Reading Labels

Before you toss an item into your cart, read every word on the food label and ingredients list. You'll be amazed at how many of the Sinister Seven find their way into food products where you'd never imagine they'd exist. You can't take anything for granted, as Marcia, one of my patients, found out. She was buying a package of rye wafers and was trying to decide between the "lite" and "hearty" varieties. Upon closer examination of the label, she discovered that the Hearty Rye Wafers contained yeast, while the Lite Rye Wafers were yeast-free.

Double-check ingredients lists on foods you assume are all-natural. There are no standards governing the use of the word *natural* on food labels, so these foods can contain fillers, preservatives, stabilizers, emulsifiers, artificial flavorings, and other food additives that can severely weaken your Immune Power.

SOME COMMON FOODS
THAT CAN CARRY SECRET THREATS

Margarine. Check the type of oil used. Some manufacturers blend cow's milk products, such as skim milk or whey, with vegetable oils. Others are *100 percent* vegetable oil. If you're soybean or corn-sensitive, make sure the margarine or oil you buy doesn't contain those oils.

Honey. Make sure it's pure honey—without additives or preservatives.

Pineapple and other canned fruits. Choose the type that's packed in its own juice rather than a heavy, sweetened syrup.

Canned or fresh crabmeat. The type abundant in most fish stores and supermarkets is really white fish flavored with crab, and it contains *wheat flour.* Wheat flour is often added to other foods as well, as a filler and/or binder.

Vegetable broth. The vegetables and herbs used to make broths and bouillon cubes or powders must be listed on the label and be recognizable to you. Stay clear of any unknown ingredients.

Seasoning blends. You might be seasoning your recipes with garlic powder, onion salt, or other spice combinations without knowing that you are doing yourself harm. Gloria, one of my patients, found she was allergic to some of the components in garlic powder—a staple on her spice rack—and had to eliminate it completely from her cooking. Many seasoning blends contain MSG, excessive sodium, BHT to preserve freshness, and other dangerous substances. Read carefully!

Salt. Salt is commonly added to a wide assortment of packaged foods to enhance their flavor. This added salt should be checked out on tomato sauce, tomato paste, club soda, broths, and many other items. Look for "sodium-free" or "low-sodium" versions of these products—they're becoming more prevalent every day.

You may be surprised to learn that some foods that contain no added salt and don't taste salty still have lots of sodium. Look for the words *soda* or *sodium*, or the symbol *Na* on the label. Some of the more common sodium additives are sodium bicarbonate, baking

SODIUM-FREE SPICES AND FLAVORINGS

Allspice	Mace	Pimiento
Almond extract	Maple extract	Rosemary
Bay leaves	Marjoram	Sage
Caraway seeds	Mustard powder	Sesame seeds
Cinnamon	Nutmeg	Thyme
Curry powder	Paprika	Turmeric
Garlic	Parsley	Vanilla extract
Ginger	Pepper	Vinegar
Lemon extract	Peppermint extract	Walnut extract

soda, most baking powders, disodium phosphate, sodium alginate, sodium benzoate, sodium hydroxide, sodium propionate, sodium sulfite, and sodium saccharin.

Immune Power Shopping Lists

To help you meet the challenge of food shopping, I've put together master shopping lists for the Elimination and Reintroduction Diets (see Part III). These will be handy as you restock your larder for Immune Power.

ELIMINATION DIET SHOPPING LIST

Grains and Flours
Brown rice
Millet
Buckwheat groats
Oats (rolled and quick-cooking)
Barley
Wild rice
Rice flour
Buckwheat flour
Rye flour
Oat flour
Barley flour
Potato flour
Chick-pea flour

Thickeners
Arrowroot

Herbs (dried or fresh)
Basil
Bay leaf
Chervil
Dillweed
Marjoram
Mint
Oregano
Parsley
Rosemary
Saffron
Sage
Savory
Tarragon
Thyme

Seed
Anise
Celery
Fennel
Mustard
Poppy
Sesame
Sunflower
Pumpkin

Leaveners
Baking powder
Baking soda
Cream of tartar

Spices
Allspice
Cardamom
Cinnamon
Cloves
Coriander
Cumin
Ginger
Mace
Nutmeg
Paprika
Pepper
Saffron
Turmeric

Seasonings or Flavor Accents
Honey
Salt

Beverages
Herbal tea
Coffee substitutes
Seltzer water

Staples
Beans
Lentils
Nuts
Raisins and currants
Dates
Figs

Tomato paste
Tomato sauce
Tomatoes
Frozen fruit juice concentrates
Nut butters
Buckwheat noodles
Mung vermicelli
Tahini (sesame paste)
Canned fruits (no sugar)
Canned juices (no additives)
Canned vegetable juices (no additives)
Waterchestnuts
Bean sprouts
Bamboo shoots
Rye wafers
Canned tuna
Canned salmon
Canned sardines

Oils
Safflower
Sunflower
Olive
Peanut
Sesame (light and dark)
Almond
Walnut
Apricot

Perishables
Goat cheese
Sheep cheese
Fruits
Vegetables
Salad greens
Poultry
Veal
Fish
Shellfish
Ginger root
Horseradish
Garlic
Shallots
Chives
Onion

REINTRODUCTION DIET SHOPPING LIST*

Grains and Flours
Wheat berries
Bulgur wheat
Cracked wheat
Couscous
Triticale
Cornmeal
Hominy grits
Whole wheat flour
Soy flour

Thickeners
Cornstarch

Seasonings or Flavor Accents
Soy sauce
Vinegar
Wine

Leaveners
Yeast

Oils
Corn
Soy
Wheat germ

Perishables
Mushrooms
Cheeses
Milk and milk products
Corn
Eggs
Tofu

Sweeteners
Sugar
Corn syrup

Other
Popping corn
Corn pasta

* In addition to the Elimination Shopping List.

Immune Power Substitutions

The following lists of substitutes should help you out when you need to eliminate one of the Sinister Seven from your meal planning.

WHEAT FLOUR SUBSTITUTES

*Thickeners**

Instead of	*Substitute*
1 tablespoon wheat flour	1 tablespoon quick-cooking tapioca
	or
	1½ teaspoons arrowroot

*Thickeners**

Instead of	*Substitute*
2 tablespoons wheat flour	1 tablespoon barley flour
	or
	1 tablespoon cornstarch
	or
	1 tablespoon potato flour
3 tablespoons wheat flour	1 tablespoon buckwheat flour
1 cup wheat flour	1 cup minus 2 tablespoons rice flour

* Not to be used for baking.

Self-Rising Flour Mix for Wheat-Flour Allergy

To be used as a substitute for wheat flour for making pancakes, biscuits, and fruit quick breads.

Sift together:
½ cup cornstarch flour,
½ cup rye, rice or potato flour
2 teaspoons baking powder

IMMUNE POWER SUBSTITUTES
FOR OTHER COMMON STAPLES

Instead of	*Substitute*
Cow's milk cheeses	Goat and sheep cheese
Cow's milk	Soy milk (if allowed)
Wine (for cooking)	Chicken or vegetable broth, tomato juice
Wheat crackers	Rye wafers, rice cakes
Wheat pasta	Mung vermicelli, buckwheat noodles, corn pasta (if allowed)
Corn	Peas, carrots, lima beans
Corn syrup (as sweetener)	Fruit juice concentrate, honey (1 tablespoon syrup equals 1 tablespoon honey)
Cornstarch	Barley flour, buckwheat flour, rice flour, potato flour, arrowroot, etc.
Cane sugar (table sugar, brown sugar, confectioner's sugar, etc.)	Honey (5 tablespoons sugar plus 1 tablespoon water equals 4 tablespoons honey), fruit juice concentrate

Immune Power Equipment

There's no need to throw out all your pots and pans when you follow the Immune Power Eating Plan, but a few basic kitchen helps are essential for nutritious, successful cooking:

- Measuring spoons
- Glass measuring cups (1-, 2-, and/or 4-cup sizes)
- Nested or graduated measuring cups (¼-, ⅓-, ½-, and 1-cup sizes)
- Nonstick saucepans (1-, 2-, and 3-quart) with covers
- Nonstick saucepots (5- and 10-quart) with covers
- Dutch oven (5- or 6-quart) with cover
- Nonstick skillets (7-, 10-, and 12-inch) with covers
- Wok
- Nonstick casseroles (1½-, 2-, and 3-quart sizes) with covers
- Shallow metal or glass baking pans (13 x 9 x 2 inch, 12 x 8 x 2 inch, and 8 x 8 inch)
- Loaf pan (9 x 5 x 3 inch)
- Muffin tins (6-cup, 2½-inch size)
- Mixing bowls (2-cup to 6-quart size)
- Steamer
- Potato ricer or masher
- Wire whisk
- Blender and/or food processor
- Garlic press
- A set of knives (8-inch chef's knife, 6-inch slicer or utility knife, and 3-inch paring knife)
- Kitchen scale
- Parchment paper (If you can't find parchment paper in your grocery store, try the cooking section of a department store, a gourmet food shop, or a mail-order cooking supplies company.)

CHAPTER 6

Immune Power Ingredients

THERE IS NOTHING limiting about the Immune Power Diet, and you don't have to be an expert chef or nutritionist to explore the culinary possibilities associated with Immune Power cooking.

However, a certain familiarity with the most common ingredients can be extremely helpful to you as you plan, shop, and prepare meals, so this chapter provides an overview of the foods you'll be eating in the Immune Power Diet. This should tell you what you need to know to start cooking the Immune Power way.

Greens

A tempting array of greens for use in making salads is available in today's markets. For some salads, you'll want to use a single variety of greens, but when few or no extras are to be added, it's best to choose a combination of two or more greens to give contrast in color, flavor, and texture.

Salad Greens (can be used interchangeably or together)

Leaf lettuce
Romaine
Oak-leaf lettuce
Chicory
Butter or Boston lettuce
Iceberg lettuce
Belgian endive

Escarole
Watercress
Spinach
Radicchio
Red-leaf lettuce
Bibb lettuce

Extra Greens to Add Interest to a Salad

Chives	Dandelion greens
Leeks	Fennel
Scallions	Mint
Beet tops	Nasturtium leaves
Parsley	Arugula
Mustard greens	

Chinese Greens to Explore

Greens	Uses
Chinese spinach	As a substitute for spinach
Chinese cabbage (Napa)	Boil, steam, stir-fry
Chrysanthemum leaves	Add to stir-fry
Water spinach	As a substitute for ordinary spinach
Chinese chives	Add to salads, omelettes, soups, pasta
Bok choy	Boil, steam, sauté, stir-fry; add to soups
Peking cabbage	Boil, steam, braise, stir-fry; add to salads; stuff leaves

When shopping for salad greens, keep the following in mind:

- Buy crisp, firm lettuce with bright-colored leaves that show no sign of wilting or decay.
- Avoid overly wet or watered lettuce.
- Check for edges that are turning brown.
- Look for well-trimmed heads—large outer leaves have to be discarded.
- Choose a head that's "heavy" for its size; lighter heads may have loose inner leaves.
- A pound of iceberg contains about 10 cups of pieces; a pound of romaine has about 16 cups; and a pound of chicory has about 12 cups.

Caring for Salad Greens

Always handle greens tenderly, so that they won't bruise. It's best to wash them the day before you plan to serve in order to give them time to chill and crisp. Wash greens quickly but thoroughly in running water. Remove wilted leaves, but do not separate the heads. Stand them upside down on a clean towel to drain for not more than thirty minutes; then gently shake off any excess moisture in a lettuce basket, salad spinner, or towel. Wrap greens in a damp towel or put them into a plastic bag or special compartment in the refrigerator until they are chilled and crisp.

Just before serving, pat off any excess moisture and tear the crisp, dry greens into bite-sized pieces (1 serving = 2 cups pieces). Use a glass, plastic, ceramic, or wooden bowl. (A wide shallow bowl is best for green salads so the leaves won't pack or crush.)

Fish

For subtle flavor and texture, nothing can approach a fresh fish, so the first rule in shopping is to buy the freshest fish available. When a recipe requires a particular fish that is not available, substitute another appropriate fresh fish (see chart on page 70).

In selecting fresh fish, reject any that have a fishy odor; this is an early sign of decomposition. A truly fresh fish will have a mild, almost sweet smell, faintly marine if it is an ocean fish. The exceptions are shark, skate, and ray, which may emit a smell of ammonia. This smell is natural and will disappear after about two days of storage.

In shopping for whole fish, look for:

- Firm, elastic flesh that springs back when pressed with a finger
- Clear, protruding eyes with black pupils
- Bright red gills
- Shiny, tightly adhering scales

In shopping for fish fillets and steaks, look for:

- A moist, translucent appearance (if the flesh is dry-looking, milky white, or discolored around the edges, it is past its prime)

In some markets, you will find that frozen fish are your only choice, but here too sharp-eyed shopping is necessary. If a dealer is careless, frozen fish may thaw and refreeze repeatedly, losing flavor and perhaps even becoming spoiled. Reject any frozen fish packages that have torn wrapping, misshapen boxes, or ice around the edges. Blood in a package indicates that a fish has thawed and been refrozen.

Of course, there will be time when the only fish available is canned—tuna and salmon are America's favorites. Be sure to buy water-packed tuna and salmon *with* bones.

Storing Fish

At home, treat your fish with great care. Ideally, fresh fish should be cooked and eaten immediately. If the fish must be stored, cover it loosely with plastic wrap and keep it in the coldest part of your refrigerator—no longer than two days. Frozen fish should be kept in a freezer rigorously maintained at 0°F. (−18°C.); the storage period should be no longer than three months in the case of fatty fish and six months for lean fish (see charts on pages 67–70).

Fish Cookery

Fish are cooked by the same methods used for meat—frying, broiling, poaching, braising, and so on. But the cooking time differs considerably. Whereas some cuts of meat are tough and require long cooking to become tender, *all* fish are naturally tender and require relatively brief cooking. The amount of fibrous connective tissue in fish is much less than in meat, and it breaks down more rapidly when exposed to heat. By the same token, too much heat quickly damages fish, causing it to shrink, toughen, and flake apart. The methods of preparing fish that we recommend for the Immune Power Diet are broiling, baking, poaching, and steaming.

Fortunately, a simple and reliable method for estimating the proper cooking time for fish has been developed by the Canadian Department of Fisheries: *the one-inch rule.* Measure the fish at its thickest point and allow 10 minutes of cooking time for every inch (2½ cm.) of thickness if the fish is fresh, 20 minutes for every inch if it is frozen. (Frozen fish may be cooked without defrosting; if you wish to defrost fish, thaw it in the refrigerator and calculate the cooking time as for fresh fish.)

There are many variables in cooking fish—inaccurate ovens, for example, or the temperature of the fish when cooking begins—so you should always test a fish for doneness too. Here's how: *For a whole fish,* cut into the thickest part of the fish with a knife; if the flesh is opaque and does not cling to the bones, it's done. Or you can check the internal temperature of a large whole fish with a rapid-response thermometer. It will register 140°F. (60°C.) when the fish is cooked to perfection. *For a steak* or *fillet*, if the flesh flakes easily when pressed with a fork, it is done.

Lean Sea Fish

The saltwater fish listed below are lean—their fat content is less than 5 percent—and almost all have firm, mild-flavored, white flesh. Their lack of fat means fewer calories, but there is a drawback too—the flesh can dry out easily during cooking. Cooking methods that supply extra moisture—poaching, steaming, sautéeing, and baking in parchment—are therefore the classic treatments for flounder, bass, and other nonoily fish.

Cod
  Whiting
  Haddock
  Pollock
  Atlantic cod
  Cusk

Flatfish
  Petrole
  Dover sole
  Pacific halibut
  Flounder
  Lemon sole
  Greenland turbot

Porgy
  Scup
  Sheepshead

Red Snapper

Drum
  White sea bass
  Croaker
  Spot
  Red drum
  Spotted sea trout

Sea Bass
  White perch
  Black sea bass
  Grouper
  Sea bass
  Striped bass

Rockfish
  Ocean perch
  Vermilion
  Rockfish

Wolfish
  Catfish

Other
  Monkfish
  Tilefish
  Dolphin

Less Lean Sea Fish

These saltwater fish contain enough fat or oil to make their flesh darker, richer, and stronger tasting than that of very lean salt-water fish. Their fat or oil content ranges from 5 to 35 percent. These fish are particularly suited to dry-heat cooking: broiling, baking, and grilling. Frying a fatty fish can yield too rich a dish; only those lowest in fat (such as salmon) should be poached.

Swordfish
Sablefish
Silversides
Herring
Shad
Smelt
Butterfish or Pacific pompano
Florida pompano
Salmon
Bluefish
Tuna
  Albacore
  Bonito
Mackerel

Fresh-Water Fish

The fat content of fresh-water fish varies widely, from 1.2 percent to 52 percent, depending on the species, habitat, diet, and whether or not the fish are spawning.

Lean	Not So Lean
Carp	Lake whitefish
White sucker	Chub
Lake herring	Lake trout
Rainbow trout	Catfish
Brown trout	
Cutthroat trout	
Burbob	
Perch	
Pike	
Bream	
Bass	
Crappie	
Rainbow smelt	

Fish Substitutes

Any fish within a group can be successfully substituted for any other fish in the group.

GROUP I

Black bass
Black bullhead
Bluegill
Crappie, black and white
Sunfish
Rock bass
White perch
Yellow bass
Yellow perch

Bluefish (snapper size)
Kingfish
Pompano
Porgy, scup, spadefish
Smelt, silversides, white-
    bait, grunion
Snapper
Spot, croaker
Surf perch

GROUP II

Bass: kelp, rock, sand, striped
Black drum
Blackfish
Catfish, bullhead
Codfish, cusk, haddock, hake, pollock
Seatrout
Grouper
Halibut (California)
Ling cod
Monkfish
Ocean whitefish
Perch: ocean, seaperch

Pike
Pompano
Porgy
Redfish (drum)
Rockfish
Seabass
Striped bass
Sheepshead, Atlantic, Pa-
    cific
Snapper
Tilefish
White seabass

GROUP III

Albacore
Bluefish
Bonito
Butterfish
Cisco
Herring
Mackerel: small, king, cero
Mahi mahi (dolphin)

Mullet
Sablefish
Salmon
Shad
Smelt
Trout
Whitefish
Yellowtail

GROUP IV

Cobia

Giant black seabass

Grouper

Marlin

Northern halibut

Shark

Snook

Sturgeon

Swordfish

Tuna

Shellfish

The term *shellfish* refers to crustaceans (crab, lobsters, and shrimp) and mollusks (clams, oysters, mussels, and scallops). Shellfish are rich in minerals and protein and low in calories, but some, particularly shrimp and lobsters, are high in cholesterol. These sea creatures can be cooked either in or out of their shells, in the traditional fish-cooking methods. Boiling is a common technique for cooking them in the shell, and they adapt well to steaming, broiling, and especially sautéeing. Shellfish need only be cooked until their protein coagulates. That means just a few minutes for the smaller shellfish and 15 to 20 minutes for the very large crabs and lobsters. Overcooking toughens their flesh.

Remember that some lump crab meat is mixed with wheat flour and sometimes egg white, and can do harm to those sensitive to these foods.

Poultry

Poultry means any type of domesticated bird—chicken, turkey, duck, and goose being the most popular. Duck and goose have a high fat content and are thus not appropriate for the Immune Power Diet, so we'll concentrate on chicken and turkey.

Chicken and turkey offer a remarkable balance of nutrients, and they're also excellent sources of top-quality protein—rich in the essential amino acids that are indispensable for building, maintaining, and replacing the body's tissues, muscles, and cells. As a bonus, both are low in saturated fats. Supermarkets now have a vast array of fresh chicken and turkey parts available, ranging from boneless cutlets and thighs to whole birds.

Cooking Poultry

One of the best things about chicken and turkey is the variety of ways in which they can be prepared. They marry well with an infinite variety of ingredients. For the Immune Power Diet we recommend broiling, poaching, and roasting. We also recommend that whenever possible, you remove the fat and skin before cooking.

Keeping Poultry Fresh

It's usually just a matter of hours after the chicken has been inspected that it appears in the supermarket case. When kept under refrigeration, the chicken will retain maximum quality in the store for seven days or more. To maintain maximum freshness and quality, tray-packed chicken should not be kept more than 2 days in the coldest part of the home refrigerator. If you plan to keep it longer, freeze it.

The same goes for turkey. The newer market forms—cutlets, thighs, tenderloins, drumsticks, and wings—are usually sold in the fresh meat department and should be treated the same as chicken. Whole turkeys are sold either fresh or frozen. Defrost the frozen ones in the refrigerator, not at room temperature. Avoid turkeys that are self-basting. The ingredients in the basting liquid can contain substances that might harm your Immune Power.

Meat

Beef and pork are not allowed on the Elimination or Reintroduction Diets. However, during the Maintenance phase, they can be served occasionally. I recommend eating red meats no more than once a week. For the average person, this may be hard to do, so I suggest that you gradually replace meats with poultry, fish, shellfish, legumes, and grains. As a first step, start thinking of meat as an accompaniment rather than the main feature of the meal. By gradually reducing the amount of beef, pork, and lamb to 2 to 4 ounces per day and stretching that portion with grains and vegetables, you can experience a smooth transition.

Select only lean, well-trimmed cuts of meat with a minimum amount of marbling (the white visible fat that runs through the red meat). The lean cuts are:

Beef: Chuck: Pot roast or steak
                      Flank steak
        Ground round or chuck
        Steaks: Porterhouse, T-bone, sirloin, and tenderloin
        Roasts: Bottom, rump, or top round
Veal: All well-trimmed cuts
Pork: Lean, well-trimmed fresh ham
        Loin rib or chop
Lamb: Leg
        Loin chop or roast
        Shank
        Shoulder chop or roast

Storing Meat

As soon as you bring meat home, open the wrappings and rewrap the meat loosely. This allows air to circulate freely, drying the surface of the meat and retarding the growth of bacteria. Store in the coldest part of the refrigerator.

To store a cooked roast, let it cool thoroughly before putting it in the refrigerator. If you don't, when the hot meat encounters the cool refrigerator air, a steamy cloud will form, and that will encourage the growth of bacteria. Cover cooked meats loosely to permit air circulation.

Cooking Meat

The cooking methods we recommend are roasting, pan-broiling, and stewing/braising.

Roasting. Some cooks prefer to start roasting at 500°F., and then reduce the heat to 325°F. after the meat is seared and has browned. However, a consistent temperature of 325°F. (or 350°F. for pork) seems to reduce shrinkage and remove more fat. Always preheat the oven and roast the meat on a rack in a shallow pan.

Take the meat out of the oven when the thermometer registers 10 degrees less than is called for. Set it on a warm platter or a carving board and cover loosely with a tent of foil. The meat will continue to cook for the next 15 minutes while the juices settle; it will also be easier to carve if it's allowed to rest for a while.

Broiling. Remove the broiler rack and preheat the broiler. If the meat is very lean, rub the rack with oil. Score the edges of the meat by making shallow cuts in the outside every 2 inches to prevent curling while it cooks. For most meats the rack should be set 3 inches below the broiler element (usually the highest rung); for very thick steaks the rack should be placed lower down.

Cook on one side until nicely brown—the cooking time will depend on the thickness of the meat—then turn and cook on the other side. When the meat is nearly done, remove it from the rack, and place, loosely covered with foil, on a carving board. As with roasts it will finish cooking in its own heat.

Pan-broiling. Use a nonstick skillet that heats evenly and will not scorch. If the meat is lean, brush the surface of the pan with oil. Heat the pan, and when the surface looks wavy, add the meat. Brown it quickly until the blood rises to the top surface, then turn and sear the other side. Pour off any fat that accumulates.

Remove to a hot platter as soon as the meat is done; it will toughen if it overcooks. Add a little broth or water to deglaze the pan and pour sauce over the pan-broiled meat.

Stewing and braising. Some of the world's great dishes are made by stewing or braising tough cuts of meat slowly and gently in aromatic liquid until they are tender. Usually the meat is browned first, then a well-seasoned liquid—broth, tomato juice, water, or a combination of these—is added, and the pot is tightly covered and set in a slow oven or over a gentle burner for several hours. The trick is to keep the liquid just at a simmer—not over 185°F.—for the entire cooking time. Boiling toughens the meat fibers.

The resulting gravy is apt to contain a considerable amount of fat. To remove every last bit of fat, let the gravy chill so that the fat comes to the top and solidifies. Reheat to serve.

Testing Meat for Doneness

Recipe directions and charts for roasting and broiling meat can give only approximations about doneness. Cooking times will vary not only according to weight but also according to shape (a long, thin roast cooks more quickly than a short, fat roast), the amount of marbling fat, and whether or not it has been boned. Always bring meat to room temperature before cooking, and preheat the oven or broiler.

When the recommended time is almost up, start testing with a microwave thermometer—by far the most accurate kind. Stick it into the center of the meat, avoiding any bone, and you'll get an immediate reading.

Here are some good old-fashioned methods for testing meat. (1) Prod it with your finger. If the meat feels soft, it is rare; if it is hard, it is well done. Medium falls somewhere in between. (2) A more persistent nudge will make juices flow. If they are red, the meat is still bloody-rare; if they are pink, it is medium: if they run clear, it is well done. Pork juices, of course, should always run clear—and to be safe, test pork with a meat thermometer.

Grains

Grains are essentially the seeds of various grassy plants. Since it is a seed, the whole grain contains all the nutrients of the plant, ready to sprout to create a new plant. Most grains especially rich in protein, the B vitamins, and vitamin E. Grains are also low in fat. Whole grains are a good source of dietary fiber.

There are several ways to use grains. Most can be cooked in water or stock with herbs or other seasonings for a tasty side dish or for use in salads, casseroles, or soups. They can also be used raw in baking. A blender will process small quantities of raw oats, wheat, or barley to add to breads, pancakes, or muffins, but a proper home grain mill is required for grinding larger amounts of grains.

General Tips for Cooking Grains

- As a general rule, use twice as much water as grain.
- Do not stir grains while they cook, because they may become sticky.
- For a richer, nuttier flavor, toast the grain before cooking. Place it in a dry pan over low heat for 10 to 15 minutes, and shake pan occasionally to prevent burning.
- Remember that the smaller the pieces of grain are, the faster they will cook.
- Using a microwave oven for cooking grains is not recommended.

Table 12: Cooking Grains

Grain (1 cup)	Description	Boiling Water	Directions	Yield
BUCKWHEAT (KASHA)	*Buckwheat groats* Seeds from a type of grass; cook for side dish, salad; grind into flour	2 cups	Simmer, covered, for 10 minutes; stir; cook covered until liquid is absorbed (3–5 minutes).	3½ cups
OATS	*Regular rolled oats* Pressed, papery grains of oat; use for cereals, baking	2 cups	Simmer, uncovered, for 5 to 8 minutes; let stand before serving.	2 cups
	Quick-cooking rolled oats	2 cups	Simmer, uncovered, for 1 minute. Cover; let stand 3 to 5 minutes.	2 cups
	Steel-cut oats Whole oat kernels cut into lengthwise pieces	2½ cups	Simmer, covered, for 15 to 20 minutes.	3 cups
RYE	*Cracked rye* Strong-tasting, bitter; grind raw for flour	2½ cups	Simmer, covered, for 10 to 15 minutes. Cover; let stand 5 minutes.	2⅔ cups
	*Rye berries** Whole rye kernels; may be ground raw for rye flour	3 cups	Simmer, covered, for 1 hour.	2½ cups
MILLET	*Millet* Bland-tasting grain; can be used in place of rice; grind for flour to add to baking	2 cups	Simmer, covered, for 25 to 30 minutes or until all water is absorbed.	3½ cups

Table 12: Cooking Grains (cont.)

Grain (1 cup)	Description	Boiling Water	Directions	Yield
BARLEY	*Pearl barley* Grains with hulls not completely removed, brownish; excellent in soups, casseroles; grind for flour	4 cups	Simmer, covered, for 45 minutes. Drain	3½ cups
	Quick-cooking barley	2 cups	Simmer, covered, for 10 to 12 minutes.	2½ cups
CORN	*Cornmeal* Finely ground corn, cook for cereal and side dishes; dry for baking	2¾ cups	Combine cornmeal and 1 cup cold water. Add to the boiling water. Simmer, covered, for 10 to 15 minutes.	4 cups
	Quick-cooking hominy grits	4 cups	Simmer, covered, for 5 to 6 minutes.	2 cups
WILD RICE	*Wild rice* A grass seed with a nutty flavor; mix with rice, soups, casseroles	3 cups	Simmer, covered, for 40 to 50 minutes.	3 cups
RICE	*Brown rice* Long-grain, parboiled	2⅔ cups	Simmer, covered, for 40 to 50 minutes.	3 to 4 cups
TRITICALE	*Triticale Berries** A high-protein, hybrid wheat; cook as cereal; grind as flour	3 cups	Simmer, covered, for 45 minutes.	2 cups

Grain (1 cup)	Description	Boiling Water	Directions	Yield
WHEAT	*Wheat berries** Hard wheat, high in gluten; grind for bread flour; chewy when cooked	3 cups	Simmer, covered, for 1 hour.	2½ cups
	Bulgur wheat Precooked cracked wheat grains; soak but don't cook to use in salads, cook as pilaf; soak to add to baking	2 cups	Simmer, covered, for 12 to 15 minutes.	3 cups
	Cracked wheat Coarsely ground unpolished wheat kernels	2½ cups	Simmer, uncovered, for 15 to 20 minutes. Cover; let stand 5 minutes.	2⅔ cups
	Ready-to-cook couscous Tiny pellets of semolina with floury coating	1½ cups	Pour boiling water over couscous; cover. Remove from heat; let stand 5 minutes.	2⅔ cups

* Soak overnight before cooking.
Note: For grains, one serving contains approximately one cup cooked grains. All grains except cornmeal and hominy grits may be cooked in broth instead of water.

Dried Legumes

All the legumes, or dried beans, are essentially seeds removed from their pods and dried. Dried beans are concentrated sources of nutrients—high in protein, carbohydrates, vitamins, and minerals. They are also low in fat.

There is an enormous variety of legumes. Each type has its own distinctive flavor, shape, and color. Flavors range from mellow and rich to nutlike, sweet, or even smoky. Some hold their shape well after cooking, while others melt into velvety purées. Beans can be added to soups, stews, and salads or baked with other vegetables and grains.

General Tips for Cooking Dried Beans

- Most (but not all) dried beans require soaking before cooking—follow directions on package.
- The amount of water and the length of time called for in cooking vary considerably (see Table 13). Some dried beans may be "drier" than others by virtue of having been in storage longer and may thus take longer to cook.
- Dried beans should cook slowly—the slower the better—so they hold their shape, become tender through and through, and taste better.
- Be sure your pot is large enough—beans will expand to three or four times their original volume.
- Do not cover the pot when you cook beans (the ingredients may boil over).
- Add salt only toward the end of cooking. Salt added early toughens beans.
- Dried beans may be cooked in a pressure cooker or a slow cooker, following the manufacturer's directions.
- Using a microwave oven to cook dried beans is not recommended. There is a good chance that the cooked beans will be tough, and there's even a possibility that they will explode.
- Cooked beans will keep in the refrigerator up to five days and may be frozen for future use.

The Basic Cooking Technique

1. Pick beans over to remove any bits of stone or foreign matter.
2. Rinse the beans.
3. Boil the beans for 5 minutes, then allow them to soak for 1 to 2 hours in cooking liquid.
4. Drain beans, add the required amount of water, stock, or other liquid, and bring the beans to a simmer. Skim any froth from the surface from time to time.

5. Beans are done when they are completely tender but not falling apart (see approximate cooking times in Table 13). Drain and rinse.

Table 13: Cooking Dried Beans*

Type of Bean	Description	Uses	Cups Liquid per Cup Beans	Cooking Time
Adzuki	Small, round, reddish-brown	Pastry fillings, sweet purées, Oriental cooking	3	45 min.– 1 hour
Black beans (also called turtle beans)	Medium-small, oval, shiny black	Mexican or Spanish dishes, soups, purées	4	1½ hours
Black-eyed peas	Medium, oval, cream with black spot	Southern dishes, with pork, with rice, casseroles	3	1 hour
Fava beans— whole	Large, round, flat off-white or tan	Casseroles, soups, salads	2½	1½ hours
Fava beans— mini	Medium, round, flat, off-white or tan	Salads, casseroles, soups, side dishes	2	1 hour
Garbanzos (also called chick-peas)	Medium, round with an indentation, creamy-beige	Hummus, falafel, and other Middle East dishes; soups, casseroles, salads, purées	4	3 hours
Great northern beans (white beans)	Medium, round to oval, white	Soups, baked beans, casseroles, salads	3	2 hours
Kidney beans	Medium, oval, pinkish to red-brown	Mexican dishes, chili, refried beans, salads, casseroles, purées	3	2 hours
Lentils–green	Small, round, flat, greenish	Stews, casseroles, pilaf, soups, salads, purées	3	45 min.
Lentils—split red	Small, round, very flat, red-orange	Casseroles, Indian dishes, soups, salads, purées	3	20–25 min.
Lima beans—large	Large, flat, oval, white or greenish	Casseroles, purées, soups	2	1½ hours
Lima beans—baby	Medium, flat, oval, white or greenish	Casseroles, soups, with lamb, side dishes, purées	2	1 hour

Table 13: Cooking Dried Beans (cont.)

Type of Bean	Description	Uses	Cups Liquid per Cup Beans	Cooking Time
Navy beans (also called pea beans)	Small to medium, round to oval, white	Casseroles, cassoulet, Boston baked beans, soups, side dishes, salads	3	2 hours
Whole peas	Medium-small, round, yellow	Scandinavian dishes, casseroles, soups, purées	3	1 hour
Split peas	Small, round, flat, green or yellow	Soups, purées	3	1 hour
Pinto beans	Medium, oval, speckled pink and white	Italian, Spanish, Mexican dishes; casseroles, chili	3	2 hours
Soybeans	Medium, round, creamy yellow	Used for making tofu, in casseroles, stewed	4	3½ hours
Soybeans—green	Medium, plump, oval, green (more tender, less starchy than regular soybeans)	Salads, casseroles, as a side dish, soups	4	3½ hours

* For 4 servings, plan to cook 1 cup raw beans.

Vegetables

From artichokes to zucchini, vegetables come in more colors and varieties than any other category of foods, and all of them can add flavor, texture, and nutrition to your meals.

Table 14 provides hints on selecting and cooking a large assortment of vegetables. However, whenever possible, eat vegetables raw; cooking causes a loss of nutrients.

General Tips for Cooking Vegetables

• Cook vegetables just until they're tender-crisp. The less time you cook them, the more vitamins are retained. Exceptions to this rule are potatoes, hard-shelled squashes, and other root vegetables.

- If you prefer your vegetables tender, cook them in liquid that can be eaten as soup. The cooking liquid contains all the vitamins.
- Vegetables will keep their natural color best if cooked in a small amount of water for a short amount of time.
- For maximum nutrient retention, cut vegetables thin for stir-frying and sautéeing so they can cook quickly.
- In a recipe containing several vegetables different shapes and sizes add textural interest and increase eating enjoyment.

Table 14: Selecting and Cooking Vegetables

Vegetable	Selection	Four Servings	Cooking Time
Artichokes	Select artichokes with tight, compact heads that feel heavy for their size. Surface brown spots are harmless.	4 medium to large	Steam: 45 min.
Asparagus	Select firm, brittle spears that are bright green almost the entire length, with tightly closed tips.	1½ to 2 pounds	Steam: 7–10 min. Simmer: 7–10 min.
Beans—green, Italian, wax	Choose crisp beans that are bright and blemish-free.	1 pound	Boil: 10–12 min. Steam: 10–15 min.
Beans, shelled—cranberry, fava, lima	Look for thick, broad, tightly closed pods that are bulging with large beans. Beans should look plump and fresh.	2½ to 3 pounds unshelled or 1 pound shelled	Boil: 10–15 min.
Beets	Select small to medium beets that are firm and have smooth skins.	1½ to 2 pounds	Simmer: 30–40 min.

Table 14: Selecting and Cooking Vegetables (cont.)

Vegetable	Selection	Four Servings	Cooking Time
Bok choy	Select crisp-looking, unblemished plants. Smaller plants are more tender.	1¼ to 1½ pounds	Steam 10–15 min. Braise: 10–15 min.
Broccoli	Look for compact clusters of tightly closed dark green flowerets. Avoid heads with thick, woody stems.	1 to 1½ pounds	Boil: 5 min. Steam: 8 min.
Brussels sprouts	Choose small, firm brussels sprouts that are compact and feel heavy for their size. They should be bright green and free of blemishes.	1¼ to 1½ pounds	Boil: 8–10 min. Steam: 8–10 min.
Cabbage—green, red, Savoy	Heads should be firm and feel heavy for their size. Outer leaves should have good color, be free of blemishes.	1 to 1½ pounds	Steam: 10–15 min. Braise: 10–12 min.
Carrots	Look for smooth, well-shaped, and brightly colored carrots, Tops should look fresh and be bright green.	1 pound	Simmer: Pieces, 7–10 min. Whole, 10–15 min.
Cauliflower	Heads should be firm, compact, creamy white, and pressed tightly together. Spreading flowerets indicate age. Leaves should be crisp and bright green.	1¼ to 1½ pounds	Flowerets: Simmer 8–12 min. Whole: Boil 20–30 min.
Celery	Select rigid, crisp, green stalks with fresh-looking leaves.	1½ pounds (1 medium-size bunch or 2 hearts)	Braise: 20–30 min.

Vegetable	Selection	Four Servings	Cooking Time
Celeriac	Select roots that are firm and relatively clean.	1 to 1½ pounds (3 small or 2 medium-size roots)	Boil: 40–50 min.
Corn	Ear should be well covered with plump young kernels, with fresh husks that are green and unwilted; silks free of decay.	4 large ears	Boil: 3–5 min.
Eggplant	Select smooth, firm eggplant, deep purple skin free of blemishes. Bright green stems.	1¼ to 1½ pounds (1 large or 2 small to medium)	Boil (cubes): 3–4 min. Steam (cubes): 5–8 min.
Garlic	Choose firm, dry bulbs with tightly closed cloves and smooth skins. Avoid bulbs with sprouting green shoots.	1 large clove	Steam: 10–15 min.
Leeks	Select leeks with clean, white bottoms and fresh-looking, crisp, green tops.	1½ pounds	Braise: 30–45 min. Steam: 20–30 min.
Onions, yellow	Firm and dry with small necks; no decay	1 pound	Braise: 30–45 min. Boil: 20–30 min.
Parsnips	Choose small to medium parsnips that are firm, smooth, well shaped. Avoid large woody parsnips.	1 pound	Whole: Boil 20–25 min. Pieces: Boil 5–10 min.
Peas, edible-pod	Look for firm crisp, bright green pods.	1 pound	Boil: 8–10 min. Steam: 8–10 min.
Peas, green (also called shell peas)	Crisp pods with fresh green color; pods full but not bulging.	2 to 2½ pounds unshelled (1 lb. unshelled yields about 1 cup shelled)	Boil: 8–10 min. Steam: 8–10 min.

Table 14: Selecting and Cooking Vegetables (cont.)

Vegetable	Selection	Four Servings	Cooking Time
Peppers, green or red bell	Look for peppers that are firm; deep color; no trace of flabbiness or decay.	3 or 4 medium to large	Bake: 30–45 min. Boil: 15–20 min.
Potatoes, russet	Firm; free from sunburned green areas; no decay; skin intact and free from blemishes.	4 medium to large	Bake: 60–75 min. Boil: 30–40 min.
Potatoes, sweet	Firm; good color; no signs of decay at ends.	4 medium to large	Bake: 45–60 min. Boil: 30–40 min.
Potatoes, thin-skinned (red and white "new")	Look for firm, well-shaped potatoes with reasonably smooth skins; avoid sprouting eyes and decay.	1½ pounds (4 medium)	Boil: 35–45 Steam: 45–55 min.
Radishes	Medium size; firm and plump; fresh red color	1 bunch	Best raw
Rutabagas	Choose small to medium rutabagas that are smooth and firm and feel heavy for their size. Lightweight rutabagas may be woody.	1½ to 2 pounds	Cubes: Braise 20–30 min Steam 20–30 min. Boil 15–20 min.
Spinach	Choose bunches having crisp, tender, deep green leaves, with few yellow leaves or blemishes.	1½ pounds	Steam: 7–10 min.
Squash (summer)	Well developed with no soft areas; firm; glossy and tender skin.	1 to 1½ pounds	Slices: Steam: 4–6 min. Whole: Boil 10–15 min.

Vegetable	Selection	Four Servings	Cooking Time
Squash (winter)	Well developed with no soft areas; firm; tough and hard skin.	1 to 1½ pounds	Braise: 15–20 min. Bake: 45–90 min. in conventional oven; 8–15 min. in microwave Steam: 8–10 min.
Sunchokes (also called Jerusalem artichokes)	Choose tubers that are firm and free of mold.	1 to 1½ pounds	Boil: 15–20 min.
Swiss chard	Look for fresh glossy, dark green leaves and heavy white or red stems.	1½ to 2 pounds	Steam: 4–6 min. Simmer: 3–5 min.
Tomatoes	Smooth; good color for stage or ripeness; firm if not fully ripe, but slightly soft if ripe; free from blemishes.	1 to 1½ pounds	Bake: 30–45 min. Broil: 8–10 min.
Turnips	Firm and smooth; free of blemishes.	1½ to 2 pounds	Simmer: 10–15 min. Steam: 20–25 min.

Nuts and Seeds

Nuts are soft, edible kernels that come surrounded by a hard shell. Most true nuts grow on trees, but not all the kernels we think of as nuts are true nuts. Some are seeds, and others, like peanuts, are actually a type of legume.

Nuts are very rich in nutrients—vitamins (especially A and B-complex), minerals (calcium, iron, phosphorus, potassium), and protein. Since they are also naturally high in fat, nuts are often processed for their oils. The fat contained in nuts is unsaturated, but nuts are still high in calories. (The one exception is the chestnut, which is very low in fat.)

When nuts are intended for snacking, serve them in the shell. Nuts in the shell are likely to be fresher, and they are less expensive.

Storing

Unshelled nuts last the longest. Store them at room temperature away from heat. Store shelled nuts in the refrigerator or, better still, the freezer. Whole nutmeats last longer than chopped nuts. Nuts also keep better if they have not been toasted or salted. Store seeds in a tightly closed container in a cool place.

Shelling

Some nuts, such as peanuts, almonds, and walnuts, are relatively easy to shell. Nuts with harder shells, such as Brazil nuts and pecans, will be easier to crack if they are soaked for 30 minutes in hot water. Soaking softens the shell slightly. Or try placing nuts in the freezer overnight to make the shell more brittle and easier to shatter.

Once a nut has been removed from the shell, it is still covered with a dark papery "skin." This skin adds flavor and nutrients and should be removed only if necessary. To lift off skins, dip nuts in hot water or toast them in the oven and then rub them together in a paper bag or a napkin.

Roasting

Nuts can be roasted either in or out of the shell. Spread on a baking sheet in a 350° oven for 15 to 20 minutes (unshelled) or 5 to 10 minutes (shelled). Watch them closely so they don't burn. Shelled nuts and seeds can also be toasted in a dry, heavy skillet on top of the stove over medium heat. Stir them to toast evenly. They may also be toasted in a 300° oven until brown.

Chopping

For best results, freeze nuts before you chop them. Then place nuts on a wooden board or in a wooden bowl and use a heavy, sharp knife or chopper to cut them into small pieces. Nuts can also be chopped in a food grinder or a food processor, but care must be taken so that they do not become too fine and pastelike. Seeds may be chopped with a knife or in a blender.

Table 15: Selecting Nuts and Seeds

Nuts and Seeds	How Sold	Uses
Almonds	Shelled whole, sliced, slivered In shell salted	Baking, pilafs, Oriental cooking, on fish, ground to paste or meal
Brazil nuts	In shell Shelled whole	Chopped, toasted, added to baking, grain dishes
Cashews	Raw whole/split Salted whole Salted fancy In shell	Indian cookery, salads, cookies ground into spread, spiced for snacking
Chestnuts	In shell (in season)	Must be roasted or boiled before using; shell, then braise or puree; use in stuffings, vegetable combinations, and desserts
Filberts (hazelnuts)	Shelled In shell	Chopped in casseroles, baking, snack mixes
Mixed nuts	In shell	For snacking
Peanuts	In shell raw/roasted Salted shelled Unsalted roasted	Soup, baking, as a garnish, ground snack mixes
Pecans	Shelled halves and pieces In shell salted	Baking, grain dishes
Pignoli (pine nuts)	Shelled whole	Stuffings, salads, pastas, snack mixes
Pistachios	In shell natural, salted or unsalted; In shell salted, red	Use natural unsalted in baking, confections, as a garnish; use salted for snacking

Table 15: Selecting Nuts and Seeds (cont.)

Nuts and Seeds	How Sold	Uses
Pumpkin seeds	Whole, shelled In shell	Snacking and in casseroles
Sunflower seeds	Hulled raw In shell	Snacking, in breads and casseroles
Walnuts	Shelled halves and pieces In shell Salted	Baking, casseroles, stuffings. Ground walnuts can be mixed with flours to dust on fish for frying and snack mixtures
Sesame seeds	Unhulled raw Hulled raw Toasted	In baking, cooking, salad dressings; on fish, chicken, vegetables

- For easy removal of whole spices, (dill seed, cloves, etc.), wrap them in a square of cheesecloth before adding to a recipe.
- Dishes meant to be served cold can be seasoned more heavily.
- Spice blends, such as curry and chili powders, should always be cooked a bit to remove the raw taste they often have.
- Season dishes meant for freezing very lightly—freezing can change flavors. Reseason the dish before reheating.

Herbs and Spices

Herbs and spices are the adornments of cooking. Sometimes their purpose is quite subtle—to highlight or sharpen the flavors in a dish. Other times, they are meant to add a lively, dominant flavor of their own. Whenever you can, cook with fresh herbs. A sprig or two added to a recipe provides an incomparable lift. You can buy fresh herbs in quantities and freeze them for later use. Just pop them—whole sprigs or chopped—into sealable plastic bags and place them in the freezer.

Dried Herbs and Spices

A little dried herb or spice can go a long way toward enhancing a dish, provided it hasn't been on your kitchen shelf for years. Here's how to make the most of these seasonings:

- Purchase dried herbs and spices frequently and in very small quantities—by the half-ounce or ounce.
- Store in small, air-tight containers away from heat. Strong or direct light can cause herbs and spices to fade, so keep containers inside a kitchen cabinet or wrap clear jars with a label that will cover most of the exposed area.
- Become accustomed to the distinctive aromas of the herbs and spices when they are new. That way, when yours begin to fade, you'll know when to replace them.
- Be adventurous! Try a new herb or spice at least once a week in the beginning of the Immune Power Diet. You can purchase very tiny samples at health food stores or specialty spice shops.

Herb Cookery

- Dried herbs are generally much more pungent than their fresh counterparts. Use one third to one half as much of a dried herb as fresh. Ground herbs are even more strongly flavored and should be used very sparingly.
- Flavors and aromas are released more readily if dried herbs are crushed lightly before using.
- Large pieces of herb, such as bay leaves or sprigs of rosemary, should be removed from a dish before it is served.
- Delicately flavored herbs such as basil, dill and *fines herbes* should be added during the last moments of cooking so the flavor will not dissipate. More pungent herbs such as thyme and rosemary should be added at the beginning of cooking.
- Add herbs and spices to poaching liquid—water, tomato juice, or broth—when cooking fish or chicken.

Spice Cookery

- The strength of a spice may change during cooking. Use spices sparingly.

- Use whole spices to flavor syrups, sauces, and drinks (ground spices cannot be removed easily and may make the mixture cloudy).
- For easy removal of whole spices, (dill seed, cloves, etc.), wrap them in a square of cheesecloth before adding to a recipe.
- Dishes meant to be served cold can be seasoned more heavily.
- Spice blends, such as curry and chili powders, should always be cooked a bit to remove the raw taste they often have.
- Season dishes meant for freezing very lightly—freezing can change flavors. Reseason the dish before reheating.

Table 16: Using Herbs and Spices

	Appetizers	Soups	Salads and Salad Dressings	Vegetables	Poultry and Fish
ALLSPICE	Cranberry Relish, Spiced Nuts, Swedish Meatballs	Asparagus, Fruit, Pea Tomato, Chicken, Minestrone	Fruit, Tomato Aspic	Sweet Potatoes, Squash, Beets, Carrots, Eggplant, Baked Beans, Spinach	Poached Fish, Spiced Shrimp, Chicken
BASIL LEAVES	Meatballs, Marinated Mushrooms	Pea, Tomato, Lentil, Minestrone, Vegetable	Herb Dressing, Seafood, Tossed Greens, Tomato Aspic, Potato	Eggplant, Carrots, Spinach, Tomatoes, Cauliflower, Peas, Potatoes, Squash	Chicken, Turkey, Shrimp, Lobster Stuffings
BAY LEAVES	Artichokes or Mushrooms, Tomato Juice, Marinated Fish	Tomato, Gumbo, Clam Chowder, Onion, Chicken, Lobster, Vegetable	Herb Dressing, Seafood, Tomato Aspic	In water when cooking most vegetables; Pickled Beets, Rice	Poached Fish, Shrimp Creole, Stewed Chicken, Spiced Shrimp
CARAWAY SEED		Pea, Potato, Borscht, Vegetable	Cucumber, Coleslaw	Beets, Potatoes, Beans, Cauliflower, Cabbage, Carrots, Squash	Tuna Casserole, Beef, Chicken, Stuffings

	Appetizers	Soups	Salads and Salad Dressings	Vegetables	Poultry and Fish
CARDAMOM SEED	Fruit Cocktail, Spiced Nuts	Fruit, Green Pea	Fruit Dressings for Fruit Salads	Squash, Rice, Baked Beans, Sweet Potatoes	Poached Fish
RED PEPPER (Cayenne)	Guacamole, Tomato Juice, Spreads	Tomato Soup, Oyster Stew, Vegetable Soup, Chowders	Cucumber, Seafood, Coleslaw, Kidney Bean	Onions, Broccoli, Eggplant, Potatoes, Asparagus	Turkey Pie, Chicken, Deviled Crab or Lobster, Crab Cakes
CELERY SALT, SEED, or FLAKES	Tomato Juice	Pea, Lentil, Celery, Tomato, Vegetable, Asparagus, Oyster	Dressing for Fruit Salads, Tomato Aspic	Potatoes, Broccoli, Onions, Tomatoes, Okra, Asparagus	Turkey, Cornish Hens, Chicken, Goose, Broiled Fish, Tuna Casseroles, Stuffings
CHILI POWDER	Guacamole	Chowders, Pea, Tomato, Pepperpot	Kidney Bean	Rice, Eggplant, Baked Beans, Onions, Tomatoes, Carrots	Seafood Casseroles, Chicken with Rice
CINNAMON	Fruit Cocktail, Spiced Nuts, Broiled Grapefruit, Cereal Nibblers	Chicken, Vegetable, Tomato, Fruit	Dressings for Fruit Salads, Mixed Fruit, Waldorf Salad	Beets, Rice, Carrots, Sweet Potatoes, Squash, Asparagus, Spinach, Broiled Bananas	Poached Fish, Spiced Shrimp, Stewed Chicken
CLOVES	Spiced Nuts, Tomato Juice, Cranberry Relish	Pea, Vegetable, Clam Chowder, Bean, Tomato	Dressings for Fruit Salads, Tomato Aspic, Frozen Fruit, Mixed Fruit	Baked Beans, Rice, Sweet Potatoes, Squash, Onions, Beets, Tomatoes	Poached Fish, Crab Cakes, Baked Fish, Spiced Shrimp, Chicken Casseroles
CURRY POWDER	Meatballs, Chicken Balls, Cereal Nibblers	Curry, Mulligatawny	French Dressing, Seafood	Squash, Rice, Vegetable Casseroles	Chicken, Turkey, Oysters, Shrimp, Lobster

Table 16: Using Herbs and Spices (cont.)

	Appetizers	Soups	Salads and Salad Dressings	Vegetables	Poultry and Fish
DILL	Meatballs, Spreads, Dips	Fish, Chicken, Potato, Pea	Herb and Cheese Dressings, Seafood Cucumber, and Potato Salads	Beans, Cabbage, Potatoes, Squash	Broiled and Poached Fish, Poultry, Shrimp
GINGER	Spiced Nuts, Beef Teriyaki, Rumaki, Spreads for Fruit or Nut Breads, Broiled Grapefruit	Carrot, Onion, Chicken, Fish Chowders	Dressings for Fruit Salads, Mixed Fruit, Frozen Fruit	Beets, Carrots, Sweet Potatoes, Squash, Baked Beans	Shellfish, Baked Fish, Turkey, Chicken Casseroles, Roast Chicken, Stir-fries
MARJORAM	Meatballs, Pizza, Tomato Juice, Mushrooms, Marinated Artichokes	Turtle, Onion, Tomato, Minestrone, Scotch Broth, Vegetable, Spinach	Tomato Aspic, Tossed Greens, Herb Dressing	Carrots, Peas, Beans, Broccoli, Cauliflower, Zucchini, Spinach, Brussels Sprouts	Spiced Shrimp, Baked Fish, Crab Cakes, Chicken, Broiled Fish, Stuffings
MUSTARD SEED or DRY MUSTARD	Dips, Meatballs, Tomato Juice	Chicken, Vegetable, Chowders, Tomato, Lentil, Potato	Rice, Italian Dressing	Cauliflower, Onions, Baked Beans, Potato, Asparagus	Cornish Hens, Seafood, Fish, Chicken, Turkey
NUTMEG and MACE	Liver Paté, Canapés, Spiced Nuts, Meatballs	Fruit Soup, Split Pea, Spinach, Chowders, Oyster Stew, Vegetable, Chicken	Dressings for Fruit Salads, Mixed Fruit, Frozen Fruit, Waldorf Salad	Sweet Potatoes, Squash, Carrots, Green Beans, Spinach, Broccoli, Asparagus	Chicken, Turkey, Cornish Hens, Fish, Seafood
OREGANO	Pizza, Meatballs, Marinated Artichokes, Tomato Juice	Tomato, Lentil, Minestrone, Vegetable, Onion, Chowders	Tuna, Salmon, Tossed Greens, Tomato Aspic	Carrots, Spinach, Beans, Potatoes, Tomatoes, Eggplant, Squash, Peas, Turnips	Broiled Fish, Baked Fish, Tuna Casseroles, Chicken, Stuffings

	Appetizers	Soups	Salads and Salad Dressings	Vegetables	Poultry and Fish
PAPRIKA	Garnish for Stuffed Celery, Canapés, Dips	Garnish for most soups	Garnish for Tuna, Chicken	Garnish for Onions, Asparagus, Potatoes, Carrots, Cauliflower,	Chicken Paprika, Garnish for Poultry and Fish, Excellent browning agent for Fish or Fried Chicken
PARSLEY FLAKES	Artichokes or Marinated Mushrooms	Garnish for most soups	Herb Dressing, Chicken, Tuna	Tomatoes, Carrots, Potatoes, Onions, Eggplant, Peas, Rice, Cauliflower	Broiled Fish, Croquettes Baked Fish, Spiced Shrimp, Chicken, Stuffings
PICKLING SPICE	Artichokes or Fish, Cauliflower, Marinated Mushrooms	Vegetable, Beef Broth, Tomato	Herb Dressing, Tomato Aspic	Beets	Boiled Shrimp, Stewed Chicken
POPPY SEED	Garnish, Spreads		Dressings for Fruit Salads, Mixed Fruit	Sweet Potatoes, Squash, Rice, Potatoes, Carrots, Turnips, Asparagus	Tuna Casseroles, Chicken Livers, Stuffings, Chicken Casseroles
POULTRY SEASONING	Chicken Spread, Meatballs	Split Pea, Minestrone, Chicken, Lentil, Bean	Seafood, Turkey, Chicken	Green Beans, Lima Beans, Onions, Eggplant	Turkey, Chicken, Stuffings
ROSEMARY	Fruit Juice, Tomato Juice, Liver Paté	Beef Broth, Chicken, Vegetable, Tomato, Pea, Minestrone	Herb Dressing, Tomato Aspic, Seafood	Carrots, Turnips, Cauliflower, Tomatoes, Lima Beans, Green Beans, Zucchini, Brussels Sprouts, Cabbage, Potatoes	Spiced Shrimp, Baked Fish, Poached Fish, Chicken, Stuffings
SAGE	Chicken Spread, Meatballs	Chicken, Vegetable, Minestrone, Tomato, Chowders	Herb Dressing	Tomatoes, Peas, Onions, Eggplant, Lima Beans, Brussels Sprouts	Turkey, Chicken, Fish, Stuffings

Table 16: Using Herbs and Spices (cont.)

	Appetizers	Soups	Salads and Salad Dressings	Vegetables	Poultry and Fish
SESAME SEED	Canapés, Grain Nibblers, Stuffed Mushrooms		Fruit Dressings for Fruit Salads, Tossed Greens	Asparagus, Tomatoes, Vegetable Casseroles	Chicken, Stuffings
THYME	Tomato Juice, Meatballs, Pizza, Liver Paté	Minestrone, Tomato, Vegetable, Manhattan Clam Chowder, Chicken, Gumbos, Bouillabaisse	Herb Dressing, Tomato Aspic	Broccoli, Zucchini, Green Beans, Onions, Lima Beans, Tomatoes, Brussels Sprouts	Baked or Broiled Fish, Spiced Shrimp, Turkey, Chicken, Stuffings

A Warning

The herb and spice blends listed in Table 17 are not *single* ingredient products. (They may also contain a great deal of salt.) Double-check to see that you have not used one of these more than once in the last four days.

Table 17: Herb and Spice Blends

Blend	Description
BOUQUET GARNI	A combination of aromatic herb branches or leaves tied in cheesecloth—usually parsley, thyme, bay leaf
CHILI POWDER	A combination of ground spices—usually cayenne pepper, cumin, allspice, salt
CRAB BOIL	A mixture of spices and herbs, including bay leaf, pepper, chilis
CURRY POWDER	Made of up to a dozen or more spices, including cumin, pepper, turmeric, fenugreek, coriander, allspice

Blend	Description
FINES HERBES	A blend of parsley, tarragon, chervil, chives
FISH SEASONING	A mixture of herbs and spices including parsley and sometimes lemon peel and salt
PICKLING SPICE	Mustard seeds, cloves, peppercorns, allspice
POULTRY SEASONING	A blend of rosemary, oregano, sage, marjoram, thyme, pepper, and sometimes ginger and/or salt

PART III

The Immune Power Menus

CHAPTER 7

Phase I: Elimination
Two 21-Day Menu Plans

YOUR JOURNEY to immune health begins with a 21-day, 1100-calorie Elimination Diet. You eat three meals a day plus snacks—based on a nutrient balance of 60 percent carbohydrate, 30 percent protein, and 10 percent fat—but the specific foods you eat are used on a four-day rotation cycle. I've found that in 21 days dangerous food toxins can be effectively cleared from the body, and a strong immune foundation can be built. Here's why. The idea of the four-day rotation principle is that you must *not eat the same food more than once every four days.* This will help determine if a particular food is causing a troublesome allergic reaction. The rotation plan also helps give the body a rest from addictive foods.

The Sinister Seven in Disguise

The goal of the Elimination Diet is to purge the Sinister Seven— cow's milk products, wheat, yeast, eggs, corn, soy products, and cane sugar—from your system. Many foods might not seem "sinister," but sometimes the Sinister Seven wear disguises—they don't always exist in pure form. For example, corn is present in some places you would never think of—baking powder, processed meats, even the glue on stamps and envelopes! Here are some clues for locating the Sinister Seven, wherever they may lurk:

Wheat is a component of the following items:

Alcoholic beverages	Bourbon
Baked goods	Bran
Beer and ale	Breads

Bulgur
Cereal
Farina
Flour
Gin
Gluten
Metamucil
Pasta
Pancakes
Semolina
Soy sauce
Vodka
Waffles
Wheat germ
Whiskey

Cow's milk is a component of the following items:

Baked goods
Butter
Buttermilk
Cheese
Chocolate
Cream
Ice cream
Lactose
Processed meat
Pudding
Sherbet
Whey
Yogurt

Corn is a component of the following items:

Alcoholic beverages
Baked goods
Baking powder
Beer and ale
Blended Whiskey
Bourbon
Corn chips
Cornstarch
Dextrose
Flour
Gin
Popcorn
Margarine
Nondairy creamer
Oil
Taco shells
Vodka

Eggs are a component of the following items:

Albumin
Baked goods
Bouillon
Egg substitutes
Mayonnaise
Pasta
Sherbet
Tartar sauce

Soybean is a component in the following items and a derivative in the following ingredients:

Baked goods (biscuits, breads,
  cakes, cookies, muffins)
Bean curd/tofu/miso
Bread/bread crumbs/breaded
  products
Brown bean sauce
Candy
Carob
Cereal
Chocolate
Cooking spray
Cow's milk substitute
Crackers
Dashi
Egg substitute
Ground bean sauce
Hoisin sauce
Ice cream

Lecithin
Margarine
Mayonnaise
Monosodium glutamate (MSG)
Nondairy creamer
Oyster sauce
Processed meats
Rice mixes
Salad dressings
Sauce mixes
Self-basting turkey
Sesame seed paste

Soups/broths
Soy sauce
Tofu
Tempeh
Processed vegetables (canned or frozen in sauce)
Vegetable shortening
Waffles (and mixes)
Wine
Worcestershire sauce
Yogurt

Yeast is found in the following:

Alcohols
Breads
Vinegars, or pickled or fermented foods
Malted foods
Dried or cured foods
Cheeses (except fresh cheeses)

In the following foods, yeast is usually used as a leavener or as an active agent in preparation:

Cakes and cake mixes
Canned refrigerator biscuits
Crackers and cookies
Flour
Hamburger and hot dog buns

Meat fried in cracker crusts
Milk fortified with vitamins derived from yeast
Pretzels
B-complex vitamins

The following substances contain yeast or yeastlike substances, because of their nature or because of their manufacture or preparation:

Antibiotics
Beer and ale
Bourbon
Brandy
Buttermilk
Candy, malted
Cereal, malted
Citric acid
Citrus juices
Dried fruits
Fermented beverages
Gin
Ginger ale

Monosodium glutamate(MSG)
Mushrooms
Root beer
Rum
Saki
Sour cream
Soy sauce
Tea, black
Truffles
Vinegars, all types
Vodka
Whiskey
Wine

Cane sugar is extremely plentiful in processed foods, and it may come in many forms. Many of these sugars are obvious—brown sugar, confectioner's sugar, invert sugar, maple raw sugar, table sugar, turbinado sugar, and white sugar—but there are also many that are not so obvious. Check food labels carefully for the following "hidden sugars" and avoid all of them. (We do allow pure honey, pure maple syrup, and juice concentrate on the Immune Power Diet.)

Corn sweeteners

Corn syrup

Corn syrup solids

Dextrose

Fructose

Glucose

Granulated fructose

High fructose corn syrup

Honey (other than pure)

Maltodextrins

Maple syrup (other than pure)

Molasses

Raisin syrup

Sucrose

The Rules

The Elimination Diet is really very easy if you keep a few simple rules in mind.

1. A particular food can be eaten only every four days. Each day you can have the same *type* of food, but not the same *variety*. Take lettuce, for example:

Day 1: Iceberg lettuce
  Day 2: Romaine lettuce
  Day 3: Red-leaf lettuce
  Day 4: Boston lettuce
  Day 5: Back to iceberg lettuce

In other words, if you have eaten iceberg lettuce one day, you can't have it again for four days. You may have iceberg and Boston lettuce on the same day, but then neither can be repeated for four days.
  Another example is grain:

Day 1: Millet
    Day 2: Brown rice
    Day 3: Buckwheat groats
    Day 4: Barley
    Day 5: Back to millet

The same would be true of onions, cooking oils, vegetables, fruits—any food at all.

2. To make rotation easier it's a good idea to eat the same food more than once a day. For example, have cooked millet for breakfast, use it in a salad for lunch, and serve it as an accompaniment for dinner. Or if you have orange juice for breakfast, have an orange at lunch and one of the chicken and orange recipes for dinner.

3. Each time you start a four-day rotation cycle, be sure you *complete that cycle* so you don't upset the nutrient balance upon which this diet is based.

4. All foods—even beverages and garnishes—must be rotated.

5. Each meal contains a "choice of beverage." No caffeine is allowed on the Immune Power Diet. You may choose among the following: coffee substitute (caffeine-free), herbal tea, mineral water, fruit juice, and salt-free seltzer. But remember: If you choose any beverage besides water, you may not consume it more often than every four days.

6. Remember that these plans are here to help you, not to make you feel restricted. If you hate spinach leaves or wild rice or bananas or you can't find kale or kiwi or papaya no matter how hard you look, feel free to substitute something you *do* like or *can* find provided it's nutritionally equivalent. (Just be sure not to eat the same food more than once every four days.) Don't be too conservative, though. Think of the Immune Power Diet as an opportunity to try new foods and expand your dietary repertoire.

7. Some of the foods and ingredients suggested in the Elimination and Reintroduction Plans may be a little difficult to locate, especially the cereals, grains, and legumes. If your local supermarket doesn't stock them, try a health food store, a specialty shop, or even the food department of a large department store.

8. All cereals—rye, millet, oat, buckwheat, brown rice—must be natural: no salt, sugar, or other additives.

9. Cook just one portion wherever possible if you are eating alone and freeze the rest in one-serving-sized portions. However, all of the recipes were tested on family members who were not on the diet and were well accepted, so plan to serve these recipes as part of a family or entertaining menu.

10. Choice of snacks and salad dressings is allowed—just add the calories yourself using the charts starting on page 267.

11. Each day's menu in the four-day rotation cycle is designed to satisfy your appetite and your nutritional needs. And it will, providing you eat each of the three meals called for. Skipping meals is not a good idea—it only makes you overly hungry and might encourage cheating. To guarantee full nourishment, I usually prescribe a vitamin-mineral regimen to supplement the foods on the menu plans. However, you should do this only under the guidance of your physician.

12. Each day's menus are followed by a nutritional analysis of all the foods consumed, first broken down according to the meal and then totaled for the day. In the analysis charts, KCAL mean calories; PRO means protein; CARB means carbohydrates; FAT means total fat, SAFA means saturated fat; MFAT means monounsaturated fat; PFAT means polyunsaturated fat; CHOL means cholesterol; CALC means calcium; IRON means iron; and SOD means sodium. Where zero is shown, none of that nutrient is present, or no data are available.

13. Men usually need more calories than women, and teenagers need more calories than full-grown adults. I've modified the Elimination and Reintroduction Diets to take this fact into account. The modifications for each menu—which are reflected by an increase in the size of the portions—are listed after the nutritional analysis. Please note that this "extra" food does not have to be eaten at the specified time. For instance, instead of having a cup of orange juice for breakfast, a man may want to save half of the juice for a snack.

The Plans

I've included two 21-day sample Elimination Diet menus—Plan A and Plan B. Choose whichever one is most appealing to you and follow it as closely as you can. If you like, when you're finished with the first plan, you may go on to the second.

Each day's menus are followed by a nutritional analysis of all the foods consumed, first broken down according to the meal and then totaled for the day. In the analysis charts, KCAL means calories; PRO means protein; CARB mean carbohydrates; FAT means total fat; SAFA means saturated fat; MFAT means monounsaturated fat; PFAT means polyunsaturated fat; CHOL means cholesterol; CALC means calcium; IRON means iron; SOD means sodium. Where zero is shown, it can mean one of two things: there is none of that nutrient present, or there is no data available.

The Elimination Diet has been carefully worked out nutritionally to be safe and healthy for more than 21 days. In fact, many of my overweight patients elect to stay on it longer in order to lose more pounds. However, if you wish to follow the Elimination Phase for several weeks or longer, you should consult your physician.

Withdrawal

The first week of the Elimination Diet can be trying. As their bodies rid themselves of accumulated toxins, some of my patients experience distressing withdrawal symptoms that make them feel worse than before. Severe headaches, extreme fatigue and lethargy, stomach upset, joint and muscle pains, acne, and skin rashes can occur.

But these very same symptoms, indicate that the Elimination Diet is working, clearing out the damage done by food toxins. And by the end of seven days—ten at the most—the discomfort usually disappears. I've found that drinking a lot of water and taking vitamin C supplements helps minimize these symptoms in the meantime.

A patient of mine named Roberta found that out. This vivacious young woman first came to me because she thought she was allergic to milk. Roberta noticed that when she stopped drinking milk, her persistent acne cleared up. This was most evident after a trip out of the country, where she didn't have her usual three glasses of milk each day. But upon her return, Roberta took up her milk-drinking habit again, and her skin problems came back.

When I tested Roberta, I found she was allergic to cow's milk products and wheat, along with a number of other foods. So I started her on the Elimination Diet and prescribed a vitamin-mineral routine to augment the diet.

Roberta started the Elimination Diet on a Sunday, and by Sunday night she thought her head would explode. By Monday morning, the headaches got so bad, she couldn't hold her head up straight. Roberta called me, frantic. She couldn't work, she couldn't walk, she couldn't sleep. I assured her that all this was temporary and asked her to give it another day. On Tuesday, Roberta called to say that her headaches were gone, and her skin was beginning to clear up. "It's a miracle, doctor," she said.

A Few Dos and Don'ts

- Never eat more than is specified in the menu. (To figure out the amount one serving of a given recipe should be, divide by the number of portions the recipe makes.)
- When fruits or vegetables are called for, use fresh or frozen ones if at all possible. Canned are too salty. If you must rely on frozen foods, be sure that there are no additives or preservatives of any kind. If you use fresh fruits and vegetables, remember that the peel is often the most nutritious part.
- Steaming is the recommended method of cooking vegetables.
- When legumes (lentils, kidney beans, chick-peas, etc.) are called for, use the dried variety. Canned beans are extremely salty.
- Use only the seasonings called for in the daily plans. Be on the lookout for hidden chemicals.
- Use salt-free tomato sauce and tomato juice.
- If you make substitutions, be sure that what you substitute is the nutritional equivalent of the original. And don't forget to rotate the new food.
- When fish is called for, you may have canned tuna and salmon instead of fresh, but be sure the canned fish has been packed in water instead of oil.

ELIMINATION PLAN A

DAY 1

BREAKFAST   1 Buckwheat Tangerine Muffin*
             1 medium orange
             Choice of beverage

LUNCH   2 cups spinach leaves
             1 medium tomato sliced
             1 medium onion sliced
             1 medium orange
             Choice of beverage

DINNER   1 serving Tomato-Broccoli Chicken*
                1 serving Cabbage and Apples*
                ½ cup steamed spinach
                Choice of beverage

MEAL	KCAL	PRO	CARB	FAT	SAFA	MFAT	PFAT	CHOL	CALC	IRON	SOD
Breakfast	196.8	2.5gm	38.0gm	4.9gm	0.4gm	0.5gm	3.3gm	0.0mg	79.5mg	0.1mg	112.5mg
Lunch	337.3	12.3gm	47.3gm	14.9gm	1.2gm	1.6gm	10.1gm	0.0mg	274.5mg	7.3mg	173.3mg
Dinner	275.9	35.7gm	23.2gm	6.0gm	1.1gm	1.3gm	2.6gm	72.5mg	234.5mg	3.2mg	213.5mg
Total	809.29	50.5gm	108.5gm	25.8gm	2.7gm	3.4gm	16.0gm	72.5mg	588.5mg	10.6mg	499.0mg

* Recipe appears in Part IV.

NOTE: Active men and teenagers should make the following changes in the size of their portions: buckwheat tangerine muffin, 1½; tomato-broccoli chicken, 1½ servings; cabbage and apples, 2 servings.

DAY 2

BREAKFAST   ½ cup boiled Barley*
                ½ cup stewed prunes
                ½ cup cantaloupe balls
                Choice of beverage

LUNCH   4 ounces sliced white-meat turkey
                ¼ cup raw green or red peppers, sliced
                ½ cup chopped celery
                2 cups Boston lettuce
                ½ cup cantaloupe balls
                Choice of beverage

DINNER   1 serving Oriental Scallops*
                1 serving Barley Medley*
                1 serving Brussels Sprouts with Lemon-Parsley Sauce*
                2 cups Boston lettuce
                Choice of beverage

MEAL	KCAL	PRO	CARB	FAT	SAFA	MFAT	PFAT	CHOL	CALC	IRON	SOD
Breakfast	270.2	4.4gm	67.2gm	0.8gm	0.1gm	0.3gm	0.1gm	0.0mg	46.3mg	2.3mg	10.8mg
Lunch	242.2	36.9gm	14.2gm	4.2gm	1.2gm	0.6gm	0.7gm	78.0mg	96.7mg	4.4mg	170.4mg
Dinner	609.0	38.9gm	91.9gm	14.0gm	1.2gm	1.3gm	8.1gm	60.2mg	270.7mg	2.2mg	378.7mg
Total	1121.4	80.2gm	173.3gm	19.0gm	2.5gm	2.2gm	8.9gm	138.2mg	413.7mg	8.9mg	559.9mg

* Recipes appear in Part IV.

NOTE: Active men and teenagers should make the following changes in the size of their portions: Oriental scallops, 1½ servings; barley medley, 1½ servings; brussels sprouts with lemon parsley sauce, 1½ servings.

DAY 3

BREAKFAST   1 cup cooked rye cereal
1 medium banana, sliced
Choice of beverage

LUNCH   1 serving Sardine Snack*
1 cup cooked green beans
2 cups romaine lettuce
1 medium banana
Choice of beverage

DINNER   1 serving Tuna Steak*
1 medium baked potato
1 cup steamed zucchini
2 cups romaine lettuce
Choice of beverage

MEAL	KCAL	PRO	CARB	FAT	SAFA	MFAT	PFAT	CHOL	CALC	IRON	SOD
Breakfast	276.5	7.2gm	64.5gm	1.4gm	0.2gm	0.0gm	0.0gm	0.0mg	26.1mg	2.2mg	1.7mg
Lunch	359.4	17.2gm	53.4gm	5.1gm	0.2gm	0.0gm	9.0gm	63.8mg	169.9mg	2.6mg	251.5mg
Dinner	445.4	40.8gm	54.8gm	8.4gm	0.0gm	0.0gm	1.0gm	0.8mg	192.0mg	4.2mg	68.4mg
Total	1081.3	65.2gm	172.7gm	14.9gm	0.4gm	0.0gm	10.0gm	64.6mg	388.0mg	9.0mg	321.6mg

* Recipe appears in Part IV.

NOTE: Active men and teenagers should make the following changes in the size of their portions: green beans, 2 cups; tuna steak, 2 servings.

DAY 4

BREAKFAST   1⅓ cups apple juice
1½ cups puffed brown rice cereal
Choice of beverage

LUNCH	3½ ounces salmon, broiled
	2 rice cakes
	1 cup alfalfa sprouts
	2 cups endive
	1 medium apple
	Choice of beverage

DINNER	1 6-ounce lamb chop, broiled
	2 cups steamed asparagus
	1 medium apple
	Choice of beverage

MEAL	KCAL	PRO	CARB	FAT	SAFA	MFAT	PFAT	CHOL	CALC	IRON	SOD
Breakfast	206.1	3.0gm	46.7gm	0.4gm	0.0gm	0.0gm	0.0gm	0.0mg	11.7mg	3.0mg	511.9mg
Lunch	392.4	35.7gm	44.7gm	9.2gm	0.1gm	0.0gm	0.0gm	47.0mg	532.7mg	4.6mg	132.0mg
Dinner	490.0	57.6gm	36.9gm	14.4gm	7.5gm	4.6gm	0.8gm	170.5mg	118.1mg	6.0mg	133.8mg
Total	1088.5	96.3gm	128.3gm	24.0gm	7.6gm	4.6gm	0.8gm	217.5mg	662.5mg	13.6mg	777.7mg

NOTE: Active men and teenagers should make the following changes in the size of their portions: apple juice, 1 cup; salmon, 5½ ounces; rice cakes, 3.

DAY 5

BREAKFAST	1½ cups hot or cold millet cereal
	½ cup cubed papaya
	Choice of beverage

LUNCH	½ cup tomato juice
	1 ounce feta cheese
	½ cup cold cooked kidney beans
	2 cups spinach leaves
	¼ cup red onion, raw
	½ cup cubed papaya
	Choice of beverage

DINNER   3 ounces roasted white-meat chicken
1 serving Millet-Onion Sauté*
1 serving Beets à l'Orange*
Choice of beverage

MEAL	KCAL	PRO	CARB	FAT	SAFA	MFAT	PFAT	CHOL	CALC	IRON	SOD
Breakfast	272.2	7.8gm	61.5gm	2.3gm	0.8gm	0.8gm	0.8gm	0.0mg	31.6mg	5.2mg	2.8mg
Lunch	462.0	21.5gm	54.5gm	21.1gm	5.4gm	1.6gm	10.3gm	25.0mg	393.1mg	9.7mg	730.5mg
Dinner	419.3	27.7gm	56.4gm	12.1gm	1.6gm	2.0gm	5.7gm	62.5mg	38.1mg	0.0mg	101.6mg
Total	1153.5	57.0gm	172.4gm	35.5gm	7.8gm	4.4gm	16.8gm	87.5mg	462.8mg	14.9mg	834.9mg

* Recipe appears in Part IV.

NOTE: Active men and teenagers should make the following changes in the size of their portions: papaya, 1 cup; tomato juice, 1½ cups; papaya, 1 cup; millet-onion-sauté, 1½ servings; beets à l'orange, 2 servings.

DAY 6

BREAKFAST   4 ounces prune juice
½ cup cooked Buckwheat*
1 2-inch wedge cantaloupe
Choice of beverage

LUNCH   1 serving Sweet Potato Salad*
1 tablespoon Honey Vinaigrette Dressing*
2 cups Boston lettuce
½ cup cantaloupe balls
Choice of beverage

DINNER   6 ounces Lemon Sautéed Veal Cutlets*
1 medium baked sweet potato
1 serving Carrots and Parsnips*
2 cups Boston lettuce
Choice of beverage

MEAL	KCAL	PRO	CARB	FAT	SAFA	MFAT	PFAT	CHOL	CALC	IRON	SOD
Breakfast	238.9	3.8gm	54.6gm	0.4gm	0.1gm	0.1gm	0.1gm	0.0mg	31.4mg	3.7mg	15.9mg
Lunch	234.8	5.1gm	45.7gm	5.0gm	0.5gm	0.6gm	3.4gm	0.0mg	93.1mg	2.4mg	106.7mg
Dinner	682.7	27.9gm	68.8gm	34.1gm	8.8gm	10.8gm	11.5gm	80.5mg	165.9mg	6.7mg	284.0mg
Total	1156.4	36.8gm	169.1gm	39.5gm	9.4gm	11.5gm	15.0gm	80.5mg	290.4mg	12.8mg	406.6mg

* Recipe appears in Part IV.

NOTE: Active men and teenagers should make the following changes in the size of their portions: prune juice, 8 ounces; sweet potato salad, 2 servings.

DAY 7

BREAKFAST   1 Rye Raisin Muffin*
1 grapefruit half
Choice of beverage

LUNCH   4 ounces sliced white-meat turkey
1 medium boiled potato
2 cups steamed cabbage
2 cups romaine lettuce
½ cup grapes, green or red
Choice of beverage

DINNER   6 medium shrimp, broiled
1 large steamed artichoke
1 cup steamed cabbage
2 cups romaine lettuce
Choice of beverage

MEAL	KCAL	PRO	CARB	FAT	SAFA	MFAT	PFAT	CHOL	CALC	IRON	SOD
Breakfast	203.7	2.7gm	40.8gm	4.7gm	0.4gm	0.5gm	3.4gm	0.0mg	39.4mg	0.1mg	114.6mg
Lunch	409.3	40.9gm	53.4gm	5.0gm	1.3gm	0.6gm	1.1gm	78.0mg	209.7mg	4.8mg	145.2mg
Dinner	113.6	11.7gm	26.1gm	1.1gm	0.0gm	0.0gm	0.2gm	28.8mg	224.4mg	4.3mg	130.1mg
Total	726.6	55.3gm	120.3gm	10.8gm	1.7gm	1.1gm	4.7gm	106.8mg	473.5mg	9.2mg	389.9mg

* Recipe appears in Part IV.

NOTE: Active men and teenagers should make the following changes in the size of their portions: rye raisin muffins, 2.

DAY 8

BREAKFAST   ½ cup cooked oatmeal*
½ cup strawberries
Choice of beverage

LUNCH   1 cup cooked Brown Rice*
Steamed vegetable plate (½ cup each of broccoli, brussels sprouts, zucchini)
2 cups escarole
1 medium apple
Choice of beverage

DINNER   5 ounces broiled sea scallops
½ medium baked butternut squash
1 serving Garlic-Steamed Broccoli*
½ cup strawberries
Choice of beverage

MEAL	KCAL	PRO	CARB	FAT	SAFA	MFAT	PFAT	CHOL	CALC	IRON	SOD
Breakfast	95.0	3.5gm	17.9gm	1.4gm	0.2gm	0.4gm	0.6gm	0.0mg	19.9mg	1.0mg	1.9mg
Lunch	397.3	12.0gm	88.3gm	2.5gm	0.2gm	0.0gm	0.2gm	0.0mg	253.6mg	5.1mg	314.8mg
Dinner	398.7	44.0gm	59.0gm	3.9gm	0.1gm	0.0gm	0.4gm	74.5mg	519.6mg	6.5mg	399.9mg
Total	891.0	59.5gm	165.2gm	7.8gm	0.5gm	0.4gm	1.2gm	74.5mg	793.1mg	12.6mg	716.6mg

* Recipe appears in Part IV. (Directions for cooking oatmeal appear in Table 12, page 77.)

NOTE: Active men and teenagers should make the following changes in the size of their portions: oatmeal, 1 cup; strawberries, 1 cup; garlic-steamed broccoli, 2 servings; strawberries, 1 cup.

DAY 9

BREAKFAST ½ cup cooked millet cereal
½ cup blueberries
Choice of beverage

LUNCH   1 cup cooked Millet*
Steamed vegetable plate (½ cup each of onions and asparagus)
1 medium tomato, sliced
2 cups bibb lettuce
½ cup blueberries
1 medium orange
Choice of beverage

DINNER   1 serving Orange Roasted Chicken*
               1 serving Millet-Onion Sauté*
               1 serving Beets à l'Orange*
               2 cups bibb lettuce
               Choice of beverage

MEAL	KCAL	PRO	CARB	FAT	SAFA	MFAT	PFAT	CHOL	CALC	IRON	SOD
Breakfast	122.3	3.0gm	28.4gm	1.0gm	0.3gm	0.3gm	0.3gm	0.0mg	9.3mg	1.8mg	4.6mg
Lunch	365.3	12.0gm	82.9gm	2.7gm	0.6gm	0.5gm	0.6gm	0.0mg	175.1mg	7.3mg	32.3mg
Dinner	434.7	29.0gm	59.1gm	12.3gm	1.6gm	2.0gm	5.7gm	62.5mg	76.6mg	2.2mg	111.5mg
Total	922.3	44.0gm	170.4gm	16.0gm	2.5gm	2.8gm	6.6gm	62.5mg	261.0mg	11.3mg	148.3mg

* Recipe appears in Part IV.

NOTE: Active men and teenagers should make the following changes in the size of their portions: blueberries, 1 cup; asparagus, 1 cup; blueberries, 1 cup; millet-onion-sauté, 1½ servings; beets à l'orange, 1½ servings.

DAY 10

BREAKFAST   ½ cup boiled Barley*
             1 medium peach
             Choice of beverage

LUNCH   1 tablespoon Fresh Garlic-Feta Spread*
             Raw vegetable plate (½ cup each of carrots, celery,
                 and red pepper)
             2 cups Boston lettuce
             1 medium tangerine
             Choice of beverage

DINNER   6 ounces Veal Chop Rosemary*
             1 cup steamed carrots
             2 cups Boston lettuce
             Choice of beverage

MEAL	KCAL	PRO	CARB	FAT	SAFA	MFAT	PFAT	CHOL	CALC	IRON	SOD
Breakfast	149.2	3.0gm	35.8gm	0.4gm	0.0gm	0.0gm	0.0gm	0.0mg	11.4mg	0.6mg	0.7mg
Lunch	169.7	8.1gm	28.8gm	4.3gm	2.1gm	0.6gm	0.2gm	12.6mg	246.1mg	7.4mg	296.8mg
Dinner	469.2	29.0gm	43.4gm	19.6gm	6.6gm	0.5gm	3.4gm	87.0mg	175.8mg	8.0mg	202.0mg
Total	788.1	40.1gm	108.0gm	24.3gm	8.7gm	1.1gm	3.6gm	99.6mg	433.3mg	16.0mg	499.5mg

* Recipe appears in Part IV.

NOTE: Active men and teenagers should make the following changes in the size of their portions: boiled barley, 1 cup; fresh garlic feta spread, 2 tablespoons; veal chop rosemary, 8 ounces; steamed carrots, 1½ cups.

DAY 11

BREAKFAST
1 Silver Dollar Rye Pancake*
1 medium banana
Choice of beverage

LUNCH
5 medium cold steamed shrimp
3 rye wafers
1 cup steamed cauliflower
2 cups romaine lettuce
1 medium banana
Choice of beverage

DINNER
4 ounces sliced white-meat turkey
1 medium baked potato
1 cup cooked cabbage
2 cups romaine lettuce
Choice of beverage

MEAL	KCAL	PRO	CARB	FAT	SAFA	MFAT	PFAT	CHOL	CALC	IRON	SOD
Breakfast	351.3	3.0gm	54.8gm	14.3gm	1.4gm	1.6gm	10.1gm	0.0mg	26.1mg	0.3mg	89.2mg
Lunch	245.3	10.8gm	50.6gm	2.1gm	0.2gm	0.0gm	0.1gm	24.0mg	141.8mg	3.3mg	169.0mg
Dinner	394.3	40.2gm	49.2gm	4.5gm	1.3gm	0.6gm	0.9gm	78.0mg	161.3mg	5.8mg	122.3mg
Total	990.9	54.0gm	154.6gm	20.9gm	2.9gm	2.2gm	11.1gm	102.0mg	329.2mg	9.4mg	380.5mg

* Recipe appears in Part IV.

NOTE: Active men and teenagers should make the following changes in the size of their portions: silver dollar rye pancakes, 2; rye wafers, 6; steamed cauliflower, 2 cups; steamed cabbage, 2 cups.

DAY 12

BREAKFAST
1 cup brown rice cereal
2 ounces pure honey
1 cup strawberries
Choice of beverage

LUNCH   1 rice cake
              1 cup alfalfa sprouts
              2 cups strawberries
              Choice of beverage

DINNER   5 ounces broiled salmon
              1 cup cooked Brown Rice*
              ½ medium baked acorn squash
              2 cups escarole
              ½ unsweetened applesauce
              Choice of beverage

MEAL	KCAL	PRO	CARB	FAT	SAFA	MFAT	PFAT	CHOL	CALC	IRON	SOD
Breakfast	355.4	2.8gm	86.5gm	0.7gm	0.0gm	0.1gm	0.3gm	0.0mg	106.9mg	3.3mg	349.0mg
Lunch	161.4	9.2gm	29.0gm	2.9gm	0.0gm	0.1gm	0.3gm	0.0mg	136.6mg	3.7mg	27.8mg
Dinner	650.3	48.3gm	89.5gm	12.0gm	0.0gm	0.0gm	0.0gm	67.1mg	760.3mg	6.1mg	458.7mg
Total	1167.1	60.3gm	205.0gm	15.6gm	0.0gm	0.2gm	0.6gm	67.1mg	1003.8mg	13.1mg	835.5mg

* Recipe appears in Part IV.

NOTE: Active men and teenagers should make the following changes in the size of their portions: strawberries, 2 cups; rice cakes, 4; strawberries, 2 cups; broiled salmon, 7 ounces; unsweetened applesauce, 1 cup.

DAY 13

BREAKFAST   ½ cup orange juice
              ½ cup cooked Buckwheat*
              ½ cup blueberries
              Choice of beverage

LUNCH   ½ cup tomato juice
              1 cup cooked Buckwheat*
              Steamed vegetable plate (1 cup each of spinach and
                  broccoli)
              1 medium orange
              Choice of beverage

DINNER   1 serving Herbed Codfish Steak*
              1 serving Millet-Onion Sauté*
              ½ cup cubed papaya
              Choice of beverage

MEAL	KCAL	PRO	CARB	FAT	SAFA	MFAT	PFAT	CHOL	CALC	IRON	SOD
Breakfast	194.1	3.3gm	43.8gm	0.4gm	0.0gm	0.0gm	0.0gm	0.0mg	15.6mg	0.2mg	5.6mg
Lunch	365.8	16.2gm	76.1gm	1.1gm	0.2gm	0.0gm	0.2gm	0.0mg	483.1mg	9.4mg	385.9mg
Dinner	633.6	55.9gm	65.4gm	18.5gm	0.6gm	0.8gm	5.3gm	0.0mg	124.7mg	0.1mg	203.9mg
Total	1193.5	75.4gm	185.3gm	20.0gm	0.8gm	0.8gm	5.5gm	0.0mg	623.4mg	9.7mg	595.4mg

* Recipe appears in Part IV.

NOTE: Active men and teenagers should make the following changes in the size of their portions: orange juice, 1 cup; blueberries, 1 cup; tomato juice, 1½ cups; herbed codfish steak, 1½ servings.

DAY 14

BREAKFAST   ½ cup boiled Barley*
              ½ cup raspberries
              Choice of beverage

LUNCH   1 tablespoon Fresh Garlic-Feta Spread*
              Steamed vegetable plate (½ cup each of carrots,
                 celery, and red pepper)
              2 cups Boston lettuce
              1 medium tangerine
              Choice of beverage

DINNER   1 serving Oriental Scallops*
              1 serving Carrots and Parsnips*
              1 serving Brussels Sprouts with Lemon-Parsley Sauce*
              Choice of beverage

MEAL	KCAL	PRO	CARB	FAT	SAFA	MFAT	PFAT	CHOL	CALC	IRON	SOD
Breakfast	118.8	2.7gm	27.3gm	0.5gm	0.0gm	0.0gm	0.0gm	0.0mg	17.4mg	1.0mg	1.3mg
Lunch	182.2	7.5gm	31.7gm	4.4gm	2.2gm	0.6gm	0.3gm	12.6mg	254.2mg	7.5mg	296.2mg
Dinner	459.5	33.6gm	53.2gm	16.8gm	1.5gm	1.8gm	10.7gm	60.3mg	268.1mg	0.0mg	385.9mg
Total	641.7	43.8gm	112.2gm	21.7gm	3.7gm	2.4gm	11.0gm	72.9mg	539.7mg	8.5mg	683.4mg

* Recipe appears in Part IV.

NOTE: Active men and teenagers should make the following changes in the size of their portions: raspberries, 1 cup; fresh garlic-feta spread, 2 tablespoons; steamed carrots, 1 cup; oriental scallops, 1½ servings.

DAY 15

BREAKFAST   1 Rye Raisin Muffin*
1 grapefruit half
Choice of beverage

LUNCH   ½ cup grapefruit juice
1 serving Sardine Snack*
1 cup steamed green beans
1 cup steamed cauliflower
Choice of beverage

DINNER   6 medium broiled shrimp
1 medium baked potato
1 cup steamed red cabbage
1 cup steamed cauliflower
Choice of beverage

MEAL	KCAL	PRO	CARB	FAT	SAFA	MFAT	PFAT	CHOL	CALC	IRON	SOD
Breakfast	203.7	2.7gm	40.8gm	4.7gm	0.4gm	0.5gm	3.4gm	0.0mg	39.4mg	0.1mg	114.6mg
Lunch	326.9	18.9gm	42.4gm	4.9gm	0.1gm	0.0gm	9.1gm	63.8mg	205.4mg	3.0mg	259.5mg
Dinner	249.3	12.0gm	51.1gm	0.9gm	0.1gm	0.0gm	0.4gm	28.8mg	127.1mg	3.7mg	58.9mg
Total	779.9	33.6gm	134.3gm	10.5gm	0.6gm	0.5gm	12.9gm	92.6mg	371.9mg	6.8mg	433.0mg

* Recipe appears in Part IV.

NOTE: Active men and teenagers should make the following changes in the size of their portions: rye raisin muffin, 2; steamed green beans, 1½ cups; steamed cauliflower, 1½ cups.

DAY 16

BREAKFAST   ½ cup apple juice
½ Grand Granola*
1 cup strawberries
Choice of beverage

LUNCH   1 cup cooked Brown Rice*
Steamed vegetable plate (1 cup each of zucchini and
green beans)
2 cups escarole
½ cup unsweetened applesauce
Choice of beverage

DINNER   1 serving Mako Shark Steak*
½ cup cooked Brown Rice*
½ medium baked acorn squash
2 cups escarole
1 medium apple
Choice of beverage

MEAL	KCAL	PRO	CARB	FAT	SAFA	MFAT	PFAT	CHOL	CALC	IRON	SOD
Breakfast	354.8	4.4gm	49.5gm	17.0gm	1.5gm	3.6gm	10.1gm	0.0mg	53.6mg	1.1mg	7.5mg
Lunch	357.4	10.6gm	78.8gm	1.7gm	0.0gm	0.0gm	0.0gm	0.0mg	215.6mg	4.2mg	297.6mg
Dinner	653.1	43.8gm	103.2gm	10.8gm	0.1gm	0.0gm	0.1gm	68.5mg	303.6mg	4.1mg	251.3mg
Total	1365.3	58.8gm	231.5gm	29.5gm	1.6gm	3.6gm	10.2gm	68.5mg	572.8mg	9.4mg	556.4mg

* Recipe appears in Part IV.

NOTE: Active men and teenagers should make the following changes in the size of their portions: apple juice, 1½ cups; unsweetened applesauce, 1 cup; mako shark steak, 1½ servings; brown rice, 1 cup.

DAY 17

BREAKFAST   1 Buckwheat Tangerine Muffin*
1 medium orange
Choice of beverage

LUNCH   2 ounces cold white-meat chicken
2 cups spinach leaves
1 medium tomato, sliced
1 tablespoon Pineapple Salad Dressing*
1 medium orange
Choice of beverage

DINNER   1 serving Tomato-Broccoli Chicken*
1 serving Cabbage and Apples*
1 cup steamed spinach
¼ medium fresh pineapple
Choice of beverage

MEAL	KCAL	PRO	CARB	FAT	SAFA	MFAT	PFAT	CHOL	CALC	IRON	SOD
Breakfast	196.8	2.5gm	38.0gm	4.9gm	0.4gm	0.5gm	3.3gm	0.0mg	79.5mg	0.1mg	112.5mg
Lunch	468.2	27.6gm	43.7gm	23.5gm	2.8gm	3.6gm	14.4gm	49.8mg	269.4mg	7.6mg	215.3mg
Dinner	388.1	38.7gm	37.0gm	6.6gm	1.2gm	1.3gm	2.7gm	72.5mg	362.4mg	6.8mg	277.3mg
Total	1003.1	68.8gm	118.7gm	35.0gm	4.4gm	5.4gm	20.4gm	122.3mg	711.3mg	14.5mg	605.1mg

* Recipes appears in Part IV.

NOTE: Active men and teenagers should make the following changes in the size of their portions: buckwheat tangerine muffin, 1½; pineapple salad dressing, 2 tablespoons; tomato-broccoli chicken, 1½ servings; cabbage and apples, 2 servings.

DAY 18

BREAKFAST	½ cup boiled Barley*
	½ cup stewed prunes
	1 cantaloupe half
	Choice of beverage

LUNCH   4 ounces sliced white-meat turkey
½ cup each sliced raw green or red pepper
2 cups Boston lettuce
½ cup melon balls
Choice of beverage

DINNER   1 serving Oriental Scallops*
1 serving Barley Medley*
2 cups Boston lettuce
½ cup cubed mango
Choice of beverage

MEAL	KCAL	PRO	CARB	FAT	SAFA	MFAT	PFAT	CHOL	CALC	IRON	SOD
Breakfast	335.7	6.0gm	82.9gm	1.3gm	0.2gm	0.5gm	0.2gm	0.0mg	66.9mg	2.7mg	27.7mg
Lunch	252.8	37.4gm	16.6gm	4.3gm	1.2gm	0.6gm	0.7gm	78.0mg	101.1mg	4.6mg	175.6mg
Dinner	526.4	35.0gm	87.0gm	6.6gm	0.4gm	0.6gm	2.7gm	60.2mg	211.8mg	2.3mg	344.3mg
Total	1114.9	78.4gm	186.5gm	12.2gm	1.8gm	1.7gm	3.6gm	138.2mg	379.8mg	9.6mg	547.6mg

* Recipe appears in Part IV.

NOTE: Active men and teenagers should make the following changes in the size of their portions: stewed prunes, ¾ cup; oriental scallops, 1½ servings; barley medley, 1½ servings.

DAY 19

BREAKFAST   1 cup cooked rye*
1 medium banana, sliced
Choice of beverage

LUNCH   1 serving Sardine Snack*
1 cup cooked green beans
2 cups romaine lettuce
1 medium banana
Choice of beverage

DINNER   1 serving Tuna Steak*
1 medium baked potato
1 cup steamed yellow summer squash
2 cups romaine lettuce
1 medium kiwi
Choice of beverage

MEAL	KCAL	PRO	CARB	FAT	SAFA	MFAT	PFAT	CHOL	CALC	IRON	SOD
Breakfast	276.5	7.2gm	64.5gm	1.4gm	0.2gm	0.0gm	0.0gm	0.0mg	26.1mg	2.2mg	1.7mg
Lunch	359.4	17.2gm	53.4gm	5.1gm	0.2gm	0.0gm	9.0gm	63.8mg	169.9mg	2.6mg	251.5mg
Dinner	494.0	41.4gm	67.1gm	8.8gm	0.0gm	0.0gm	1.0gm	0.8mg	211.6mg	4.6mg	284.6mg
Total	1130.9	65.8gm	185.0gm	15.3gm	0.4gm	0.0gm	10.0gm	64.6mg	407.6mg	9.4mg	537.8mg

* Recipe appears in Part IV. (Directions for cooking rye appear in Table 12, page 77.)

NOTE: Active men and teenagers should make the following changes in the size of their portions: sardine snack, 1½ servings; cooked green beans, 1½ cups; tuna steak, 1½ servings; steamed yellow summer squash, 1½ cups.

DAY 20

BREAKFAST   ½ cup apple juice
1½ cups puffed brown rice
Choice of beverage

LUNCH   3½ ounces poached salmon
2 rice cakes
1 cup alfalfa sprouts
1 cup endive
½ cup unsweetened applesauce
Choice of beverage

DINNER 1 broiled lamb chop (6 ounces)
½ medium baked acorn squash
1 cup steamed asparagus
1 medium apple
Choice of beverage

MEAL	KCAL	PRO	CARB	FAT	SAFA	MFAT	PFAT	CHOL	CALC	IRON	SOD
Breakfast	226.0	3.0gm	51.6gm	0.4gm	0.0gm	0.0gm	0.0gm	0.0mg	14.6mg	3.2mg	513.1mg
Lunch	353.5	34.8gm	35.3gm	8.8gm	0.0gm	0.0gm	0.0gm	47.0mg	486.2mg	3.6mg	127.4mg
Dinner	531.8	55.9gm	50.9gm	14.0gm	7.3gm	4.6gm	0.6gm	170.5mg	135.0mg	6.5mg	127.4mg
Total	1111.3	94.5gm	137.8gm	23.2gm	7.3gm	4.6gm	0.6gm	217.5mg	635.8mg	13.3mg	767.9mg

NOTE: Active men and teenagers should make the following changes in the size of their portions: apple juice, 1 cup; puffed brown rice, 2 cups; rice cakes, 3; endive, 2 cups; unsweetened applesauce, 1 cup.

DAY 21

BREAKFAST ½ cup cooked millet cereal
1 papaya half
Choice of beverage

LUNCH ½ cup tomato juice
½ cup cooked chick-peas
1 serving Spinach Salad*
½ cup papaya
Choice of beverage

DINNER 3 ounces roasted white-meat chicken
1 serving Millet-Onion Sauté*
1 serving Beets à l'Orange*
1 cup strawberries
Choice of beverage

MEAL	KCAL	PRO	CARB	FAT	SAFA	MFAT	PFAT	CHOL	CALC	IRON	SOD
Breakfast	140.2	3.4gm	32.9gm	0.9gm	0.3gm	0.3gm	0.3gm	0.0mg	41.0mg	1.8mg	4.8mg
Lunch	621.7	30.2gm	90.8gm	19.4gm	1.7gm	4.0gm	11.8gm	0.0mg	356.4mg	13.9mg	433.5mg
Dinner	464.3	28.6gm	66.9gm	12.6gm	1.6gm	2.1gm	6.0gm	62.5mg	59.1mg	0.6mg	103.1mg
Total	1226.2	62.2gm	190.6gm	32.9gm	3.6gm	6.4gm	18.1gm	62.5mg	456.5mg	16.3mg	541.4mg

* Recipe appears in Part IV.

NOTE: Active men and teenagers should make the following changes in the size of their portions: papaya, 1; tomato juice, 1½ cups; papaya, 1; millet-onion-sauté, 1½ servings; beets à l'orange, 2 servings; strawberries, 2 cups.

ELIMINATION PLAN B

DAY 1

BREAKFAST   ½ cup apple juice
½ cup Grand Granola*
Choice of beverage

LUNCH   3 ounces water-packed tuna
¾ cup cooked green peas
1 cup chopped cucumber
1 medium tomato, sliced
2 cups romaine lettuce
1 medium apple
Choice of beverage

DINNER   1 serving Salmon Steak*
½ cup cooked green peas
1 cup steamed cauliflower
2 cups romaine lettuce
1 serving Baked Peaches*
Choice of beverage

MEAL	KCAL	PRO	CARB	FAT	SAFA	MFAT	PFAT	CHOL	CALC	IRON	SOD
Breakfast	309.8	3.5gm	39.0gm	16.4gm	1.5gm	3.5gm	9.8gm	0.0mg	32.6mg	0.5mg	6.0mg
Lunch	369.5	34.7gm	56.7gm	2.2gm	0.1gm	0.0gm	0.1gm	53.6mg	178.5mg	6.3mg	416.7mg
Dinner	415.5	40.6gm	67.3gm	11.4gm	0.3gm	1.3gm	0.6gm	53.6mg	634.6mg	3.3mg	158.9mg
Total	1094.8	78.8gm	163.0gm	30.0gm	1.9gm	4.8gm	10.5gm	107.2mg	847.7mg	10.1mg	581.6mg

* Recipe appears in Part IV.

NOTE: Active men and teenagers should make the following changes in the size of their portions: apple juice, 1 cup; water-packed tuna, 4½ ounces; cooked green peas, 1 cup.

DAY 2

BREAKFAST   1 Orange Rice Muffin*
1 small orange
Choice of beverage

LUNCH   4 ounces sliced white-meat turkey
2 rice cakes
1 cup alfalfa sprouts
2 cups Boston lettuce
1 medium, orange sliced
Choice of beverage

DINNER   1 serving Hawaiian Chicken*
1 cup cooked Brown Rice*
1 cup steamed zucchini
2 cups Boston lettuce
1 medium kiwi
Choice of beverage

MEAL	KCAL	PRO	CARB	FAT	SAFA	MFAT	PFAT	CHOL	CALC	IRON	SOD
Breakfast	260.3	3.5gm	52.2gm	4.9gm	0.4gm	0.5gm	3.4gm	0.0mg	77.1mg	8.1mg	88.3mg
Lunch	363.6	43.0gm	37.8gm	5.2gm	1.2gm	0.5gm	0.6gm	78.0mg	140.5mg	3.9mg	84.3mg
Dinner	468.3	35.5gm	70.9gm	4.8gm	0.8gm	1.0gm	0.6gm	73.0mg	141.7mg	4.1mg	353.6mg
Total	1092.2	82.0gm	160.9gm	19.8gm	2.4gm	2.0gm	4.6gm	151.0mg	359.3mg	8.1mg	526.2mg

* Recipe appears in Part IV. (Hawaiian Chicken is variant of Orange Baked Chicken.)

NOTE: Active men and teenagers should make the following changes in the size of their portions: orange muffin, 2; rice cakes, 3; steamed zucchini, 1½ cups.

DAY 3

BREAKFAST   3 rye wafers
1 tablespoon cashew butter
1 cup sliced strawberries
Choice of beverage

LUNCH   1 serving Fennel and Cucumber Salad*
3 rye wafers
2 cups escarole
Choice of beverage

DINNER | 1 6-ounce lean veal chop, broiled
1 serving Brussels Sprouts with Lemon-Parsley Sauce*
1 cup steamed broccoli
2 cups watercress
Choice of beverage

NOTE: You may use commercially prepared cashew butter, but check the label carefully for preservatives, sugar, corn syrup, etc. If you prefer to make your own, simply toss a cup of cashews into the blender or food processor and process until smooth.

MEAL	KCAL	PRO	CARB	FAT	SAFA	MFAT	PFAT	CHOL	CALC	IRON	SOD
Breakfast	206.5	5.7gm	28.0gm	9.2gm	1.6gm	4.7gm	1.6gm	0.0mg	35.5mg	1.8mg	131.0mg
Lunch	125.7	4.4gm	19.1gm	3.6gm	0.2gm	0.3gm	2.0gm	0.0mg	107.3mg	2.1mg	222.1mg
Dinner	532.2	59.5gm	33.4gm	21.1gm	8.0gm	5.4gm	5.8gm	170.5mg	397.6mg	7.5mg	212.6mg
Total	864.4	69.6gm	80.5gm	33.9gm	9.8gm	10.4gm	9.4gm	170.5mg	540.4mg	11.4mg	565.7mg

* Recipe appears in Part IV.

NOTE: Active men and teenagers should make the following changes in the size of their portions: rye wafers, 6; cashew butter, 2 tablespoons; sliced strawberries, 2 cups; rye wafers, 6; brussels sprouts with lemon-parsley sauce, 2 servings.

DAY 4

BREAKFAST | 1 cup cooked barley cereal
1 cup blueberries
Choice of beverage

LUNCH | ½ cup cooked red kidney beans*
½ cup artichoke heart
2 cups spinach leaves
1 cup each sliced green and red pepper
1 cup celery slices
Choice of beverage

DINNER
1 serving Beans Indienne*
1 serving Barley Medley*
1 cup steamed cabbage
1 cup steamed spinach
Choice of beverage

MEAL	KCAL	PRO	CARB	FAT	SAFA	MFAT	PFAT	CHOL	CALC	IRON	SOD
Breakfast	255.7	5.1gm	59.8gm	1.1gm	0.0gm	0.0gm	0.0gm	0.0mg	16.7mg	1.3mg	10.2mg
Lunch	384.2	19.8gm	55.3gm	15.3gm	1.2gm	1.6gm	10.1gm	0.0mg	314.9mg	9.8mg	362.0mg
Dinner	620.0	28.1gm	117.2gm	12.5gm	1.1gm	0.7gm	8.0gm	0.0mg	373.6mg	7.0mg	190.3mg
Total	1259.9	53.0gm	232.3gm	28.9gm	2.3gm	2.3gm	18.1gm	0.0mg	705.2mg	18.1mg	562.5mg

* Recipe appears in Part IV. (Directions for cooking kidney beans appear in Table 13, page 81.)

NOTE: Active men and teenagers should make the following changes in the size of their portions: blueberries, 1½ cups; cooked red kidney beans, 1 cup; beans Indienne, 1½ servings; barley medley, 1½ servings.

DAY 5

BREAKFAST
1 cup cooked oatmeal*
¼ cup sunflower seeds
½ cup unsweetened applesauce
Choice of beverage

LUNCH
1 tablespoon Easy Feta Cheese Spread*
½ cup radishes
1 cup carrot slices
2 cups romaine lettuce
1 medium apple
Choice of beverage

DINNER　　　1 serving Shrimp Pocket*
　　　　　　　1 cup steamed cauliflower
　　　　　　　2 cups romaine lettuce
　　　　　　　1 medium apple
　　　　　　　Choice of beverage

MEAL	KCAL	PRO	CARB	FAT	SAFA	MFAT	PFAT	CHOL	CALC	IRON	SOD
Breakfast	404.3	15.2gm	46.9gm	19.7gm	2.5gm	4.2gm	11.8gm	0.0mg	66.4mg	4.4mg	206.5mg
Lunch	158.3	3.5gm	37.7gm	1.2gm	0.1gm	0.0gm	0.0gm	0.3mg	143.9mg	3.1mg	75.2mg
Dinner	326.5	30.2gm	45.0gm	5.5gm	2.2gm	0.6gm	0.4gm	184.0mg	328.2mg	2.3mg	344.7mg
Total	889.1	48.9gm	129.6gm	26.4gm	4.8gm	4.8gm	12.2gm	184.0mg	538.5mg	9.8mg	626.4mg

* Recipe appears in Part IV. (Directions for cooking oatmeal appear in Table 12, page 77.)

NOTE: Active men and teenagers should make the following changes in the size of their portions: easy feta cheese spread, 2 tablespoons; radishes, ¾ cup; shrimp pocket, 2 servings.

DAY 6

BREAKFAST　　½ cup orange juice
　　　　　　　1 serving Silver Dollar Rice Pancake*
　　　　　　　1 tablespoon Pineapple Topping*
　　　　　　　Choice of beverage

LUNCH　　　　3½ ounces cold salmon
　　　　　　　2 rice cakes
　　　　　　　1 cup chopped zucchini
　　　　　　　2 steamed endives
　　　　　　　½ unsweetened pineapple slices
　　　　　　　Choice of beverage

DINNER　　　4 ounces sliced white-meat turkey
　　　　　　　1 serving Sweet Potato with Pineapple*
　　　　　　　1 cup steamed asparagus
　　　　　　　2 cups Boston lettuce
　　　　　　　Choice of beverage

MEAL	KCAL	PRO	CARB	FAT	SAFA	MFAT	PFAT	CHOL	CALC	IRON	SOD
Breakfast	313.2	2.7gm	48.3gm	13.9gm	1.2gm	1.6gm	10.1gm	0.0mg	33.8mg	0.1mg	88.8mg
Lunch	368.2	32.6gm	42.2gm	8.3gm	0.0gm	0.0gm	0.0gm	47.0mg	557.5mg	3.9mg	135.0mg
Dinner	431.1	42.7gm	47.7gm	9.2gm	1.7gm	3.3gm	2.1gm	78.0mg	159.3mg	5.0mg	113.7mg
Total	1112.5	78.0gm	138.2gm	31.4gm	2.9gm	4.9gm	12.2gm	125.0mg	750.6mg	9.0mg	337.5mg

* Recipe appears in Part IV.

NOTE: Active men and teenagers should make the following changes in the size of their portions: silver dollar rice pancakes, 2 servings; pineapple topping, 2 tablespoons; rice cakes, 3.

DAY 7

BREAKFAST   1 cup cooked rye*
1 medium sliced banana
Choice of beverage

LUNCH   Steamed vegetable plate (½ cup each of broccoli, brussels sprouts, and carrots)
2 rye crackers
1 ounce pumpkin seeds
1 medium banana
Choice of beverage

DINNER   5 ounces broiled flounder
½ medium baked acorn squash
1 serving Broccoli with Pumpkin Seeds*
2 cups escarole
Choice of beverage

MEAL	KCAL	PRO	CARB	FAT	SAFA	MFAT	PFAT	CHOL	CALC	IRON	SOD
Breakfast	276.5	7.2gm	64.5gm	1.4gm	0.2gm	0.0gm	0.0gm	0.0mg	26.1mg	2.2mg	1.7mg
Lunch	399.3	15.1gm	60.1gm	15.1gm	2.7gm	4.8gm	5.8gm	0.0mg	167.6mg	6.1mg	163.2mg
Dinner	555.4	58.5gm	41.6gm	20.4gm	1.5gm	2.5gm	3.9gm	0.0mg	442.5mg	5.3mg	380.9mg
Total	1231.2	80.8gm	166.2gm	36.9gm	4.4gm	7.3gm	9.7gm	0.0mg	636.2mg	13.6mg	545.8mg

* Recipe appears in Part IV. (Directions for cooking rye appear in Table 12, page 77.)

NOTE: Active men and teenagers should make the following changes in the size of their portions: pumpkin seeds, 2 ounces; baked acorn squash, 1 medium; broccoli with pumpkin seeds, 2 servings.

DAY 8

BREAKFAST   ½ cup cooked millet cereal
1 cup strawberries
Choice of beverage

LUNCH   1 serving Tasty Baked Chick-Peas*
1 cup boiled Millet*
1 medium steamed artichoke
1 serving Three Berries*
Choice of beverage

DINNER   1 serving Chicken Stir-Fry*
1 cup boiled Millet*
1 cup steamed spinach
1 cup steamed red cabbage
Choice of beverage

MEAL	KCAL	PRO	CARB	FAT	SAFA	MFAT	PFAT	CHOL	CALC	IRON	SOD
Breakfast	126.7	3.4gm	28.7gm	1.3gm	0.3gm	0.3gm	0.5gm	0.0mg	26.0mg	2.3mg	1.8mg
Lunch	534.6	24.4gm	83.7gm	11.1gm	1.1gm	1.3gm	5.7gm	0.0mg	154.7mg	4.7mg	71.8mg
Dinner	322.7	22.5gm	58.8gm	3.4gm	0.9gm	0.8gm	1.1gm	24.3mg	349.4mg	10.4mg	185.7mg
Total	984.0	50.3gm	171.2gm	15.8gm	2.3gm	2.4gm	7.3gm	24.3mg	530.1mg	17.4mg	259.3mg

* Recipe appears in Part IV.

NOTE: Active men and teenagers should make the following changes in the size of their portions: strawberries, 2 cups; three berries, 2 servings; chicken stir-fry, 2 servings; steamed spinach, 2 cups; steamed red cabbage, 2 cups.

DAY 9

BREAKFAST   ½ cup apple juice
½ cup Grand Granola*
Choice of beverage

LUNCH   1 serving Cauliflower-Fruit Slaw*
2 cups romaine lettuce
2 unsweetened apricot halves
Choice of beverage

DINNER 1 serving Veal Burger*
1 medium baked potato
1 medium broiled tomato with oregano
2 cups romaine lettuce
½ cup unsweetened applesauce
Choice of beverage

MEAL	KCAL	PRO	CARB	FAT	SAFA	MFAT	PFAT	CHOL	CALC	IRON	SOD
Breakfast	309.8	3.5gm	39.0gm	16.4gm	1.5gm	3.5gm	9.8gm	0.9mg	32.6mg	0.5mg	6.0mg
Lunch	96.0	3.1gm	18.4gm	2.3gm	0.1gm	0.2gm	1.7gm	0.0mg	104.0mg	1.7mg	19.6mg
Dinner	588.6	37.9gm	64.5gm	19.9gm	8.2gm	0.0gm	0.1gm	116.1mg	134.3mg	4.7mg	120.7mg
Total	994.4	44.5gm	121.9gm	38.6gm	9.8gm	3.7gm	11.6gm	117.0mg	270.9mg	6.9mg	146.3mg

* Recipe appears in Part IV.

NOTE: Active men and teenagers should make the following changes in the size of their portions: apple juice, 1½ cups; veal burger, 1½ servings.

DAY 10

BREAKFAST 1 Cashew Rice Cake*
1 medium tangerine
Choice of beverage

LUNCH 5 medium shrimp
3 rice cakes
1 cup steamed asparagus
2 cups steamed endive
1 cup fresh cherries
Choice of beverage

DINNER 1 serving Caribbean Shrimp Kabobs*
1 cup cooked Brown Rice*
2 cups Boston lettuce
1 serving Orange Peaches*
Choice of beverage

MEAL	KCAL	PRO	CARB	FAT	SAFA	MFAT	PFAT	CHOL	CALC	IRON	SOD
Breakfast	107.3	1.7gm	22.7gm	1.9gm	0.2gm	0.7gm	0.2gm	0.0mg	15.8mg	0.1mg	12.4mg
Lunch	268.8	14.0gm	52.6gm	2.9gm	0.4gm	0.0gm	0.2gm	24.0mg	163.9mg	3.8mg	44.4mg
Dinner	475.3	30.1gm	74.8gm	7.3gm	0.4gm	0.4gm	2.6gm	171.4mg	182.5mg	3.2mg	514.5mg
Total	851.4	45.8gm	150.1gm	12.1gm	1.0gm	1.1gm	3.0gm	195.4mg	362.2mg	7.1mg	571.3mg

* Recipe appears in Part IV.

NOTE: Active men and teenagers should make the following changes in the size of their portions: cashew rice cake, 2; caribbean shrimp kabobs, 1½ servings; orange peaches, 2 servings.

DAY 11

BREAKFAST
1 Silver Dollar Buckwheat Pancake*
2 teaspoons Raisin Topping*
½ medium mango
Choice of beverage

LUNCH
½ cup pineapple juice
Steamed vegetable plate (½ cup each of broccoli, brussels sprouts, and carrots)
1 cup cooked Buckwheat*
½ medium cooked acorn squash
Choice of beverage

DINNER
6 ounces broiled sea scallops
½ cup cooked Buckwheat*
1 serving Carrots with Basil*
2 cups escarole
Choice of beverage

MEAL	KCAL	PRO	CARB	FAT	SAFA	MFAT	PFAT	CHOL	CALC	IRON	SOD
Breakfast	229.1	1.7gm	37.1gm	9.5gm	0.9gm	1.1gm	6.7gm	0.0mg	25.9mg	0.1mg	59.2mg
Lunch	539.9	15.2gm	124.5gm	1.2gm	0.1gm	0.1gm	0.3gm	0.0mg	259.7mg	6.4mg	6.9mg
Dinner	405.4	44.6gm	38.0gm	9.5gm	0.6gm	0.8gm	5.1gm	91.4mg	329.3mg	6.9mg	495.8mg
Total	1174.4	61.5gm	199.6gm	20.2gm	1.6gm	2.0gm	12.1gm	91.4mg	650.9mg	13.4mg	637.5mg

* Recipe appears in Part IV.

NOTE: Active men and teenagers should make the following changes in the size of their portions: silver dollar buckwheat pancake, 2; raisin topping, 4 teaspoons; pineapple juice, 1 cup; cooked acorn squash, 1 medium.

DAY 12

BREAKFAST
½ cup grapefruit juice
½ cup barley cereal
2 unsweetened dates
Choice of beverage

LUNCH
4 ounces cold white-meat chicken, sliced
½ cup cooked green peas
½ cup sliced red pepper
1 cup shredded cabbage
1 grapefruit half
Choice of beverage

DINNER
1 serving Roast Chicken with Spinach-Barley Stuffing*
1 cup steamed zucchini
1 cup red-leaf lettuce
1 cup red or green grapes
Choice of beverage

MEAL	KCAL	PRO	CARB	FAT	SAFA	MFAT	PFAT	CHOL	CALC	IRON	SOD
Breakfast	186.9	3.0gm	45.0gm	0.4gm	0.0gm	0.0gm	0.0gm	0.0mg	19.1mg	1.2mg	3.7mg
Lunch	338.7	38.5gm	27.0gm	8.7gm	2.3gm	3.0gm	1.9gm	99.0mg	89.9mg	3.2mg	116.8mg
Dinner	368.1	27.5gm	48.1gm	9.1gm	1.9gm	2.5gm	3.3gm	62.5mg	120.5mg	1,7mg	188.7mg
Total	893.7	69.0gm	120.1gm	18.2gm	4.2gm	5.5gm	5.2gm	161.5mg	229.5mg	6.1mg	309.2mg

* Recipe appears in Part IV.

NOTE: Active men and teenagers should make the following changes in the size of their portions: grapefruit juice, 1 cup; white meat chicken, 6 ounces; cooked green peas, 1 cup; steamed zucchini, 2 cups.

DAY 13

BREAKFAST
½ cup cooked oatmeal*
1 medium apple, sliced
Choice of beverage

LUNCH
3½ ounces cold poached salmon
1 medium boiled potato
1 cup cold cooked green beans
2 cups romaine lettuce
1 medium apple, sliced
Choice of beverage

DINNER   4 ounces white-meat turkey, sliced
              1 medium sweet potato
              1 cup green beans
              2 cups romaine lettuce
              1 serving Baked Peaches*
              Choice of beverage

MEAL	KCAL	PRO	CARB	FAT	SAFA	MFAT	PFAT	CHOL	CALC	IRON	SOD
Breakfast	153.9	3.3gm	33.7gm	1.7gm	0.3gm	0.4gm	0.5gm	0.0mg	19.0mg	1.0mg	1.2mg
Lunch	433.5	33.2gm	59.1gm	8.6gm	0.1gm	0.0gm	0.1gm	47.0mg	568.0mg	4.1mg	136.3mg
Dinner	468.0	41.0gm	62.4gm	6.9gm	1.4gm	1.8gm	1.0gm	78.0mg	222.5mg	4.9mg	239.6mg
Total	1055.4	77.5gm	155.2gm	17.2gm	1.8gm	2.2gm	1.6gm	125.0mg	809.5mg	10.0mg	377.1mg

* Recipe appears in Part IV. (Directions for cooking oatmeal appear in Table 12, page 77.)

NOTE: Active men and teenagers should make the following changes in the size of their portions: oatmeal, 1 cup; cold cooked green beans, 2 cups; sliced white-meat turkey, 6 ounces; baked peaches, 2 servings.

DAY 14

BREAKFAST   ½ cup orange juice
             1 rice cake
             Choice of beverage

LUNCH   ½ cup cooked lentils*
             ¾ cup cooked Brown Rice*
             1 cup steamed zucchini
             1 medium orange, sliced
             Choice of beverage

DINNER   1 lean lamb chop, broiled (6 ounces)
             1 serving Lentils and Rice*
             1 serving Beets à l'Orange*
             1 medium kiwi
             Choice of beverage

MEAL	KCAL	PRO	CARB	FAT	SAFA	MFAT	PFAT	CHOL	CALC	IRON	SOD
Breakfast	131.9	2.4gm	23.9gm	3.5gm	0.2gm	2.0gm	0.6gm	0.0mg	31.7mg	0.1mg	12.6mg
Lunch	344.6	13.1gm	73.1gm	2.1gm	15.0gm	0.0gm	0.0gm	0.0mg	153.1mg	4.2mg	213.0mg
Dinner	638.7	56.0gm	52.4gm	23.0gm	7.5gm	5.1gm	3.7gm	170.5mg	81.6mg	3.7mg	277.6mg
Total	1115.2	71.5gm	149.4gm	28.6gm	22.7gm	7.1gm	4.3gm	170.5mg	266.4mg	8.0mg	503.2mg

* Recipe appears in Part IV. (Directions for cooking lentils appear in Table 13, page 81.)

NOTE: Active men and teenagers should make the following changes in the size of their portions: orange juice, 1 cup; rice cakes, 3; cooked brown rice, 1¼ cups; steamed zucchini, 1½ cups; beets à l'orange, 2 servings.

DAY 15

BREAKFAST   ½ cup pineapple juice
1 cup cooked Buckwheat*
Choice of beverage

LUNCH   1 cup cooked Buckwheat*
Steamed vegetable plate (½ cup each of broccoli, brussels sprouts, and carrots)
2 cups Boston lettuce
1 medium banana
Choice of beverage

DINNER   1 serving Veal and Onion Dinner*
½ medium baked butternut squash
1 serving Brussels Sprouts with Lemon-Parsley Sauce*
2 slices unsweetened pineapple
Choice of beverage

MEAL	KCAL	PRO	CARB	FAT	SAFA	MFAT	PFAT	CHOL	CALC	IRON	SOD
Breakfast	262.3	4.4gm	57.0gm	0.1gm	0.0gm	0.0gm	0.0gm	0.0mg	21.1mg	0.3mg	1.2mg
Lunch	405.7	10.9gm	89.8gm	1.6gm	0.3gm	0.1gm	0.3gm	0.0mg	186.6mg	4.8mg	88.1mg
Dinner	727.7	43.3gm	104.9gm	26.9gm	8.9gm	0.8gm	5.4gm	116.0mg	207.7mg	2.4mg	182.0mg
Total	1395.7	58.6gm	111.2gm	28.6gm	9.2gm	0.9gm	5.7gm	116.0mg	415.4mg	7.5mg	271.3mg

* Recipe appears in Part IV.

NOTE: Active men and teenagers should make the following changes in the size of their portions: pineapple juice, 1 cup; veal and onion dinner, 1½ servings; brussels sprouts with lemon-parsley sauce, 1½ servings.

DAY 16

BREAKFAST   ½ cup cooked millet cereal
1 cup strawberries
Choice of beverage

LUNCH   2 cups spinach leaves
½ cup each sliced green and red pepper
1 grapefruit half
Choice of beverage

DINNER   1 serving Tuna Steak*
1 cup cooked Millet*
1 serving Steamed Broccoli with Pumpkin Seeds*
1 cup strawberries
Choice of beverage

MEAL	KCAL	PRO	CARB	FAT	SAFA	MFAT	PFAT	CHOL	CALC	IRON	SOD
Breakfast	126.7	3.4gm	28.7gm	1.3gm	0.3gm	0.3gm	0.5gm	0.0mg	26.0mg	2.3mg	1.8mg
Lunch	264.0	9.8gm	30.4gm	14.7gm	1.2gm	1.6gm	10.1gm	0.0mg	201.8mg	6.5mg	171.9mg
Dinner	608.2	50.9gm	70.9gm	18.3gm	2.0gm	3.1gm	5.6gm	60.6mg	356.0mg	4.0mg	73.1mg
Total	998.9	64.1gm	130.0gm	34.3gm	3.5gm	5.0gm	16.1gm	60.6mg	583.8mg	12.8mg	92.8mg

* Recipe appears in Part IV.

NOTE: Active men and teenagers should make the following changes in the size of their portions: strawberries, 2 cups; tuna steak, 1½ servings; steamed broccoli with pumpkin seeds, 1½ servings.

DAY 17

BREAKFAST   1 Cinnamon-Oat-Honey Muffin*
1 cantaloupe half
Choice of beverage

LUNCH   4 ounces sliced white-meat turkey
1 cup steamed green beans
1 medium tomato, sliced
1 cup sliced celery
2 cups romaine lettuce
½ cup cantaloupe balls
Choice of beverage

DINNER   1 serving Seviche*
1 medium boiled potato
1 cup steamed green beans
2 cups romaine lettuce
Choice of beverage

MEAL	KCAL	PRO	CARB	FAT	SAFA	MFAT	PFAT	CHOL	CALC	IRON	SOD
Breakfast	210.8	4.1gm	39.0gm	6.2gm	0.5gm	0.8gm	3.4gm	0.0mg	58.4mg	0.5mg	136.6mg
Lunch	317.5	40.9gm	30.5gm	4.8gm	1.2gm	0.6gm	0.7gm	78.0mg	238.2mg	5.2mg	250.6mg
Dinner	247.5	15.0gm	41.6gm	4.0gm	0.2gm	0.2gm	1.8gm	20.4mg	198.6mg	2.7mg	212.1mg
Total	775.8	60.0gm	111.1gm	15.0gm	1.9gm	1.6gm	8.6gm	98.4mg	495.2mg	8.4mg	599.3mg

* Recipe appears in Part IV.

NOTE: Active men and teenagers should make the following changes in the size of their portions: sliced white-meat turkey, 6 ounces; steamed green beans, 2 cups; seviche, 2 servings.

DAY 18

BREAKFAST   ½ cup orange juice
1½ cups puffed brown rice cereal
1 medium orange, sliced
Choice of beverage

LUNCH   2 rice cakes
2 cups Boston lettuce
1 medium orange
Choice of beverage

DINNER   1 serving Caribbean Shrimp Kabobs*
1 cup cooked Brown Rice*
1 cup steamed asparagus
2 cups Boston lettuce
1 medium mango half
Choice of beverage

MEAL	KCAL	PRO	CARB	FAT	SAFA	MFAT	PFAT	CHOL	CALC	IRON	SOD
Breakfast	285.8	4.9gm	66.1gm	0.5gm	0.0gm	0.0gm	0.0gm	0.0mg	69.8mg	2.9mg	510.7mg
Lunch	181.0	5.3gm	34.5gm	3.7gm	0.0gm	0.0gm	0.0gm	0.0mg	100.7mg	2.3mg	33.3mg
Dinner	555.3	34.9gm	92.5gm	8.1gm	0.6gm	0.5gm	2.9gm	171.4mg	231.8mg	4.5mg	523.9mg
Total	1022.1	45.1gm	193.1gm	12.3gm	0.6gm	0.5gm	2.9gm	171.4mg	402.3mg	9.7mg	1067.9mg

* Recipe appears in Part IV.

NOTE: Active men and teenagers should make the following changes in the size of their portions: orange juice, 1½ cups; rice cakes, 3; Caribbean shrimp kabob, 1½ servings.

DAY 19

BREAKFAST   ½ cup pineapple juice
2 rye wafers
1 tablespoon cashew butter
1 unsweetened pineapple slice
Choice of beverage

LUNCH   4 ounces cold cooked lobster
2 rye wafers
1 cup sliced carrots
1 cup escarole
½ cup unsweetened pineapple tidbits
Choice of beverage

DINNER   1 serving Lamb Shanks*
1 serving Carrots and Parsnips*
2 cups steamed kale
¼ fresh pineapple
Choice of beverage

NOTE: You may use commercially prepared cashew butter, but check the label carefully for preservatives, sugar, corn syrup, etc. If you prefer to make your own, simply toss a cup of cashews into the blender or food processor and process until smooth.

MEAL	KCAL	PRO	CARB	FAT	SAFA	MFAT	PFAT	CHOL	CALC	IRON	SOD
Breakfast	142.0	2.2gm	27.8gm	3.0gm	0.5gm	1.5gm	0.5gm	0.0mg	34.8mg	1.0mg	45.0mg
Lunch	261.4	24.4gm	37.0gm	2.3gm	0.0gm	0.0gm	0.0gm	96.4mg	174.9mg	3.0mg	340.6mg
Dinner	805.9	47.4gm	100.7gm	27.1gm	7.8gm	1.7gm	10.3gm	118.7mg	562.7mg	3.8mg	293.1mg
Total	1209.3	74.0gm	165.5gm	32.4gm	8.3gm	3.2gm	10.8gm	215.1mg	772.4mg	7.8mg	678.7mg

* Recipe appears in Part IV.

NOTE: Active men and teenagers should make the following changes in the size of their portions: pineapple juice, 1 cup; lamb shanks, 1½ servings.

DAY 20

BREAKFAST ½ cup pear juice
½ cup barley cereal
1 cup raspberries
Choice of beverage

LUNCH 3½ ounces water-packed tuna
½ cup each shredded white and red cabbage
½ cup each green and red pepper slices
½ cup raspberries
Choice of beverage

DINNER 1 serving Salmon Steak*
1 cup boiled barley
2 cups steamed broccoli
1 medium pear
Choice of beverage

MEAL	KCAL	PRO	CARB	FAT	SAFA	MFAT	PFAT	CHOL	CALC	IRON	SOD
Breakfast	228.4	3.6gm	55.2gm	0.9gm	0.0gm	0.0gm	0.0gm	0.0mg	37.1mg	1.9mg	6.9mg
Lunch	206.1	30.9gm	18.4gm	1.4gm	0.0gm	0.0gm	0.0gm	62.4mg	78.6mg	3.3mg	485.7mg
Dinner	584.2	45.2gm	112.2gm	10.5gm	0.2gm	0.2gm	0.2gm	53.6mg	867.9mg	5.0mg	167.5mg
Total	1018.7	79.7gm	185.8gm	12.8gm	0.2gm	0.2gm	0.2gm	116.0mg	983.6mg	10.2mg	660.1mg

* Recipe appears in Part IV.

NOTE: Active men and teenagers should make the following changes in the size of their portions: pear juice, 1 cup; raspberries, 2 cups; salmon steak, 1½ servings.

DAY 21

BREAKFAST 1 serving Silver Dollar Buckwheat Pancakes*
2 tablespoons pure honey
Choice of beverage

LUNCH ½ cup cooked chick-peas*
1 serving Cauliflower-Fruit Slaw*
1 cup mashed cooked turnip
2 cups romaine lettuce
Choice of beverage

DINNER   1 serving Oriental Scallops*
1 serving Millet-Onion Sauté*
1 cup steamed eggplant
1 cup cooked turnip greens
Choice of beverage

MEAL	KCAL	PRO	CARB	FAT	SAFA	MFAT	PFAT	CHOL	CALC	IRON	SOD
Breakfast	274.3	2.7gm	39.9gm	15.6gm	1.3gm	1.7gm	10.2gm	0.0mg	69.6mg	0.5mg	88.4mg
Lunch	467.0	23.7gm	81.6gm	7.1gm	0.5gm	2.6gm	3.4gm	0.0mg	266.4mg	8.2mg	88.6mg
Dinner	475.0	38.8gm	66.3gm	11.5gm	0.6gm	0.9gm	5.3gm	60.2mg	439.8mg	2.7mg	394.6mg
Total	1216.3	65.2gm	187.8gm	34.2gm	2.4gm	5.2gm	18.9gm	60.2mg	775.8mg	11.4mg	571.6mg

* Recipe appears in Part IV. (Directions for cooking chick-peas appear in Table 12, on page 81.)

NOTE: Active men and teenagers should make the following changes in the size of their portions: Cauliflower-fruit slaw, 2 servings; oriental scallops, 1½ servings; millet-onion-sauté, 1½ servings.

CHAPTER 8

Phase II: Reintroduction
A 14-Day Menu Plan

Now you're ready to begin the Reintroduction Diet, when you systematically reintroduce specific foods to your diet to see if any of them causes a bad reaction. At this point, you will be more tuned into your body's signals, and you should be able to notice even the most subtle symptoms. A twinge here, an ache there, a slight soreness in a joint, or a rumbling in the tummy—our bodies send us hundreds of these clues each day.

As you challenge your body by reintroducing (one at a time) each of the Sinister Seven—cow's milk and products, wheat, yeast, eggs, corn, soy products, and cane sugar—your immune system might rebel by bringing on the old headaches, cramps, or other aches again. Observe closely and pay attention to those signals. During this period, you must assume that anything wrong with you is due to something you've eaten—especially if you had experienced the symptom before and it disappeared during the preceding 21 days. Once you gather all these clues, you're on your way to solving your own immune mystery and tailoring a diet plan cued into your immune system.

For best results, I suggest you do the following as you gear up for the Reintroduction Phase:

1. Reintroduce *one* of the Sinister Seven every other day.

2. Reintroduce each of the Sinister Seven target foods in as pure a form as possible. For instance, when reintroducing wheat, try to eat 100 percent pure wheat cereal, bread, or pasta. Don't eat wheat products that contain other Sinister Seven foods, such as pancakes made with wheat flour *and* eggs.

3. Reintroduce the target food for that day at least two but no more than three different times throughout the day. Keep the quan-

tities of the target food to a minimum, since you will be following the Elimination Diet on alternate days.

4. Make sure you note your reactions, which may occur in five minutes or five hours. These are just some of the things to check for: headache, nausea, flatulence, itchiness, soreness, inflammation, rash, fatigue, depression, general feeling of unwellness.

5. Once you have reintroduced a Sinister Seven food, if you notice no adverse reactions you may continue to use it.

A hypothetical Reintroduction schedule could look like this:

Day 1	Reintroduce Wheat	* Cream of wheat for breakfast * Bulgur instead of rice or potato * Thicken sauce with flour
Day 2	Elimination Diet	
Day 3	Reintroduce Corn	* Cornmeal for breakfast * Serving of corn on the cob * Thicken sauce with cornstarch
Day 4	Elimination Diet	
Day 5	Reintroduce Sugar	* Add a teaspoon of sugar to anything twice a day
Day 6	Elimination Diet	
Day 7	Reintroduce Eggs	* Soft-boiled egg for breakfast * Hard-cooked egg for lunch
Day 8	Elimination Diet	
Day 9	Reintroduce Soy	* Add tofu to your salad * Add soy sauce to a stir-fry * Baste chicken with soy sauce
Day 10	Elimination Diet	
Day 11	Reintroduce Cow's Milk	* Drink a glass of milk * Have low-fat cottage cheese on your salad * Spoon yogurt or sour cream onto your baked potato
Day 12	Elimination Diet	
Day 13	Reintroduce Yeast	* Add mushrooms to your salad * Make a salad dressing with vinegar
Day 14	Elimination Diet	

The above list should serve simply as an example—not a hard-and fast schedule. You may introduce the Sinister Seven in any order you like, and you have many choices when it comes to reintroducing a given ingredient. (For instance, if you can't stand yogurt, you don't have to eat it!) For those who appreciate a little more guidance, on the following pages we have included a more detailed 14-day sample Reintroduction Plan. Your "choice of beverage" is the same as for the Elimination Diet (see list page 105).

Each day's menus are followed by a nutritional analysis of all the foods consumed, first broken down according to the meal and then totaled for the day. In the analysis charts, KCAL means calories; PRO means protein; CARB means carbohydrates; FAT means total fat; SAFA means saturated fat; MFAT means monounsaturated fat; PFAT means polyunsaturated fat; CHOL means cholesterol; CALC means calcium; IRON means iron; and SOD means sodium.

The most important thing to remember about reintroduction is to relax! It's not difficult to follow the plan; it just takes a few minutes to plan your meals. You're *in control* of what you eat. Once you realize that, your problems will be over.

REINTRODUCTION PLAN

DAY 1
(Reintroducing Wheat)

BREAKFAST   1 Plain Whole Wheat Muffin*
1 grapefruit half
Choice of beverage

LUNCH   3 ounces cooked whole wheat pasta
½ cup Spaghetti Sauce*
2 cups iceberg lettuce
1 grapefruit half
Choice of beverage

DINNER   5 ounces broiled fillet of sole
1 cup steamed broccoli
1 medium broiled tomato
2 cups escarole
Choice of beverage

NOTE: The muffin and the pasta contain wheat.

MEAL	KCAL	PRO	CARB	FAT	SAFA	MFAT	PFAT	CHOL	CALC	IRON	SOD
Breakfast	201.2	3.7gm	29.2gm	8.9gm	0.8gm	3.0gm	4.3gm	0.0mg	42.6mg	0.1mg	112.8mg
Lunch	469.6	15.3gm	92.4gm	6.4gm	0.4gm	0.5gm	3.4gm	0.0mg	60.6mg	0.6mg	765.4mg
Dinner	235.1	17.6gm	27.5gm	8.1gm	0.7gm	0.8gm	5.0gm	0.0mg	322.6mg	4.4mg	71.0mg
Total	704.7	36.6gm	149.1gm	23.4gm	1.9gm	4.3gm	12.7gm	0.0mg	425.8mg	5.1mg	949.2mg

* Recipe appears in Part IV.

NOTE: Active men and teenagers should make the following changes in the size of their portions: whole wheat muffin, 1½; cooked whole wheat pasta, 4 ounces; broiled fillet of sole, 7 ounces.

DAY 2
(Elimination Day)

BREAKFAST
1 cup pear juice
1 cup rye cereal
1 teaspoon caraway seeds
Choice of beverage

LUNCH
1 serving Carrot and Spinach Salad*
1 tablespoon Vinaigrette Dressing*
2 rye crackers
1 medium pear
Choice of beverage

DINNER
1 serving Minted Chicken Breast*
½ cup cooked green peas
1 cup steamed carrots
2 cups romaine lettuce
1 medium pear
Choice of beverage

MEAL	KCAL	PRO	CARB	FAT	SAFA	MFAT	PFAT	CHOL	CALC	IRON	SOD
Breakfast	239.7	3.7gm	58.6gm	0.8gm	0.0gm	0.2gm	0.1gm	0.0mg	36.9mg	1.9mg	10.6mg
Lunch	221.3	4.7gm	45.4gm	4.4gm	0.2gm	0.4gm	2.2gm	0.0mg	124.8mg	2.3mg	106.3mg
Dinner	455.5	39.6gm	66.7gm	5.2gm	0.9gm	0.2gm	1.1gm	73.0mg	216.6mg	5.6mg	202.3mg
Total	916.5	48.0gm	170.7gm	10.4gm	1.1gm	0.8gm	3.4gm	73.0mg	378.3mg	9.8mg	319.2mg

* Recipe appears in Part IV.

NOTE: Active men and teenagers should make the following changes in the size of their portions: carrot and spinach salad, 2 servings; minted chicken breast, 1½ servings; cooked green peas, 1 cup.

DAY 3
(Reintroducing Eggs)

BREAKFAST
½ cup pineapple juice
1 serving Scrambled Eggs with Feta Cheese*
Choice of beverage

LUNCH 1 serving Antipasto Plate*
2 rice cakes
2 unsweetened pineapple slices
Choice of beverage

DINNER 6 ounces roast veal
½ cup cooked Brown Rice*
½ cup cooked green pepper
2 cups iceberg lettuce
1 medium kiwi
Choice of beverage

NOTE: In addition to the scrambled eggs, the antipasto contains eggs.

MEAL	KCAL	PRO	CARB	FAT	SAFA	MFAT	PFAT	CHOL	CALC	IRON	SOD
Breakfast	167.4	7.4gm	17.9gm	7.2gm	2.7gm	2.5gm	0.7gm	280.3mg	84.5mg	0.3mg	150.2mg
Lunch	369.2	38.2gm	30.6gm	11.4gm	2.0gm	2.2gm	1.7gm	308.7mg	88.0mg	0.5mg	203.0mg
Dinner	555.7	50.9gm	41.8gm	20.0gm	9.1gm	8.3gm	0.4gm	171.7mg	78.1mg	7.1mg	270.1mg
Total	1092.3	96.5gm	90.3gm	38.6gm	13.8gm	13.0gm	2.8gm	760.7mg	250.6mg	7.9mg	623.3mg

* Recipe appears in Part IV.

NOTE: Active men and teenagers should make the following changes in the size of their portions: pineapple juice, 1 cup; scrambled egg with feta cheese, 2 servings.

DAY 4
(Elimination Day)

BREAKFAST ½ cup apricot juice
½ cup oatmeal*
1 medium banana, sliced
Choice of beverage

LUNCH 3½ ounces cold poached salmon
1 medium boiled potato
1 cup cold cooked green beans
2 cups Boston lettuce
1 medium banana
Choice of beverage

DINNER 6 ounces broiled sea scallops
1 medium baked potato
1 cup steamed green beans
1 cup steamed kale
2 cups Boston lettuce
Choice of beverage

MEAL	KCAL	PRO	CARB	FAT	SAFA	MFAT	PFAT	CHOL	CALC	IRON	SOD
Breakfast	252.4	4.7gm	58.5gm	1.9gm	0.4gm	0.4gm	0.5gm	0.0mg	25.3mg	1.6mg	6.1mg
Lunch	457.1	34.0gm	64.7gm	8.6gm	0.2gm	0.0gm	0.1gm	47.0mg	529.1mg	4.9mg	137.5mg
Dinner	447.6	51.7gm	60.1gm	3.8gm	0.0gm	0.0gm	0.1gm	91.4mg	519.9mg	11.9mg	543.6mg
Total	1157.1	90.4gm	183.3gm	14.3gm	0.6gm	0.4gm	0.7gm	138.4mg	1074.3mg	18.4mg	687.2mg

* Directions for cooking oatmeal appear in Table 12, page 77.

NOTE: Active men and teenagers should make the following changes in the size of their portions: apricot juice, 1 cup; oatmeal, 1 cup; baked potato, 1 large.

DAY 5
(Reintroducing Cow's Milk)

BREAKFAST ½ cup low-fat plain yogurt sprinkled with 2 teaspoons all-bran cereal
½ cup unsweeetened applesauce
1 grapefruit half
Choice of beverage

LUNCH 2 ounces low-fat cottage cheese
1 cup steamed beet greens
1 medium tomato, sliced
1 cup chopped celery
2 cups red-leaf lettuce
1 medium apple
Choice of beverage

DINNER 1 serving Tuna Steak*
½ cup cooked mustard greens
1 cup each chopped celery and tomatoes
1 cup red-leaf lettuce
1 medium unpeeled apple

NOTE: The yogurt and the cottage cheese contain cow's milk.

MEAL	KCAL	PRO	CARB	FAT	SAFA	MFAT	PFAT	CHOL	CALC	IRON	SOD
Breakfast	634.3	7.5gm	153.7gm	5.1gm	2.6gm	1.4gm	0.2gm	14.4mg	188.1mg	1.9mg	117.2mg
Lunch	228.6	14.1gm	44.4gm	2.1gm	0.4gm	0.2gm	0.0gm	2.5mg	332.9mg	5.8mg	677.2mg
Dinner	442.7	44.1gm	53.1gm	9.5gm	0.1gm	0.0gm	1.1gm	60.6mg	456.0mg	9.5mg	337.3mg
Total	1305.6	65.7gm	251.2gm	16.7gm	3.1gm	1.6gm	1.3gm	77.5mg	977.0mg	17.2mg	1131.7mg

* Recipe appears in Part IV.

NOTE: Active men and teenagers should make the following changes in the size of their portions: low-fat plain yogurt, 1 cup; low-fat cottage cheese, 4 ounces; tuna steak, 1½ servings.

DAY 6
(Elimination Day)

BREAKFAST 2 rye wafers
1 teaspoon almond butter
1 teaspoon honey
1 cantaloupe half
Choice of beverage

LUNCH 1 serving Chick-Pea Soup*
2 rye crackers
1 medium carrot
1 cantaloupe half
Choice of beverage

DINNER 1 serving Orange Baked Chicken*
1 medium baked sweet potato
1 cup steamed spinach
2 cups romaine lettuce
1 cantaloupe half
Choice of beverage

NOTE: You may use commercially prepared almond butter, but check the label carefully for preservatives, sugar, corn syrup, etc. If you prefer to make your own, simply toss a cup of almonds into the blender or food processor and process until smooth.

MEAL	KCAL	PRO	CARB	FAT	SAFA	MFAT	PFAT	CHOL	CALC	IRON	SOD
Breakfast	127.9	2.8gm	22.3gm	3.8gm	0.3gm	2.1gm	0.7gm	0.0mg	28.5mg	0.7mg	93.3mg
Lunch	328.2	9.2gm	74.8gm	8.5gm	0.6gm	0.8gm	4.2gm	0.0mg	112.7mg	1.3mg	515.0mg
Dinner	469.5	38.3gm	72.7gm	5.1gm	1.0gm	1.3gm	0.9gm	73.0mg	409.1mg	9.5mg	371.2mg
Total	925.6	50.3gm	169.8gm	17.4gm	1.6gm	4.2gm	11.2gm	73.0mg	550.3mg	3.1mg	979.5mg

* Recipe appears in Part IV.

NOTE: Active men and teenagers should make the following changes in the size of their portions: rye wafers, 4; almond butter, 2 teaspoons; chick-pea soup, 2 servings, orange baked chicken, 1½ servings.

DAY 7
(Reintroducing Yeast)

BREAKFAST ½ cup pineapple juice
2 rice cakes
2 tablespoons cashew butter
½ cup unsweetened pineapple tidbits
Choice of beverage

LUNCH 3 ounces water-packed tuna
2 rice cakes
1 medium red pepper, sliced
2 large black olives
2 unsweetened pineapple slices
1 small dill pickle
Choice of beverage

DINNER
1 serving Fish Fillets in Wine Sauce*
1 cup cooked Brown Rice*
½ cup steamed brussels sprouts
2 cups iceberg lettuce
1 medium tangerine
Choice of beverage

NOTE: The dill pickle and the wine sauce contain yeast. You may use commercially prepared cashew butter, but check the label carefully for preservatives, sugar, corn syrup, etc. If you prefer to make your own, simply toss a cup of cashews into the blender or food processor and process until smooth.

MEAL	KCAL	PRO	CARB	FAT	SAFA	MFAT	PFAT	CHOL	CALC	IRON	SOD
Breakfast	400.5	8.1gm	59.5gm	16.6gm	3.1gm	9.3gm	2.7gm	0.0mg	52.6mg	2.3mg	8.5mg
Lunch	320.3	28.1gm	41.3gm	5.7gm	0.0gm	0.0gm	0.0gm	53.6mg	82.5mg	2.9mg	562.6mg
Dinner	567.1	43.5gm	74.2gm	11.6gm	0.9gm	1.0gm	6.9gm	0.0mg	176.3mg	2.6mg	382.1mg
Total	1287.9	79.7gm	175.0gm	33.9gm	4.0gm	10.3gm	9.6gm	53.6mg	311.4mg	7.8mg	953.2mg

* Recipe appears in Part IV.

NOTE: Active men and teenagers should make the following changes in the size of their portions: pineapple juice, 1 cup; rice cakes, 3; cashew butter, 3 tablespoons; water-packed tuna, 4 ounces; fish fillets in wine sauce, 1½ servings.

DAY 8
(Elimination Day)

BREAKFAST
½ cup cooked oatmeal*
½ cup fresh sliced peaches
Choice of beverage

LUNCH
3½ ounces broiled salmon
1 medium boiled potato
1 cup green beans
2 cups Boston lettuce
Orange Peaches*
Choice of beverage

DINNER   1 serving Veal Chop Rosemary*
1 serving Potato Pancakes*
1 serving Beets à l'Orange*
2 cups Boston lettuce
Choice of beverage

MEAL	KCAL	PRO	CARB	FAT	SAFA	MFAT	PFAT	CHOL	CALC	IRON	SOD
Breakfast	109.0	3.6gm	22.0gm	1.2gm	0.2gm	0.4gm	0.5gm	0.0mg	13.6mg	0.9mg	1.2mg
Lunch	379.1	33.2gm	44.7gm	8.2gm	0.0gm	0.0gm	0.1gm	47.0mg	527.1mg	119.3mg	464.0mg
Dinner	383.0	25.8gm	22.1gm	20.4gm	6.7gm	0.9gm	4.3gm	87.0mg	61.5mg	2.2mg	122.3mg
Total	871.1	62.6gm	88.8gm	29.8gm	6.9gm	1.3gm	4.9gm	134.0mg	602.2mg	122.4mg	587.5mg

* Recipe appears in Part IV. (Directions for cooking oatmeal appear in Table 12, page 77.)

NOTE: Active men and teenagers should make the following changes in the size of their portions: oatmeal, 1 cup; broiled salmon, 5 ounces; veal chop rosemary, 1½ servings; potato pancakes, 1½ servings.

DAY 9
(Reintroducing Corn)

BREAKFAST   ½ cup grapefruit juice
1½ cups puffed corn cereal
1 grapefruit half
Choice of beverage

LUNCH   1 corn taco
1 medium tomato, sliced
1 cup broccoli, steamed
1 cup escarole
1 cup cubed mango
Choice of beverage

DINNER   1 cup fresh or frozen whole kernel corn
1 serving Broccoli with Pumpkin Seeds*
2 cups escarole
Choice of beverage

MEAL	KCAL	PRO	CARB	FAT	SAFA	MFAT	PFAT	CHOL	CALC	IRON	SOD
Breakfast	194.8	3.9gm	43.8gm	0.9gm	0.2gm	0.3gm	0.6gm	0.0mg	57.8mg	8.9mg	360.8mg
Lunch	182.2	7.4gm	37.1gm	3.0gm	0.0gm	0.1gm	0.0gm	0.0mg	179.1mg	3.1mg	99.3mg
Dinner	317.6	17.9gm	50.8gm	10.2gm	1.5gm	2.5gm	3.9gm	0.0mg	353.7mg	2.6mg	43.7mg
Total	694.6	29.2gm	131.7gm	14.1gm	1.7gm	2.9gm	4.5gm	0.0mg	590.6mg	14.6mg	503.0mg

* Recipe appears in Part IV.

NOTE: Active men and teenagers should make the following changes in the size of their portions: grapefruit juice, 1 cup; corn taco, 2; sliced tomato, 2; steamed broccoli with pumpkin seeds, 1½ servings.

DAY 10
(Elimination Day)

BREAKFAST | 1 cup cooked rye* mixed with 1 teaspoon caraway seeds
1 medium pear, sliced
Choice of beverage

LUNCH | 1 serving Chick-Pea Soup*
2 rye crackers
2 radishes
½ medium yellow summer squash, steamed and sliced
Choice of beverage

DINNER | 1 serving Lemon Dill Chicken*
½ cup cooked lima beans
1 serving Carrots with Basil*
1 medium onion, sliced
½ medium yellow summer squash, steamed and sliced
1 medium pear
Choice of beverage

MEAL	KCAL	PRO	CARB	FAT	SAFA	MFAT	PFAT	CHOL	CALC	IRON	SOD
Breakfast	272.3	7.1gm	62.9gm	1.8gm	0.0gm	0.3gm	0.2gm	0.0mg	52.3mg	2.6mg	0.9mg
Lunch	221.6	7.1gm	49.3gm	7.8gm	0.5gm	0.6gm	4.1gm	0.0mg	86.2mg	1.5mg	465.9mg
Dinner	490.7	36.2gm	65.1gm	11.3gm	1.6gm	1.9gm	6.0gm	73.0mg	171.3mg	3.9mg	116.8mg
Total	984.6	50.4gm	177.3gm	20.9gm	2.1gm	2.8gm	10.3gm	73.0mg	309.8mg	8.0mg	583.6mg

* Recipe appears in Part IV. (Directions for cooking rye appear in Table 12, page 77.)

NOTE: Active men and teenagers should make the following changes in the size of their portions: chick-pea soup, 2 servings; lemon dill chicken, 1½ servings; cooked lima beans, 1 cup.

DAY 11
(Reintroducing Soy)

BREAKFAST   ½ cup apple juice
            1 Apple Rice Muffin*
            Choice of beverage

LUNCH   6 medium cold steamed shrimp
            2 rice cakes
            1 serving Bean Sprout Salad*
            1 medium apple
            Choice of beverage

DINNER   5 medium shrimp, steamed
            1 serving Oriental Spaghetti*
            1 cup steamed tofu
            1 cup steamed brussels sprouts
            ½ cup unsweetened applesauce
            Choice of beverage

NOTE: The bean sprout salad, the tofu, and the spaghetti contain soy.

MEAL	KCAL	PRO	CARB	FAT	SAFA	MFAT	PFAT	CHOL	CALC	IRON	SOD
Breakfast	310.6	2.1gm	64.6gm	5.0gm	0.5gm	0.5gm	3.4gm	0.0mg	40.8mg	0.5mg	96.2mg
Lunch	244.9	10.7gm	46.4gm	3.8gm	0.5gm	0.9gm	1.0gm	24.0mg	73.0mg	0.8mg	340.4mg
Dinner	484.6	31.4gm	60.1gm	19.3gm	2.7gm	2.1gm	5.8gm	24.0mg	419.3mg	7.2mg	481.3mg
Total	1040.1	44.2gm	171.1gm	28.1gm	3.7gm	3.5gm	10.2gm	48.0mg	533.1mg	8.5mg	917.9mg

* Recipe appears in Part IV. (Apple Rice Muffins are a variant of Orange Rice Muffins.)

NOTE: Active men and teenagers should make the following changes in the size of their portions: apple juice, 1 cup; apple rice muffin, 1½; cold steamed shrimp, 10 medium; bean sprout salad, 1½ servings; unsweetened applesauce, 1 cup.

DAY 12
(Elimination Day)

BREAKFAST   ½ cup boiled Barley*
            ½ cup stewed prunes
            Choice of beverage

LUNCH   1 serving Sweet Potato Salad*
1 tablespoon Honey Vinaigrette Dressing*
2 cups Boston lettuce
1 medium peach, sliced
Choice of beverage

DINNER   1 broiled lamb chop (6 ounces)
½ cup boiled Barley*
1 cup steamed asparagus
2 cups Boston lettuce
¼ medium fresh pineapple
Choice of beverage

MEAL	KCAL	PRO	CARB	FAT	SAFA	MFAT	PFAT	CHOL	CALC	IRON	SOD
Breakfast	307.5	4.4gm	77.7gm	0.7gm	0.0gm	0.3gm	0.1gm	0.0mg	51.4mg	2.8mg	4.0mg
Lunch	330.6	5.0gm	52.1gm	13.2gm	1.1gm	1.5gm	9.5gm	0.0mg	89.6mg	2.3mg	199.0mg
Dinner	505.7	56.3gm	40.2gm	14.2gm	7.3gm	4.6gm	0.7gm	170.5mg	112.8mg	7.6mg	137.3mg
Total	1143.8	65.7gm	170.0gm	28.1gm	8.4gm	6.4gm	10.3gm	170.5mg	253.8mg	12.7mg	340.3mg

* Recipe appears in Part IV.

NOTE: Active men and teenagers should make the following changes in the size of their portions: boiled barley, 1 cup; sweet potato salad, 1½ servings; broiled lamb chop, 2; boiled barley, 1 cup.

DAY 13
(Reintroducing Sugar)

BREAKFAST   ½ cup orange juice
1 grapefruit half with 1 teaspoon table sugar
Choice of beverage

LUNCH   4 ounces water-packed tuna
1 medium tomato, sliced
1 cup chopped celery
2 cups romaine lettuce
Choice of beverage

DINNER   5 ounces broiled red snapper
          1 cup steamed broccoli
          1 medium tomato, sliced
          2 cups romaine lettuce
          ½ cup strawberries with 1 teaspoon table sugar
          Choice of beverage

NOTE: The table sugar is sprinkled on the fresh fruit.

MEAL	KCAL	PRO	CARB	FAT	SAFA	MFAT	PFAT	CHOL	CALC	IRON	SOD
Breakfast	103.0	1.4gm	25.3gm	0.2gm	0.0gm	0.0gm	0.0gm	0.0mg	23.0mg	0.2mg	1.3mg
Lunch	223.6	36.0gm	17.0gm	1.6gm	0.0gm	0.0gm	0.0gm	71.1mg	163.3mg	4.6mg	683.5mg
Dinner	275.6	36.6gm	30.3gm	2.6gm	0.1gm	0.1gm	0.2gm	78.0mg	309.6mg	5.6mg	127.1mg
Total	602.2	74.0gm	72.6gm	4.4gm	0.1gm	0.1gm	0.2gm	149.1mg	495.9mg	10.4mg	811.9mg

NOTE: Active men and teenagers should make the following changes in the size of their portions: orange juice, 1 cup; water-packed tuna, 6½ ounces; broiled red snapper, 7 ounces; strawberries, 1 cup.

DAY 14
(Elimination Day)

BREAKFAST 1 cup cooked rye cereal
           1 medium banana, sliced
           Choice of beverage

LUNCH   1 serving Sardine Snack*
           1 cup cooked green beans
           2 cups raw spinach leaves
           1 medium banana
           Choice of beverage

DINNER   1 serving Minted Chicken Breast*
½ cup cooked green peas
1 cup steamed carrots
2 cups chicory
1 medium pear
Choice of beverage

MEAL	KCAL	PRO	CARB	FAT	SAFA	MFAT	PFAT	CHOL	CALC	IRON	SOD
Breakfast	276.5	7.2gm	64.5gm	1.4gm	0.2gm	0.0gm	0.0gm	0.0mg	26.1mg	2.2mg	1.7mg
Lunch	359.4	17.2gm	53.4gm	5.1gm	0.2gm	0.0gm	9.0gm	63.8mg	169.9mg	2.6mg	251.5mg
Dinner	455.5	39.6gm	66.7gm	5.2gm	0.9gm	0.2gm	1.1gm	73.0mg	216.6mg	5.6mg	202.3mg
Total	1091.4	64.0gm	184.6gm	11.7gm	1.3gm	0.2gm	10.1gm	136.8mg	412.6mg	10.4mg	455.5mg

* Recipe appears in Part IV.

NOTE: Active men and teenagers should make the following changes in the size of their portions: banana, 1 large; sardine snack, 2 servings; minted chicken breast, 1½ servings; cooked green peas, 1 cup.

CHAPTER 9

Phase III: Maintenance
A Plan for Life

YOUR JOURNEY to total Immune Power is almost at an end! The trick now is to remain at your peak of immune health by building positive food habits into your life forever. How? By eating a well-balanced diet based on the principles of nutrition I have outlined in this book.

Just remember to eliminate completely any of the foods to which you have had a poor reaction and rotate all foods so that you don't eat the same food within four days. Once you discover what your danger foods are, you needn't eliminate them totally from your diet. Unless you have a severe allergic reaction, you can eventually start eating each of those foods again, providing you do so in moderation. While following the first two phases of the Immune Power Eating Plan, your body was cleansed of toxins, erasing the cumulative effects of overdosing on danger foods. This actually reduced the severity of the immune response, allowing your body to rebuild its own strength. By breaking the sensitivity cycle, you became more resistant to moderate doses of your danger foods.

Allergists have found that if you eat your danger foods no more than once every four days, your body usually avoids the negative responses that these foods would otherwise trigger. This limited frequency gives your body a chance to dilute and absorb the toxins produced, and since your immune system is so much stronger after the Elimination and Reintroduction diets, your reaction to sensitive foods will be milder.

The Maintenance Diet is meant to be flexible, so you can customize your meals to suit *your* needs. It's more a way of life than a "diet"—an eating plan that will promote better lifelong health. You plan your own menus based on a daily intake of 60 percent complex carbohydrates, 30 percent protein, and 10 percent fat, and including a good amount of fiber (see Chapter 4 for inspiration). Remember:

- *Complex Carbohydrates.* Pasta, rice, and other grains, plus dried beans, potatoes, vegetables, and fruit are excellent sources of nutrients *and* energy. These should comprise the major part of your daily diet.
- *Protein.* The best source of protein is animal foods (meat, poultry, fish, eggs, milk, cheese), but these foods are usually high in fat and cholesterol, so you should limit the amount of animal protein you eat and increase the amount of protein you get from plant sources, particularly grains and legumes (see Chapter 4).
- *Fat.* Keep the amount of fat in your diet to a minimum. In addition to cutting out fatty foods, following the guidelines given in Table 4 (page 36), your cooking techniques can help minimize fat (see Chapter 5).
- *Fiber.* Find fiber in whole-grain breads, crackers, and cereals, as well as in raw and cooked fruits and vegetables.

A Few Guidelines for Maintaining Your Immune Health

- If your reaction to your danger foods has not been severe, you may eat them in moderate amounts once every four days. If your reaction was severe, eliminate the food totally.
- If you need to eliminate one of the Sinister Seven, see the substitutions listed on pages 62–63, and the Immune Power Recipes that follow.
- *Distribute your food.* Eat three small meals and two snacks throughout the day.
- *Limit sweets.* Cakes, cookies, pies, candy, and ice cream are all chockful of sugar and often high in fat too.
- *Limit your salt intake.* Experiment with herbs and spices to add flavor and zing to your meals (see Chapter 6 for ideas).

The Future

You now have the tools, knowledge, and motivation you need to optimize your health and happiness. With these in hand, it's now time to continue on your own.

A little nervous about going solo? Don't be. Actually, you're very well prepared to continue, having just completed the advanced course in fine-tuning your immune system. You possess a deep understanding of the far-reaching effects of the food-health connection. When you combine these ideas with those behind my original Immune Power Diet, you'll begin to enjoy the rewards of a healthier, more pleasurable life.

Of course, there might be setbacks from time to time, but don't despair. Just turn to the pages of this book and review those ideas that will set you on the right path.

Soon, total immune health will become *your* way of life instead of a goal you're trying to reach. You'll experience a continual state of vitality and well-being, not a once-in-a while energy "high." And better yet, you'll be cooking as well as you feel!

PART IV

The Immune Power Recipes

CHAPTER 10

Tips for Following the Immune Power Recipes

THE RECIPES that follow were selected to add variety and interest to your Immune Power Menus, and all were developed to eliminate the Sinister Seven—cow's milk and products, wheat, brewer's and baker's yeast, eggs, corn, soy products, and cane sugar. If you know that you have a problem with any of the foods called for in a recipe, eliminate it from the recipe if possible, or substitute another equivalent food.

Each recipe is followed by a nutritional analysis, usually broken down according to a serving size.

Some of these recipes have ingredients that are labeled *optional*. Optional ingredients have not been figured into the nutritional analysis of the recipe, but you may refer to the charts in the Appendix to get the information you need.

A Few Dos and Don'ts

- Use only low-fat, low-salt products—especially canned tomatoes, tomato sauce, tomato juice, and sardines. We recommend that you make your own chicken broth (recipe on page 163), but there are some low-sodium broths that may be used occasionally.
- When oil is called for, we have not specified which kind of oil, since no one kind of oil may be eaten more often than once every four days. Keep track of which oil you use in preparing meals. You may find it easier to keep track if you use the same one at all three meals on a given day.
- We recommend the use of fresh vegetables whenever possible. Frozen vegetables are acceptable for most recipes, but canned

vegetables are generally much too salty for this diet (or for any diet, for that matter). Steaming is the best cooking method, and vegetables are especially nutritious if they are not peeled.

- Fresh fruits are always best as well, but if you do have to rely on canned ones occasionally, choose unsweetened fruit packed in its own juice.
- Use cornstarch-free baking powder.
- We recommend that in recipes that require legumes (lentils, kidney beans, chick-peas, etc.) you use the dried variety, rather than canned, and cook them according to the instructions in Table 13 (page 81) or on the package (adjust seasonings to fit the Immune Power Plan). Canned beans are extremely high in sodium. If you must use canned beans or chick-peas once in a while, drain them well and rinse them thoroughly. And remember that the nutritional analysis of the recipe will be different from the one given here.
- If you are on a low-sodium diet, omit tuna, sardines, and feta cheese. Substitutions may be made for tuna and sardines, but the feta should simply be omitted.
- In some of the fish recipes, we refer to cooking fish in parchment and sealing the fish with the "drugstore wrap." By that we mean the way they used to seal packages in drugstores: Place the fish on the middle of the parchment; pick up two opposite ends and fold them together repeatedly until the package is sealed; then fold the other ends under the package.

CHAPTER 11

Soups

Vegetable Broth
MAKES 5 CUPS

2 leeks, chopped
2 stalks celery, chopped
2 medium onions, chopped
2 carrots, chopped
1 garlic clove, cut in half

4 sprigs fresh parsley
1 dried bay leaf
½ teaspoon thyme
1½ quarts water

Combine all ingredients in a large pot. Bring to a boil; skim off any foam. Reduce heat and simmer, covered, 45 minutes. Strain and discard vegetables. Keep broth refrigerated or freeze it in small portions for future use.

NOTES: • Vegetable broth may be used in place of chicken broth in all your cooking.
• There is no nutritional analysis for this recipe, since it is difficult to assess how much of the nutritional value is imparted to the broth and how much is discarded.

Chicken Broth
MAKES FOUR 1-CUP SERVINGS

1 (3-pound) stewing chicken, cut in pieces

8 cups water

Place chicken and water in a large pot and bring to a boil. Boil 5 minutes. Skim, then reduce heat and simmer for 2 to 3 hours. Remove chicken and strain broth through cheesecloth or a fine-mesh colander. Cool at room temperature. Cover and refrigerate overnight to allow fat to rise to the surface and harden. Remove fat. Keep broth refrigerated or freeze it in small portions for future use.

NOTES: • Save chicken for use in other recipes.
• We recommend the use of this homemade chicken broth in all of your cooking. Commercial chicken broth is far too salty.
• There is no nutritional analysis for this recipe because there are too many variables in the chicken, among them the fat content, the water content, and the kind of feed the chicken was given. What's more, since the original ingredients are discarded, it is difficult to assess the nutritional value of what is left—the broth.

Veal Broth
MAKES FOUR 1-CUP SERVINGS

1 pound veal for stew,
* cut into 2-inch pieces*

3 pounds veal bones, split
3 quarts cold water

Combine meat, bones, and water in a large pot and bring to a boil. Boil five minutes. Skim. Reduce heat and simmer for 2½ hours. Remove meat and bones and strain broth through cheesecloth or a fine-mesh colander. Cool at room temperature and cover tightly. Refrigerate overnight so that fat will rise to the surface and harden. Remove fat. Keep broth refrigerated or freeze it in small portions for future use.

NOTES: • Veal broth makes an excellent clear soup, to be served as an appetizer or a between-meal snack. It may also serve as a base for other soups. If the Elimination Diet permits, it may be substituted for Chicken Broth.
• Save the veal meat for later use, either served hot or chilled and used in a salad.
• There is no nutritional analysis for veal broth because of the variables, including the fat content of the veal and the nature of the feed the animal was given. What's more, since the original ingredients are discarded, it's difficult to assess the nutritional value of what is left—the broth.

Chick-Pea Soup
MAKES FIVE 1-CUP SERVINGS

¾ cup chopped onion
2 carrots, diced
2 tablespoons oil
4 cups cooked chick-peas

1 tablespoon lemon juice
1 bay leaf
¼ teaspoon black pepper
4 cups water

Sauté onion and carrots in hot oil in a large saucepan until onion is transparent. Add chick-peas. Stir in the remaining ingredients. Cook, covered, over low heat 25 to 30 minutes or until vegetables are tender. Add more water if soup is too thick. Remove bay leaf. Purée soup in blender. Reheat before serving.

NOTE: Do not use canned chick-peas; they're much too high in salt.

Variation: Add another cup of whole cooked chick-peas to the purée for chunky-style soup.

Per serving: 159 calories; 4.8 gm protein; 7.2 gm fat; 36.7 gm carbohydrates; 0.6 gm fiber; 0.5 gm saturated fat; 0.6 gm monounsaturated fat; 4.1 gm polyunsaturated fat; 0 mg cholesterol; 372 mg sodium; 51.5 mg calcium

Lentil Soup
MAKES 4½ CUPS

1¼ cups (8 ounces) uncooked
    lentils
4 cups Chicken Broth (see page
    163)
¾ cup chopped onion

2 garlic cloves, minced
2 teaspoons oil
1 teaspoon ground cumin
¼ teaspoon black pepper (op-
    tional)

Wash lentils and put them, with chicken broth, in a large saucepan. Bring to a boil. Remove from heat and let stand, uncovered, one hour. Stir in the remaining ingredients. Bring to a boil and simmer 20 to 25 minutes or until lentils are cooked.

Per cup: 67.8 calories; 1.7 gm protein; 2.3 gm fat; 7.9 gm carbohydrates; 0.2 gm fiber; 0.2 gm saturated fat; 0.2 gm monounsaturated fat; 1.5 gm polyunsaturated fat; 0 mg cholesterol; 160.2 mg sodium; 29.7 mg calcium

Split-Pea Soup
MAKES 4½ CUPS

1 cup uncooked split green peas
4½ cups water
¾ cup chopped onion
2 medium potatoes, cubed

½ cup chopped celery
1 teaspoon dried dill
¼ teaspoon salt (optional)
¼ teaspoon pepper

Place peas and water in a large saucepan over medium heat. Bring to a boil; remove from heat. Let stand, uncovered, one hour. Add remaining ingredients and bring to a boil. Simmer gently for about 40 minutes or until peas are tender.

Per cup: 115.2 calories; 5 gm protein; 0.3 gm fat; 26.1 gm carbohydrates; 0.3 gm fiber; 0 gm saturated fat; 0 gm monounsaturated fat; 0 gm polyunsaturated fat; 0 mg cholesterol; 115 mg sodium; 28.9 mg calcium

Senegalese Soup
MAKES 2 SERVINGS

1 medium onion, chopped
1 medium carrot, thinly sliced
1 stalk celery, chopped
2 garlic cloves, minced
2 tablespoons oil
1 tablespoon curry powder
1 tablespoon potato flour

1 tablespoon salt-free tomato
  paste
6 cloves
1 small cinnamon stick
2 cups Chicken Broth (see page
  163)
½ cup cooked slivered chicken

Sauté onion, carrot, celery, and garlic in hot oil in a medium saucepan for five minutes. Remove from heat. Stir in curry, flour, tomato paste, spices, and broth. Return to heat; simmer 25 to 30 minutes. Remove cloves and cinnamon stick. Add chicken and heat through.

Per cup: 430 calories; 38.9 gm protein; 23.2 gm fat; 16 gm carbohydrates; 1.1 gm fiber; 3.8 gm saturated fat; 5 gm monounsaturated fat; 12 gm polyunsaturated fat; 95.6 mg cholesterol; 292 mg sodium; 92.5 mg calcium

CHAPTER 12

Salads

Alfalfa-Tomato Salad
MAKES I SERVING

1 medium tomato, sliced
½ medium cucumber, thinly
*   sliced*
1 tablespoon unsweetened pine-
*   apple juice*

½ teaspoon lime juice
⅛ teaspoon crushed dried mint
Alfalfa sprouts

Arrange tomato and cucumber slices on a large plate. Stir together juices and mint and pour mixture over vegetables. Top with alfalfa sprouts. Cover and chill.

Per serving: 82.3 calories; 2.5 gm protein; 0.8 gm fat; 21.1 gm carbohydrates; 2 gm fiber; 0.1 gm saturated fat; 0 gm monounsaturated fat; 0.2 gm polyunsaturated fat; 0 mg cholesterol; 33.8 mg sodium; 48.8 mg calcium

Banana Salad
MAKES I SERVING

1 banana, sliced
1 tablespoon lemon juice
¼ cup chopped celery
1 tablespoon diced pimiento

2 tablespoons chopped salt-free
*   peanuts*
½ cup cold Brown Rice (see
*   page 78)*

In a small bowl, toss banana slices with lemon juice. Add the remaining ingredients and toss lightly.

NOTE: Serve on a bed of 3 lettuce leaves if desired.

Per serving: 400.3 calories; 10.7 gm protein; 11.3 gm fat; 65.1 gm carbohydrates; 1.9 gm fiber; 1.4 gm saturated fat; 4.4 gm monounsaturated fat; 2.9 gm polyunsaturated fat; 0 mg cholesterol; 30.5 mg sodium; 62.3 mg calcium

Broccoli and Celery Salad
MAKES 3 SERVINGS

1½ cup broccoli flowerets
½ cup chopped celery
1 tablespoon chopped pimiento

1 teaspoon dark sesame oil
1 teaspoon lemon juice

Steam broccoli flowerets 2 to 3 minutes and chill. In a small bowl, toss together broccoli, celery, and pimiento. Mix oil and lemon juice. Pour dressing over vegetables and toss lightly. Serve.

NOTE: Serve on a bed of lettuce if desired.

Per serving: 208.6 calories; 9.2 gm protein; 5.8 gm fat; 22.2 gm carbohydrates; 0.5 gm fiber; 0.7 gm saturated fat; 1.8 gm monounsaturated fat; 2.2 gm polyunsaturated fat; 0 mg cholesterol; 79 mg sodium; 315 mg calcium

Carrot and Squash Salad
MAKES 2 SERVINGS

½ cup cooked carrots, cut in thin strips
½ cup seeded yellow squash, cut in thin strips
½ cup seeded zucchini, cut in thin strips

2 tablespoons Vinaigrette Dressing I (see page 235)
4 large lettuce leaves

Place vegetables in a large bowl. Add dressing and toss gently until vegetables are well coated. Serve on lettuce leaves.

Per serving: 64 calories; 1.7 gm protein; 2.9 gm fat; 7.8 gm carbohydrates; 1.1 gm fiber; 0.2 gm saturated fat; 0.3 gm monounsaturated fat; 2.1 gm polyunsaturated fat; 0 mg cholesterol; 11.9 mg sodium; 26.7 mg calcium

Dilled Carrot and Zucchini Salad
MAKES 1 SERVING

1 medium carrot, sliced
1 medium zucchini, sliced
2 teaspoons oil

⅛ teaspoon dried dill
2 lettuce leaves

Steam carrot and zucchini just until crisp-tender, 2 to 3 minutes; toss in a small bowl with oil and dill. Chill. Serve on lettuce leaves.

Per serving: 135.7 calories; 2.7 gm protein; 9.3 gm fat; 12.3 gm carbohydrates; 1.9 gm fiber; 0.9 gm saturated fat; 1.1 gm monounsaturated fat; 6.8 gm polyunsaturated fat; 0 mg cholesterol; 29.1 mg sodium; 47.3 mg calcium

Carrot and Spinach Salad
MAKES 1 SERVING

2 cups spinach leaves
½ cup grated carrots

2 tablespoons chopped radishes

Toss together all ingredients until lightly mixed.

Variation: Add 1 tablespoon Vinaigrette Dressing I (page 235).

Per serving: 72 calories; 4.6 gm protein; 0.52 gm fat; 13.9 gm carbohydrates; 1.6 gm fiber; 0 gm saturated fat; 0 gm monounsaturated fat; 0 gm polyunsaturated fat; 0 mg cholesterol; 122.5 mg sodium; 137.5 mg calcium

Carrot and Raisin Salad
MAKES 1 SERVING

1 tablespoon raisins
1 large carrot, shredded

Dash ground ginger

Plump raisins by letting them soak for 10 to 15 minutes in warm water; rinse well. In a small bowl, stir together carrot, raisins, and ginger. Chill. Serve on lettuce.

NOTE: Serve on shredded lettuce if desired.

Per serving: 87.8 calories; 1.7 gm protein; 0.3 gm fat; 21.2 gm carbohydrates; 2 gm fiber; 0 gm saturated fat; 0 gm monounsaturated fat; 0.1 gm polyunsaturated fat; 0 mg cholesterol; 48.6 mg sodium; 42.1 mg calcium

Carrot-Pineapple Salad
MAKES 1 SERVING

1 tablespoon raisins
2 tablespoons unsweetened
  crushed pineapple

1 large carrot, shredded
2 lettuce leaves

Plump raisins by soaking them in warm water for 10 to 15 minutes; rinse well. In a small bowl stir together pineapple, carrot, and raisins. Chill. Serve on lettuce leaves.

Per serving: 97 calories; 1.8 gm protein; 0.3 gm fat; 23.7 gm carbohydrates; 2 gm fiber; 0 gm saturated fat; 0 gm monounsaturated fat; 0.1 gm polyunsaturated fat; 0 mg cholesterol; 48.9 mg sodium; 46.5 mg calcium

Cauliflower-Fruit Slaw
MAKES 4 SERVINGS

1½ cups cooked cauliflower
  flowerets, coarsely chopped
  (fresh or frozen)
1 orange, peeled and diced

2 medium unpeeled apples,
  chopped
1 tablespoon oil

In a small bowl, toss together all ingredients. Chill. Toss again before serving.

Per serving: 61.5 calories; 1.3 gm protein; 1.9 gm fat; 11.1 gm carbohydrates; 0.7 gm fiber; 0.1 gm saturated fat; 0.2 gm monounsaturated fat; 1.7 gm polyunsaturated fat; 0 mg cholesterol; 8.1 mg sodium; 24.8 mg calcium

Fennel and Cucumber Salad
MAKES 4 SERVINGS

1 cucumber, seeded and cut into
  thin strips
1 fennel bulb, cut into thin strips

1 tablespoon lemon juice
1 tablespoon oil
1 tablespoon chopped mint

In a small bowl, toss together all ingredients until well mixed. Chill.

NOTE: Serve on a bed of lettuce if desired.

Per serving: 38.2 calories; 0.8 gm protein; 2.8 gm fat; 2 gm carbohydrates; 0.4 gm fiber; 0.2 gm saturated fat; 0.3 gm monounsaturated fat; 2 gm polyunsaturated fat; 0 mg cholesterol; 80.6 mg sodium; 18.8 mg calcium

Feta-Tomato Salad
MAKES I SERVING

4 large romaine leaves
½ tomato, thinly sliced
2 tablespoons crumbled feta cheese

¼ teaspoon dried oregano leaves
1 lime wedge

Tear romaine into bite-sized pieces and place on serving plate. Place tomato slices on romaine and sprinkle with crumbled cheese and oregano. Squeeze lime over all.

Per serving: 61.1 calories; 3.2 gm protein; 3.2 gm fat; 6.1 gm carbohydrates; 0.5 gm fiber; 2.1 gm saturated fat; 0.6 gm monounsaturated fat; 0.2 gm polyunsaturated fat; 12.5 mg cholesterol; 165.7 mg sodium; 96.2 mg calcium

Marinated White Beans
MAKES 2 SERVINGS

1 garlic clove, crushed
¼ cup oil
¼ cup lemon juice
2 tablespoons chopped fresh parsley

¼ teaspoon dried tarragon, crushed
2 cups cooked white (Great Northern) beans (see page 81)

Mix together all ingredients except beans. Place beans in a small bowl and then pour marinade over. Cover and refrigerate several hours or overnight.

NOTE: Do not use canned beans; they're much too high in salt.

Per serving: 462.2 calories; 14.3 gm protein; 28.2 gm fat; 41.5 gm carbohydrates; 0 gm fiber; 2.5 gm saturated fat; 3.2 gm monounsaturated fat; 20.2 gm polyunsaturated fat; 0 mg cholesterol; 14.4 mg sodium; 102.2 mg calcium

Lima Bean Vinaigrette
MAKES 2 SERVINGS

1½ cups cooked baby lima beans (fresh or frozen)
¼ cup chopped scallions
½ cup chopped sweet red pepper

2 tablespoons chopped parsley
Approx. 2 tablespoons Vinaigrette Dressing II (see page 235)

In a small bowl, mix together lima beans, scallions, red pepper, and parsley. Toss with Vinaigrette Dressing. Cover and refrigerate to chill. If desired, add more dressing to taste.

Per serving: 213.2 calories; 5.6 gm protein; 11.1 gm fat; 5.0 gm carbohydrates; 3.9 gm fiber; 0.6 gm saturated fat; 0.06 gm monounsaturated fat; 4.3 gm polyunsaturated fat; 0 mg cholesterol; 16.5 mg sodium; 34.4 mg calcium

Sweet Potato Salad
MAKES 4 SERVINGS

1 pound sweet potatoes, baked and cooled
½ cup cold cooked green peas (fresh or frozen)
½ cup crushed unsweetened pineapple

3 tablespoons chopped fresh parsley
⅓ cup Honey Vinaigrette Dressing (see page 236)
8 lettuce leaves (optional)

Peel and slice sweet potatoes and place in a small bowl. Add remaining ingredients; toss lightly. If desired, serve on lettuce leaves.

Per serving: 170.7 calories; 3.1 gm protein; 2.7 gm fat; 35.3 gm carbohydrates; 28 gm fiber; 0.25 gm saturated fat; 0.3 gm monounsaturated fat; 1.9 gm polyunsaturated fat; 0 mg cholesterol; 66.6 mg sodium; 45.4 mg calcium

Wild Rice Salad
MAKES 4 SERVINGS

*1 large unpeeled Delicious apple,
  diced*
2 tablespoons chopped pecans
¼ cup golden raisins
2 teaspoons lemon juice
*¾ cup cooked Wild Rice (see
  page 78)*

¾ cup chopped celery
*1 tablespoon orange juice con-
  centrate*
¾ cup green grapes, cut in half
8 lettuce leaves

Toss together apple, pecans, raisins, and lemon juice until apple is
well coated with lemon juice. Add the rice, celery, orange juice,
and grapes. Toss to mix. Chill. Serve on lettuce leaves.

Per serving: 99.3 calories; 1.1 gm protein; 2.5 gm fat; 20.2 gm carbohydrates;
1.1 gm fiber; 0.2 gm saturated fat; 1.4 gm monounsaturated fat; 0.6 gm
polyunsaturated fat; 0 mg cholesterol; 21.6 mg sodium; 20.8 mg calcium

Barley Salad
MAKES 4 SERVINGS

½ cup uncooked barley
*1½ cups Chicken Broth (see
  page 163)*
*¾ cup cooked Wild Rice (see
  page 78)*
½ cup chopped celery

½ cup green grapes, cut in half
¼ cup chopped Bermuda onion
¼ cup chopped almonds
4 teaspoons lemon juice
1 tablespoon oil
1 garlic clove, mashed

In a medium saucepan, cook barley in chicken broth for about 45
minutes or until done. Drain and cool. Combine with rice in a large
bowl. Add celery, grapes, onion, and almonds and toss lightly. Stir
together lemon juice, oil, and garlic and pour over barley mixture.
Toss lightly. Chill 30 minutes before serving.

Per serving: 266.4 calories; 6.3 gm protein; 6.5 gm fat; 27.6 gm carbohydrates;
0.7 gm fiber; 0.7 gm saturated fat; 3.1 gm monounsaturated fat; 3.4 gm
polyunsaturated fat; 0 mg cholesterol; 83.0 mg sodium; 50 mg calcium

Buckwheat and Vegetable Salad
MAKES 4 SERVINGS

2 cups cooked Buckwheat (see
page 77)
¾ cup cooked peas, fresh or fro-
zen
¾ cup halved cherry tomatoes
½ cup peeled and diced
cucumber

3 tablespoons oil
1 tablespoon lemon juice
1 teaspoon curry powder
½ teaspoon onion powder

In a large bowl, toss together buckwheat, peas, tomatoes, and cu-cumbers. Mix together oil, lemon juice, curry powder, and onion powder. Pour dressing over vegetables and toss gently.

NOTE: Serve on lettuce leaves if desired.

Per serving: 192.2 calories; 4.5 gm protein; 17 gm fat; 26.8 gm carbohydrates; 1.4 gm fiber; 0.6 gm saturated fat; 0.8 gm monounsaturated fat; 5.1 gm polyunsaturated fat; 0 mg cholesterol; 29.6 mg sodium; 14.9 mg calcium

Buckwheat Noodle Salad
MAKES 5 SERVINGS

2 cups buckwheat noodles,
cooked according to package
instructions
1 sweet red pepper, chopped
½ cup cooked cold peas (fresh or
frozen)
2 garlic cloves, minced

1 tablespoon toasted sesame
seeds
3 tablespoons sesame oil
2 tablespoons lemon juice
¼ teaspoon cayenne pepper
10 lettuce leaves

Mix all ingredients except lettuce in a large bowl and toss lightly. Marinate 30 minutes in refrigerator. Serve on lettuce leaves.

NOTE: Toast seeds in a shallow baking pan at 200° for 10 to 15 minutes or until golden brown.

Per serving: 302.3 calories; 6.7 gm protein; 16.1 gm fat; 34.1 gm carbohydrates; 1.2 gm fiber; 1.9 gm saturated fat; 5.4 gm monounsaturated fat; 5.8 gm polyunsaturated fat; 0 mg cholesterol; 25.8 mg sodium; 16 mg calcium

Tuna Salad
MAKES I SERVING

1 cup bite-size chicory pieces
1 (3½-ounce) can water-packed
tuna
1 pimiento, cut into strips (about
1 tablespoon)

¼ cup sliced water chestnuts
1 tablespoon unsweetened pine-
apple juice
1 tablespoon oil

Line a serving plate with chicory. Flake tuna and place on chicory. Arrange pimiento and water chestnuts on tuna. Stir together juice and oil and pour over all. Cover and chill.

Per serving: 404.7 calories; 50.7 gm protein; 17 gm fat; 13.4 gm carbohydrates; 1.5 gm fiber; 1.3 gm saturated fat; 1.6 gm monounsaturated fat; 11.4 gm polyunsaturated fat; 64 mg cholesterol; 83 mg sodium; 18 mg calcium

Grapefruit-Sole Salad
MAKES I SERVING

1 cup shredded lettuce
4 ounces cooked, flaked fillet of
sole, chilled
1 pink grapefruit, peeled and di-
vided into sections

½ cup chopped celery
2 tablespoons Tomato Salad
Dressing (see page 236)

Arrange lettuce on a chilled serving plate. Place fish, grapefruit, and celery on lettuce. Drizzle Tomato Salad Dressing over all.

Variation: Other fish may be substituted for the sole. See list on page 69.

Per serving: 222 calories; 36.6 gm protein; 1.5 gm fat; 23.5 gm carbohydrates; 1 gm fiber; 0 gm saturated fat; 0 gm monounsaturated fat; 0.1 gm polyunsaturated fat; 0 mg cholesterol; 219 mg sodium; 86.8 mg calcium

Chicken Salad
MAKES 6 SERVINGS

2 cups slivered cooked white-meat chicken
2 cups chopped celery
1 cup cold cooked Millet (see page 77)
1 cup drained mandarin orange segments
½ cup cold cooked peas (fresh or frozen)

½ cup sliced almonds
1 medium sweet red pepper, chopped
1 medium carrot, shredded
Approx. ½ cup Tropical Salad Dressing (see page 237)

Toss together all ingredients except salad dressing in a large bowl. Add salad dressing and toss lightly. (You may want to add a little more dressing.)

Per serving: 267.1 calories; 31 gm protein; 8.6 gm fat; 17.6 gm carbohydrates; 1.6 gm fiber; 1.3 gm saturated fat; 4.3 gm monounsaturated fat; 1.7 gm polyunsaturated fat; 73 mg cholesterol; 115.5 mg sodium; 72.1 mg calcium

Chicken Salad Brazil
MAKES 2 SERVINGS

½ cup cooked white-meat chicken, cubed
2 tablespoons chopped celery
2 tablespoons chopped Brazil nuts
1 teaspoon grated onion

1 teaspoon lemon juice
1 teaspoon grated lemon rind
1 tablespoon Pineapple Salad Dressing (see page 236)
4 lettuce leaves

Place all ingredients except lettuce in a large bowl and toss lightly. Serve on lettuce leaves.

Per serving: 261.6 calories; 29.4 gm protein; 14.6 gm fat; 3.7 gm carbohydrates; 0.1 gm fiber; 3.7 gm saturated fat; 5.1 gm monounsaturated fat; 4.8 gm polyunsaturated fat; 73 mg cholesterol; 76.6 mg sodium; 53.1 mg calcium

Polynesian Chicken Salad
MAKES 6 SERVINGS

2 cups slivered cooked white-meat chicken
2 cups chopped celery
1 cup cold cooked Brown Rice (see page 78)
1 cup drained pineapple chunks (use pineapple canned in its own juice)
½ cup cold cooked peas (fresh or frozen)

½ cup sliced almonds
1 medium sweet red pepper, chopped
1 medium carrot, shredded
2 tablespoons toasted sesame seeds
Approx. ½ cup Tropical Salad Dressing (see page 237)

Toss together all ingredients except salad dressing in a large bowl. Add salad dressing and toss lightly. (You may want to add more dressing.)

NOTE: Toast seeds in a shallow baking pan at 200° for 10 to 15 minutes or until golden brown.

Per serving: 336.1 calories; 39.8 gm protein; 10.9 gm fat; 19.1 gm carbohydrates; 1.6 gm fiber; 1.6 gm saturated fat; 4.6 gm monounsaturated fat; 2 gm polyunsaturated fat; 91.1 mg cholesterol; 137 mg sodium; 78.1 mg calcium

Seviche
MAKES 6 SERVINGS

½ pound sea scallops, cut into quarters
Approx. ⅓ cup lemon juice
½ cup chopped fresh tomatoes
½ cup chopped celery

1 tablespoon oil
2 tablespoons sliced green olives
1 tablespoons chopped onion
1 (4-ounce) can chopped chilies
½ teaspoon dried oregano leaves

Mix together scallops and lemon juice in a glass bowl until scallops are covered (if juice does not cover scallops, add more). Cover and refrigerate 3 hours or until scallops are white and opaque, indicating that they are fully "cooked." Add the remaining ingredients and toss gently until well mixed. Chill.

Per serving: 77.5 calories; 9.1 gm protein; 3.3 gm fat; 3.6 gm carbohydrates; 0.1 gm fiber; 0.2 gm saturated fat; 0.2 gm monounsaturated fat; 1.7 gm polyunsaturated fat; 20 mg cholesterol; 191.8 mg sodium; 54.3 mg calcium

Lobster Salad Plate
MAKES I SERVING

Shredded lettuce
1 small lobster tail, freshly
  cooked, chilled, and flaked
½ cup frozen artichoke hearts,
  cooked and chilled

2 stalks celery, cut into 2-inch
  pieces
Lime wedge

Arrange lettuce on a chilled salad plate. Place lobster, artichoke, and celery on lettuce. Serve with a squeeze of lime juice.

NOTE: If you are not using lobster tail, use 3 ounces *freshly cooked* and chilled lobster meat.

Per serving: 156.6 calories; 21.1 gm protein; 2.6 gm fat; 14.2 gm carbohydrates; 2.8 gm fiber; 0 gm saturated fat; 0 gm monounsaturated fat; 0.1 gm polyunsaturated fat; 200 mg cholesterol; 122.1 mg sodium; 99.9 mg calcium

Orange-Lobster Salad
MAKES I SERVING

3 lettuce leaves
1 small lobster tail, freshly
  cooked, chilled, and flaked
½ cup fresh orange segments,
  cut into quarters

1 tablespoon orange juice
Dash curry powder

Arrange lettuce leaves on a chilled salad plate. Toss together remaining ingredients. Spoon onto lettuce.

NOTE: If you are not using lobster tail, use 3 ounces *freshly cooked* and chilled lobster meat.

Per serving: 165.3 calories; 19.7 gm protein; 2.4 gm fat; 16.7 gm carbohydrates; 1.7 gm fiber; 0 gm saturated fat; 0 gm monounsaturated fat; 0.2 gm polyunsaturated fat; 200 mg cholesterol; 17.4 mg sodium; 103.5 mg calcium

CHAPTER 13

Fish and Shellfish

Codfish Steaks
MAKES 2 SERVINGS

2 (6-ounce) codfish steaks
1 medium tomato, sliced
1 small onion, sliced

2 teaspoons lemon juice
½ teaspoon dried oregano leaves

Place each steak on a large piece of parchment paper and top each with half of the remaining ingredients. Fold parchment up over fish and seal each package in a drugstore wrap (see page 162). Place in a shallow baking dish and bake at 350° for 25 to 30 minutes or until done.

Variation: Halibut steaks may be substituted for codfish.

Per serving: 350.6 calories; 35 gm protein; 9.5 gm fat; 13.4 gm carbohydrates; 1.7 gm fiber; 0 gm saturated fat; 0 gm monounsaturated fat; 0.2 gm polyunsaturated fat; 50 mg cholesterol; 198.9 mg sodium; 95.3 mg calcium

Herbed Codfish Steak
MAKES I SERVING

1 (6-ounce) codfish steak
Ground celery seeds

Ground coriander seeds
Dash of dried chervil

Place steak on broiler pan; sprinkle with herbs. Broil 5 inches from flame, 8 to 10 minutes or until fish flakes easily when tested with a fork.

Per serving: 156 calories; 35 gm protein; 0.6 gm fat; 0 gm carbohydrates; 0 gm fiber; 0 gm saturated fat; 0 gm monounsaturated fat; 0 gm polyunsaturated fat; 50 mg cholesterol; 140 mg sodium; 20 mg calcium

Mako Shark Steak
MAKES I SERVING

1 (4-ounce) mako shark steak
4 fresh or frozen broccoli spears
 (frozen spears should be
 thawed)

½ cup sliced water chestnuts
1 tablespoon chopped pimiento
¼ teaspoon dried chervil
1 tablespoon water

Place steak on a large piece of parchment paper. Layer broccoli, water chestnuts, pimiento, and chervil over steak; sprinkle with water. Fold parchment up over the fish and seal package in a drugstore wrap (see page 162). Place in a shallow baking dish and bake at 400° for 35 to 40 minutes or until done.

Variation: Fresh tuna steak may be substituted for mako shark.

Per serving: 349.9 calories; 36.5 gm protein; 9.5 gm fat; 31.3 gm carbohydrates; 4 gm fiber; 0 gm saturated fat; 0 gm monounsaturated fat; 0.1 gm polyunsaturated fat; 68.5 mg cholesterol; 98.3 mg sodium; 140.4 mg calcium

Salmon Steak
MAKES I SERVING

1 (6-ounce) salmon steak
½ cup thinly sliced cucumber

¼ teaspoon dried dill
1 lime wedge

Place steak on a large piece of parchment paper and top with cucumber and dill. Squeeze lime over all. Fold parchment up over the fish and seal package in a drugstore wrap (see page 162). Place in a shallow baking dish and bake at 400° for 20 to 25 minutes or until done.

Per serving: 219.7 calories; 31.2 gm protein; 8.5 gm fat; 30.4 gm carbohydrates; 0.2 gm fiber; 0 gm saturated fat; 0 gm monounsaturated fat; 0 gm polyunsaturated fat; 53.6 mg cholesterol; 134 mg sodium; 485.6 mg calcium

Vegetable-Stuffed Fish
MAKES 6 SERVINGS

*1 (3- to 5-pound) whole fish,
butterflied*
1 lemon, thinly sliced
1 medium tomato, sliced
*1 small green pepper, cut into
rings*
1 medium onion, cut into rings

1 tablespoon chopped fresh parsley
½ teaspoon dried oregano
½ teaspoon dried basil
Oil
*Lemon slices and fresh parsley
sprigs for garnish*

Open fish out in a large shallow baking pan. Place alternate layers of vegetables and lemon on one side of fish. Sprinkle with herbs. Close fish and secure with toothpicks. Rub fish lightly with oil. Bake at 400° for about 20 to 25 minutes or until fish flakes easily when tested with a fork. Garnish with lemon slices and sprigs of parsley.

NOTES: • Fish may be bluefish, striped bass, fresh water bass, red snapper, salmon, or any one of your favorite whole fish.
• To butterfly a fish, remove the backbone with a sharp knife without splitting the fish in half.

Per serving: Vegetable-Stuffed Fish (Blue & Striped Bass): 147 calories; 23.3 gm protein; 3.9 gm fat; 4 gm carbohydrates; 0.4 gm fiber; 0.2 gm saturated fat; 0.2 gm monounsaturated fat; 1.7 gm polyunsaturated fat; 0 mg cholesterol; 83 mg sodium; 14 mg calcium
Vegetable-Stuffed Fish (Fresh Water Bass): 159 calories; 22.8 gm protein; 5.5 gm fat; 4 gm carbohydrates; 0.4 gm fiber; 0.2 gm saturated fat; 0.2 gm monounsaturated fat; 1.7 gm polyunsaturated fat; 0 mg cholesterol; 2.9 mg sodium; 14.3 mg calcium
Vegetable-Stuffed Fish (Red Snapper): 147 calories; 24 gm protein; 3.5 gm fat; 4 gm carbohydrates; 0.4 gm fiber; 0.2 gm saturated fat; 0.2 gm monounsaturated fat; 1.7 gm polyunsaturated fat; 0 mg cholesterol; 82 mg sodium; 33.4 mg calcium
Vegetable-Stuffed Fish (Salmon): 357 calories; 33.8 gm protein; 22.2 gm fat; 4 gm carbohydrates; 0.4 gm fiber; 0.2 gm saturated fat; 0.2 gm monounsaturated fat; 1.7 gm polyunsaturated fat; 46.6 mg cholesterol; 3 mg sodium; 31 mg calcium

Salmon-Filled Fillet
MAKES I SERVING

1 small piece salmon (3x2x1   *1 (4-ounce) fish fillet*
inches)

Place salmon at one end of fish fillet; roll up. Place fish, seam side down, in a small ramekin. Bake at 350° for 15 to 20 minutes or until done.

NOTE: This recipe works well with any number of lean fish. See list on page 69–70.

Per serving: 223.6 calories; 33.2 gm protein; 9 gm fat; 0 gm carbohydrates; 0 gm fiber; 0 gm saturated fat; 0 gm monounsaturated fat; 0 gm polyunsaturated fat; 13.4 mg cholesterol; 234.7 mg sodium; 127.7 mg calcium

Tuna Steak
MAKES I SERVING

1 (4-ounce) tuna steak   *1 small scallion, chopped*
1 small zucchini, sliced   *2 tablespoons grapefruit juice*

Place tuna steak on a large piece of parchment paper and top with the remaining ingredients. Fold parchment up over the fish and seal in a drugstore wrap (see page 162). Place in a shallow baking dish and bake at 375° for 15 to 20 minutes or until done.

Variation: Other fish may be substituted for tuna. See substitutes list on page 72.

Per serving: 239 calories; 34.1 gm protein; 7.8 gm fat; 8.2 gm carbohydrates; 0.8 gm fiber; 0 gm saturated fat; 0 gm monounsaturated fat; 0.9 gm polyunsaturated fat; 60.6 mg cholesterol; 44.7 mg sodium; 57.2 mg calcium

Caribbean Shrimp Kabobs
MAKES 4 SERVINGS

¼ cup lime juice
1 tablespoon oil
1 garlic clove, mashed
¼ teaspoon hot red pepper flakes
12 large shrimp, shelled and
  cleaned
1 large zucchini, cut into ½-inch
  chunks

8 canned pineapple chunks
  (choose pineapple canned in
  its own juice)
½ package frozen artichoke
  hearts, thawed
8 large black pitted olives

Stir together lime juice, oil, garlic, and pepper in a large bowl. Add shrimp and toss lightly. Let shrimp marinate for 10 to 15 minutes. Thread shrimp, zucchini, pineapple, artichoke, and olives on skewers, beginning and ending with shrimp. Place skewers on broiler rack and broil the kabobs 3 inches from heat for 4 to 5 minutes, turning and basting frequently.

NOTE: If desired, serve on cooked Brown Rice (see page 78) and garnish with orange slices.

Variations: • Substitute lemon juice for lime juice.
  • Substitute chunks of swordfish for shrimp.

Per serving: With shrimp: 196.4 calories; 23.5 gm protein; 5.9 gm fat; 14.5 gm carbohydrates; 0.2 gm fiber; 0.4 gm saturated fat; 0.4 gm monounsaturated fat; 2.6 gm polyunsaturated fat; 171.4 mg cholesterol; 229 mg sodium; 115.5 mg calcium
With swordfish: 227 calories; 24 gm protein; 9.5 gm fat; 12.7 gm carbohydrates; 0.2 gm fiber; 0.4 gm saturated fat; 0.4 gm monounsaturated fat; 2.6 gm polyunsaturated fat; 0 mg cholesterol; 68.4 mg sodium; 65.2 mg calcium

Shrimp Pocket
MAKES I SERVING

*4 large shrimp, shelled and
  cleaned*
*1 tablespoon crumbled feta
  cheese*
2 tomato slices

1 cup frozen Italian green beans
*¼ teaspoon dried oregano leaves,
  crushed*
1 teaspoon lime juice

Place shrimp on a large piece of parchment paper; top with the remaining ingredients. Fold parchment up over shrimp and seal package in a drugstore wrap (see page 162). Place in a shallow baking dish and bake at 400° for 20 to 25 minutes or until done.

Per serving: 195.3 calories; 26.2 gm protein; 4.4 gm fat; 14.3 gm carbohydrates; 2.5 gm fiber; 2.1 gm saturated fat; 0.6 gm monounsaturated fat; 0.3 gm polyunsaturated fat; 184 mg cholesterol; 326.8 mg sodium; 209.7 mg calcium

Oriental Scallops
MAKES I SERVING

1 tablespoon lemon juice
¼ teaspoon ground ginger
⅛ teaspoon dry mustard

4 ounces fresh large scallops
*1 medium green pepper, cut into
  1-inch pieces*

Stir together lemon juice, ginger, and mustard in a small bowl; add scallops. Toss lightly until scallops are well covered. Let stand in refrigerator one hour. Drain, reserving marinade. Thread scallops and green pepper alternately on skewer. Broil 5 inches from heat for 7 to 8 minutes per side, basting occasionally with reserved marinade.

Per serving: 152 calories; 27.1 gm protein; 2 gm fat; 7.7 gm carbohydrates; 0.8 gm fiber; 0 gm saturated fat; 0.1 gm monounsaturated fat; 0.2 gm polyunsaturated fat; 60.2 mg cholesterol; 302.7 mg sodium; 138.2 mg calcium

CHAPTER 14

Poultry

Chicken Stir-Fry
MAKES 6 SERVINGS

½ cup Chicken Broth (see page 163)
1 garlic clove, minced
1 chicken breast, skinned, boned, and cut into thin strips
4 cups sliced cabbage
1 cup chopped scallions

3 celery stalks, cut into 1-inch pieces
2 green peppers, cut into 1-inch pieces
1 small piece fresh ginger, grated

Pour ¼ cup of the broth into a wok or large skillet and add garlic. Heat stock and garlic almost to the boil. Add chicken and cook, stirring constantly, for a few minutes, until chicken is opaque. Remove chicken from pan with a slotted spoon. Add remaining broth to the pan. Stir in cabbage, scallions, and celery. Stir-fry for 3 to 5 minutes. Add green pepper and ginger and continue to cook, stirring frequently, just until vegetables are crisp-tender. Return chicken to wok and heat through.

Per serving: 85.2 calories; 10.6 gm protein; 1.2 gm fat; 8.6 gm carbohydrates; 0.7 gm fiber; 0.3 gm saturated fat; 0.3 gm monounsaturated fat; 0.3 gm polyunsaturated fat; 24.3 mg cholesterol; 47.2 mg sodium; 39.4 mg calcium

Orange Baked Chicken
MAKES 2 SERVINGS

*1 chicken breast, boned,
skinned, and split in half*

1 tablespoon orange juice concentrate

Brush chicken breast with orange juice concentrate and place in small shallow baking pan. Bake at 350° for 15 to 20 minutes or until done.

Variation: For Hawaiian Chicken, substitute pineapple juice concentrate for the orange juice.

Per serving: With orange: 153.3 calories; 26.8 gm protein; 3 gm fat; 2.7 gm carbohydrates; 0 gm fiber; 0.8 gm saturated fat; 1 gm monounsaturated fat; 0.6 gm polyunsaturated fat; 73 mg cholesterol; 63.2 mg sodium; 15.2 mg calcium
With pineapple: 142 calories; 26.9 gm protein; 3 gm fat; 7.9 gm carbohydrates; 0 gm fiber; 0.8 gm saturated fat; 1 gm monounsaturated fat; 0.6 gm polyunsaturated fat; 73 mg cholesterol; 63.7 mg sodium; 20 mg calcium

Roast Chicken with Spinach-Barley Stuffing
MAKES 6 SERVINGS

2 cups cooked Barley (see page 78)
1 (10-ounce) package frozen spinach, cooked and well drained

¼ cup crumbled feta cheese
¼ cup sunflower seeds
½ teaspoon dried dill
1 (5- to 6-pound) roasting chicken

Stir together barley, spinach, cheese, seeds, and dill; mix well. Stuff bird loosely. Tie legs together and fold wings back. Place bird, breast side up, in a shallow roasting pan. Roast at 350° for about 2¼ hours or until leg moves easily and juices are no longer pink. Allow ½ cup stuffing and 4 ounces chicken (without skin) per serving.

Per serving: 468.6 calories; 53.3 gm protein; 14.3 gm fat; 33.5 gm carbohydrates; 0.8 gm fiber; 4.0 gm saturated fat; 2.4 gm monounsaturated fat; 21.7 gm polyunsaturated fat; 89.8 mg cholesterol; 883.3 mg sodium; 185.6 mg calcium

Orange Roasted Chicken
MAKES 12 SERVINGS

*1 (4- to 5-pound) roasting
chicken*
*1 unpeeled orange, cut into
small chunks*

*1 onion, peeled and cut into
small chunks*
¼ cup orange juice

Remove all fat pads from chicken. Fill body and neck cavity of
chicken with orange and onion chunks and 2 tablespoons orange
juice. Truss. Place chicken, breast side up, in shallow roasting pan.
Roast at 350° for 30 minutes. Turn chicken on side in pan and roast
20 minutes. Turn chicken on other side and roast 20 minutes. Turn
chicken breast side up again and finish roasting, allowing 17 to 20
minutes per pound total, until leg moves easily. Baste frequently
with remaining orange juice. Remove chicken skin before serving.
Skim off fat from pan juices, thicken them with potato flour if desired, and pour over chicken.

Per serving: 123.5 calories; 20.1 gm protein; 3.2 gm fat; 2.3 gm carbohydrates; 0
gm fiber; 1 gm saturated fat; 1.2 gm monounsaturated fat; 0.6 gm
polyunsaturated fat; 62.5 mg cholesterol; 55.6 mg sodium; 14 mg calcium

Cornish Hens with Barley Stuffing
MAKES 2 SERVINGS

*1 cup cooked Barley (see page
78)*
*¼ cup cooked Wild Rice (see
page 78)*
¼ cup pumpkin seeds

1 teaspoon oil
¼ teaspoon dried thyme
¼ teaspoon salt (optional)
2 (1½-pound) Cornish hens

Stir together barley, rice, seeds, oil, and seasonings; mix well. Stuff
birds loosely. Tie legs together and fold wings back. Place birds,
breast side up, in a shallow roasting pan. Roast at 350° for about
1¼ hours or until leg moves easily and juices are no longer pink.
Allow one bird (skin removed) per serving.

Per serving: 565 calories; 53.7 gm protein; 17.4 gm fat; 74 gm carbohydrates; 1.0
gm fiber; 2.6 gm saturated fat; 3.7 gm monounsaturated fat; 5.7 gm
polyunsaturated fat; 73 mg cholesterol; 341 mg sodium; 20.6 mg calcium

Oriental Chicken Stir-Fry
MAKES 6 SERVINGS

½ cup Chicken Broth (see page 63)
1 garlic clove, minced
1 chicken breast, skinned, boned, and cut into thin strips
4 cups bok choy, sliced
3 stalks celery, cut into 1-inch pieces

1 medium onion, sliced
1 sweet red pepper, cut into 1-inch pieces
1 green pepper, cut into 1-inch pieces
1 small piece fresh ginger, grated

Pour ¼ cup broth into a wok or large skillet; add garlic. Heat stock and garlic almost to the boil. Add chicken and cook, stirring constantly, for a few minutes, until chicken is opaque. Remove chicken from pan with a slotted spoon. Add remaining broth and stir in bok choy, celery, and onion. Stir-fry for 3 to 5 minutes. Add the remaining ingredients and continue to cook, stirring frequently, just until vegetables are crisp-tender. Return chicken to wok and heat through.

Variation: Add 1 cup steamed pea pods just before serving.

Per serving: 74.3 calories; 10.2 gm protein; 1.2 gm fat; 5.8 gm carbohydrates; 1 gm fiber; 0.3 gm saturated fat; 0.3 gm monounsaturated fat; 0.3 gm polyunsaturated fat; 24.3 mg cholesterol; 62.3 mg sodium; 39.3 mg calcium
With pea pods: 95.3 calories; 11.6 gm protein; 1.3 gm fat; 9.6 gm carbohydrates; 2 gm fiber; 0.3 gm saturated fat; 0.3 gm monounsaturated fat; 0.3 gm polyunsaturated fat; 24.3 mg cholesterol; 85.6 mg sodium; 45.6 mg calcium

Minted Chicken Breasts
MAKES 2 SERVINGS

*1 chicken breast, skinned,
boned, and split in half*
*¼ cup Chicken Broth (see page
163)*

¼ cup chopped onion
2 tablespoons lemon juice
¼ teaspoon dried mint
1 cup alfalfa sprouts

Place chicken, broth, onion, lemon juice, and mint in a small skillet
or saucepan and bring mixture to a boil. Lower the heat, cover, and
simmer for 15 to 20 minutes or until chicken is done. Sprinkle with
alfalfa sprouts before serving.

Per serving: 159.7 calories; 28 gm protein; 3.2 gm fat; 3.4 gm carbohydrates; 0.5
gm fiber; 0.8 gm saturated fat; 1 gm monounsaturated fat; 0.7 gm
polyunsaturated fat; 73 mg cholesterol; 86.4 mg sodium; 25.5 mg calcium

Curried Chicken and Rice
MAKES 3 SERVINGS

2 tablespoons raisins
*1 cup cooked Brown Rice (see
page 78)*
*½ cup cooked Wild Rice (see
page 78)*
*½ cup Chicken Broth (see page
163)*

*½ cup cooked white-meat
chicken, cubed*
*1 medium unpeeled apple,
chopped*
1 teaspoon grated orange rind
1 teaspoon curry powder

Plump raisins by soaking them for 10 to 15 minutes in warm water.
Rinse well. Stir together all ingredients in a 1-quart saucepan. Heat
through over low heat.

Per serving: 257 calories; 21 gm protein; 2.9 gm fat; 36.3 gm carbohydrates; 0.9
gm fiber; 0 gm saturated fat; 0.7 gm monounsaturated fat; 0.4 gm
polyunsaturated fat; 48.6 mg cholesterol; 159.7 mg sodium; 29.5 mg calcium

Lemon Dill Chicken
MAKES 2 SERVINGS

1 chicken breast, skinned, boned, and split in half
¼ cup chopped onion
1½ teaspoons dried dill

1 teaspoon grated lemon rind
⅛ teaspoon ground nutmeg
½ cup water
4 teaspoons fresh lemon juice

Place chicken and onion in a shallow baking dish; sprinkle with dill, lemon rind, and nutmeg. Mix water and lemon juice and pour over chicken. Cover and let chicken marinate in refrigerate several hours or overnight. Bake at 375° for 20 to 25 minutes or until chicken is done, basting every 5 minutes.

Per serving: 154.7 calories; 27.1 gm protein; 3.2 gm fat; 3 gm carbohydrates; 0.1 gm fiber; 0.9 gm saturated fat; 1 gm monounsaturated fat; 0.6 gm polyunsaturated fat; 73 mg cholesterol; 65 mg sodium; 34.1 mg calcium

Chicken Roll-Ups
MAKES 2 SERVINGS

1 chicken breast, skinned, boned, and split in half
½ cup cooked Millet (see page 77)
1 tablespoon chopped broad-leaf parsley.

2 teaspoons lemon juice
1 teaspoon grated onion
Dash black pepper
1 cup Chicken Broth (see page 163)
2 tablespoons potato flour

Flatten chicken halves with a flat mallet. Stir together millet, parsley, lemon juice, onion, and pepper. Spoon one half of millet mixture onto end of each piece of chicken; roll up and fasten with a toothpick. Place chicken and broth in a small skillet and bring to a boil. Lower heat, cover, and simmer for 15 to 20 minutes or until chicken is done, turning chicken once. Remove chicken and keep warm. Stir potato flour into pan juices. Cook, stirring constantly, until thickened, about 3 minutes. Spoon sauce over chicken.

Per serving: 323 calories; 31 gm protein; 3.8 gm fat; 21.1 gm carbohydrates; 0.6 gm fiber; 0.9 gm saturated fat; 1.1 gm monounsaturated fat; 0.7 gm polyunsaturated fat; 73 mg cholesterol; 159.3 mg sodium; 63.6 mg calcium

Chicken Cacciatore
MAKES 2 SERVINGS

*1 chicken breast, skinned,
  boned, and split in half*
1 teaspoon oil
1 small onion, sliced

*1 small green pepper, cut into
  thin strips*
*1 (8-ounce) can salt-free tomato
  sauce*

Brown chicken lightly in hot oil in a small skillet. Stir in the remaining ingredients and bring mixture to a boil. Simmer 10 to 15 minutes or until done.

NOTE: Serve over ½ cup hot cooked Brown Rice (see page 78) or Millet (see page 77) if desired.

Per serving: 230.3 calories; 29.5 gm protein; 5.5 gm fat; 14 gm carbohydrates; 0.7 gm fiber; 1.1 gm saturated fat; 1.3 gm monounsaturated fat; 2.4 gm polyunsaturated fat; 73 mg cholesterol; 97.3 mg sodium; 25.6 mg calcium

Chicken and Vegetables
MAKES 4 SERVINGS

*1 (3½-pound) stewing chicken,
  cut in pieces*
1 quart water
½ teaspoon dried sage
*4 medium potatoes, peeled and
  quartered*

*8 small whole white onions,
  peeled*
*1½ to 2 cups fresh green beans,
  cooked, or 1 (10-ounce) package frozen green beans,
  thawed*

Place chicken, water, and sage in 3-quart Dutch oven. Bring to a boil and simmer 45 minutes. Add potatoes and onions and simmer another 15 to 20 minutes. Remove chicken and vegetables from broth. Chill broth and remove skin from chicken. Remove fat from chilled broth. Return fat-free broth, chicken, potatoes, onions, and green beans to Dutch oven and heat through. Serve in soup dishes.

Per serving: 268.3 calories; 28.6 gm protein; 10.5 gm fat; 7.4 gm carbohydrates; 1.5 gm fiber; 3.1 gm saturated fat; 4.4 gm monounsaturated fat; 2.2 gm polyunsaturated fat; 38 mg cholesterol; 5.7 mg sodium; 34.4 mg calcium

Tomato-Broccoli Chicken
MAKES 2 SERVINGS

1 chicken breast, skinned,
  boned, and split in half
1 teaspoon oil
2 tablespoons chopped onion
2 small tomatoes, chopped

1½ to 2 cups fresh broccoli,
  chopped, or 1 (10-ounce)
  package frozen chopped broccoli, thawed
1 teaspoon crushed oregano

Brown chicken in hot oil in a skillet. Remove chicken. Add the remaining ingredients and cook 3 to 5 minutes. Return chicken to skillet and cover. Cook over medium heat until chicken is done, 15 to 20 minutes.

NOTE: Serve over ½ cup hot cooked Brown Rice (see page 78) or Millet (see page 77) if desired.

Per serving: 224.5 calories; 31.9 gm protein; 5.7 gm fat; 13 gm carbohydrates; 4 gm fiber; 1.1 gm saturated fat; 1.3 gm monounsaturated fat; 2.5 gm polyunsaturated fat; 72.5 mg cholesterol; 104.5 mg sodium; 97.5 mg calcium

Quick-Stir Turkey Dinner
MAKES 2 SERVINGS

¼ pound turkey breast, skinned,
  boned, and cut into ½-inch
  strips
1 tablespoon oil
1 medium carrot, cut into thin
  strips
¼ pound fresh broccoli flowerets

1 small onion, thinly sliced
¼ pound zucchini, sliced
1 large fresh tomato, cut into
  wedges
½ cup Chicken Broth (see page
  163)
1 teaspoon dried basil

Cook turkey strips in hot oil in a wok or large skillet until turkey loses its pinkness. Stir in the remaining ingredients. Cover and simmer 6 to 8 minutes, stirring occasionally, until vegetables are crisp-tender.

Per serving: 147.3 calories; 5.8 gm protein; 7.6 gm fat; 17.3 gm carbohydrates; 2.4 gm fiber; 0.7 gm saturated fat; 0.8 gm monounsaturated fat; 5.4 gm polyunsaturated fat; 82 mg cholesterol; 80.9 mg sodium; 80.9 mg calcium

Turkey and Wild Rice Casserole
MAKES 2 SERVINGS

¼ cup chopped onion
1 tablespoon oil
¾ cup Wild Rice (page 78)
¾ cup diced cooked white-meat
turkey

2 tablespoons sliced almonds
¼ teaspoon salt
Dash black pepper
¾ cup Chicken Broth (see page 163)

Sauté onion in hot oil in a large skillet until transparent. Stir in cooked rice and all other remaining ingredients. Pour mixture into a 1-quart casserole and cover. Bake at 350° for 45 minutes. Remove cover and continue to bake 10 to 15 minutes more or until all liquid is absorbed.

Per serving: 246.2 calories; 19.6 gm protein; 13 gm fat; 12.5 gm carbohydrates; 0.5 gm fiber; 1.5 gm saturated fat; 3.8 gm monounsaturated fat; 6.4 gm polyunsaturated fat; 36.3 mg cholesterol; 344.6 mg sodium; 46.9 mg calcium

CHAPTER 15

Veal and Lamb

Veal and Wild Rice Dinner
MAKES 2 SERVINGS

¼ pound fresh chestnuts
¼ pound lean ground veal
¼ cup chopped onion
1 tablespoon finely chopped
  celery
1 tablespoon chopped green
  pepper

1 tablespoon chopped fresh parsley
2 teaspoons oil
1 cup cooked Wild Rice (see
  page 78)
¼ teaspoon black pepper
¼ cup sliced almonds

With a sharp knife, cut an X in the top of the chestnuts. Cover
chestnuts with water and boil for 20 minutes. Drain. In a small
baking pan, bake chestnuts at 350° for about 20 minutes. Peel skin
from chestnuts while they're still warm; cut into fourths. Sauté veal
in large nonstick skillet until browned. Drain off fat. Remove veal
and set aside. In the same skillet, sauté onion, celery, pepper, and
parsley in hot oil until onion is limp. Add veal and cook 1 minute.
Stir in wild rice, black pepper, chestnuts, and almonds and heat
through.

Variation: Bake two acorn squash halves at 325° for 1 hour. Fill
cavities with veal and wild rice mixture and bake 20 to 25 minutes
longer or until squash is cooked.

Per serving: 455.8 calories; 21.9 gm protein; 23.1 gm fat; 39.4 gm carbohydrates;
1 gm fiber; 5.7 gm saturated fat; 7.9 gm monounsaturated fat; 3.4 gm
polyunsaturated fat; 58 mg cholesterol; 54.6 mg sodium; 76.7 mg calcium

Veal and Onion Dinner
MAKES 4 SERVINGS

1 medium onion, chopped
1 tablespoon oil
1 pound lean ground veal
2 cups cooked Buckwheat (see page 77)

1 cup each fresh carrots and peas, cooked, or 1 (10-ounce) package frozen carrots and peas, thawed
1 teaspoon dried marjoram
1 teaspoon dried mint
Dash black pepper

In a saucepan, sauté onion in oil until onion is transparent. Drain off fat. Stir in veal. Cook over medium heat until veal is browned. Stir in the remaining ingredients. Cover and cook 10 to 12 minutes or until heated through.

Per serving: 381.7 calories; 34.9 gm protein; 19.1 gm fat; 31.6 gm carbohydrates; 2.2 gm fiber; 8.1 gm saturated fat; 0 gm monounsaturated fat; 0 gm polyunsaturated fat; 116 mg cholesterol; 142.7 mg sodium; 42.2 mg calcium

Lemon-Sautéed Veal Cutlets
MAKES 6 SERVINGS

¼ cup potato meal or potato flour
1½ pounds veal cutlets
6 tablespoons oil

¼ cup fresh lemon juice
¼ cup chopped fresh parsley
Lemon slices for garnish

With a flat mallet, pound veal until ¼ inch thick. Dust veal on both sides with potato meal, shaking off any excess. Heat oil in a large skillet; add veal and brown on both sides. Add lemon juice and parsley and cook 1 minute. Remove veal and keep warm. Cook remaining sauce until reduced by half. Spoon sauce over veal and garnish with lemon slices.

Per serving: 416 calories; 33.6 gm protein; 40 gm fat; 4.8 gm carbohydrates; 0 gm fiber; 1.2 gm saturated fat; 4.0 gm monounsaturated fat; 10.3 gm polyunsaturated fat; 148 mg cholesterol; 56 mg sodium; 10.4 mg calcium

Veal Chop Juniper
MAKES I SERVING

1 (7-ounce) loin veal chop　　*¼ teaspoon juniper berries,*
1 teaspoon oil　　　　　　　　*ground*
⅓ cup water

Trim all fat from chop. Brown chop on both sides in hot oil in small skillet. Add water and juniper berries. Simmer 8 to 10 minutes or until chop is done. Remove chop and keep warm. Cook liquid until it is reduced by half. Pour sauce over chop.

Per serving: 269.8 calories; 23 gm protein; 18.5 gm fat; 0 gm carbohydrates; 0 gm fiber; 6.5 gm saturated fat; 0.5 gm monounsaturated fat; 3.3 gm polyunsaturated fat; 87 mg cholesterol; 70 mg sodium; 10 mg calcium

Veal Chop Rosemary
MAKES I SERVING

1 (7-ounce) loin veal chop　　*¼ teaspoon dried rosemary,*
1 teaspoon oil　　　　　　　　*crushed*
⅓ cup water

Trim all fat from chop. Brown chop on both sides in hot oil in a small skillet. Drain off fat. Add water and rosemary and simmer 8 to 10 minutes or until chop is done. Remove chop; keep warm. Boil liquid until it is reduced by half. Pour sauce over chop.

Variation: Substitute dried marjoram, oregano, or tarragon for rosemary.

Per serving: 269.9 calories; 23 gm protein; 18.5 gm fat; 0 gm carbohydrates; 0 gm fiber; 6.5 gm saturated fat; 0.5 gm monounsaturated fat; 3.3 gm polyunsaturated fat; 87 mg cholesterol; 68 mg sodium; 10 mg calcium

Veal Burger
MAKES I SERVING

¼ pound lean ground veal   *¼ teaspoon toasted sesame seeds*

Form the veal into a patty. Brown on both sides in a nonstick skillet. Reduce heat, cover, and cook to desired degree of doneness. Sprinkle with sesame seeds before serving.

NOTE: Toast seeds in a shallow baking pan at 200° for 10 to 15 minutes or until golden brown.

Per serving: 310.7 calories; 30.8 gm protein; 19 gm fat; 0 gm carbohydrates; 0 gm fiber; 8.1 gm saturated fat; 0 gm monounsaturated fat; 0 gm polyunsaturated fat; 116.1 mg cholesterol; 90.9 mg sodium; 14.3 mg calcium

Osso Buco
MAKES 3 SERVINGS

2 veal shanks
3 tablespoons potato flour
1 tablespoon oil
3 cups Chicken Broth (see page 163)
1 cup canned salt-free tomatoes, drained and chopped

2 garlic cloves, minced
¼ cup lemon juice
2 tablespoons grated lemon rind
2 tablespoons chopped fresh parsley

Coat veal shanks with flour and brown in hot oil in Dutch oven. Add broth, tomatoes, and garlic. Cover and cook over low heat for 1¼ hours or until meat is tender. Cool. Skim off all fat. Add juice, rind, and parsley. Cook over medium heat until heated through.

Per serving: 272.1 calories; 25.4 gm protein; 11.8 gm fat; 17.9 gm carbohydrates; 0 gm fiber; 3.7 gm saturated fat; 3.9 gm monounsaturated fat; 3.8 gm polyunsaturated fat; 60 mg cholesterol; 343.3 mg sodium; 43 mg calcium

Lamb Kabobs
MAKES I SERVING

1 tablespoon oil
1½ teaspoons apple juice concentrate
¼ teaspoon dry mustard
¼ teaspoon dried dill
4 ounces boneless lamb, cut into 3 cubes

6 cherry tomatoes
3 pieces zucchini, about 1 inch thick
3 artichoke quarters

In a large bowl, stir together oil, apple juice concentrate, mustard, and dill. Add lamb, tomatoes, zucchini, and artichoke and toss lightly until well coated. Remove lamb and vegetables; reserve marinade. Thread lamb and vegetables alternately on skewer. Broil 5 inches from heat for 10 to 15 minutes, turning and basting frequently with reserved marinade.

NOTE: Serve over ½ cup hot cooked Brown Rice (see page 78) or Millet (see page 77) if desired.

Per serving: 562 calories; 60.8 gm protein; 35.9 gm fat; 18.2 gm carbohydrates; 5.5 gm fiber; 1.2 gm saturated fat; 1.0 gm monounsaturated fat; 11.1 gm polyunsaturated fat; 76.6 mg cholesterol; 99.5 mg sodium; 40 mg calcium

Lamb Chop with Mint Sauce
MAKES I SERVING

1 (5-ounce) loin lamb chop
2 tablespoons apple juice concentrate

1 tablespoon water
¼ teaspoon lemon juice
½ teaspoon dried mint leaves

Trim all fat from chop. Broil chop on both sides to desired degree of doneness. Combine the remaining ingredients in a small saucepan and bring mixture to a boil. Cook sauce until liquid is reduced by half. Pour over chop.

Per serving: 359.3 calories; 23.2 gm protein; 25.6 gm fat; 14.2 gm carbohydrates; 0 gm fiber; 1.1 gm saturated fat; 0 gm monounsaturated fat; 0.97 gm polyunsaturated fat; 70 mg cholesterol; 57.5 mg sodium; 17.3 mg calcium

Lamb Shanks
MAKES 2 SERVINGS

2 lamb shanks
1 garlic clove, slivered
1 tablespoon oil
1½ cups water
1 medium leek, chopped

2 medium peeled potatoes, quartered
2 medium carrots, cut into 2-inch chunks
½ teaspoon curry powder
Potato flour (optional)

Remove all membrane and fat from lamb. With a sharp knife, pierce the skin of the lamb and insert slivers of garlic into meat. Brown lamb on all sides in hot oil in a Dutch oven; drain off fat. Add water. Cover and bring to a boil. Reduce heat and simmer for 1 hour. Add vegetables and curry powder and cook another hour more or until meat is tender. (You may need to add more water.) Skim off all fat before serving. Thicken pan juices with potato flour if desired, and pour over meat.

Per serving: 508 calories; 35 gm protein; 18 gm fat; 50.5 gm carbohydrates; 1.8 gm fiber; 7.1 gm saturated fat; 0.8 gm monounsaturated fat; 5.2 gm polyunsaturated fat; 118.7 mg cholesterol; 124.2 mg sodium; 82.7 mg calcium

Grecian Lamb
MAKES I SERVING

2 teaspoons oil
4 ounces boneless lamb, cut into ½-inch strips
1 garlic clove, minced
1 medium tomato, diced

1 cup French-style green beans
½ teaspoon dried rosemary, crushed
½ cup hot cooked Barley (see page 78)

Heat oil in a large skillet and brown lamb in it. Stir in garlic, tomato, beans, and rosemary. Cook over medium heat, stirring occasionally, for about 12 minutes or until lamb is cooked to desired degree of doneness. Serve over barley.

Per serving: 453 calories; 32 gm protein; 31.2 gm fat; 7.7 gm carbohydrates; 1.7 gm fiber; 0.3 gm saturated fat; 1.1 gm monounsaturated fat; 7.1 gm polyunsaturated fat; 70 mg cholesterol; 79 mg sodium; 92 mg calcium

CHAPTER 16

Main-Dish Grains and Legumes

Beans Indienne
MAKES 2 SERVINGS

1 small onion, chopped
1 garlic clove, minced
1 tablespoon oil
¼ teaspoon curry powder
Dash cayenne pepper
*1 cup cooked red kidney beans
  (see page 81)*

*1 cup cooked white (Great
  Northern) beans (see page 81)*
*2 tablespoons cooking liquid
  from beans*
*2 cups hot cooked Brown
  Rice(see page 78)*

Sauté onion and garlic in hot oil in a small skillet until onion is transparent; stir in curry powder and cayenne pepper. Add beans and stir to mix. Cook over low heat, stirring occasionally, for 5 to 10 minutes or until heated through. Add bean liquid or water to moisten. Serve over brown rice.

NOTE: Do not use canned kidney beans; they're much too high in salt.

Variation: Substitute hot cooked Millet (see page 77) for the rice.

Per serving: 241 calories; 15.1 gm protein; 7.5 gm fat; 40.9 gm carbohydrates; 0.3 gm fiber; 0.6 gm saturated fat; 0.3 gm monounsaturated fat; 5.1 gm polyunsaturated fat; 0 mg cholesterol; 6.3 mg sodium; 52.8 mg calcium

Barley Medley
MAKES 4 SERVINGS

1½ cups uncooked barley
3 small shallots, chopped
1 tablespoon oil
½ sweet red pepper, chopped

2 stalks celery, chopped
3½ cups water
¼ teaspoon salt

Wash and drain barley. Sauté shallots in hot oil in a 2-quart saucepan over medium heat, stirring constantly. Add the barley and the remaining ingredients and bring mixture to a boil. Cover, reduce heat, and cook 35 to 40 minutes, stirring occasionally, until barley is cooked.

Per serving: 305 calories; 6.2 gm protein; 4.2 gm fat; 62.4 gm carbohydrates; 0.3 gm fiber; 0.4 gm saturated fat; 0.4 gm monounsaturated fat; 2.5 gm polyunsaturated fat; 0 mg cholesterol; 30 mg sodium; 26.8 mg calcium

Chili Beans
MAKES 2 SERVINGS

2 cups cooked red kidney beans
  (see page 81)
1 (8-ounce) can salt-free tomato
  sauce

½ cup chopped onion
½ cup chopped green pepper
1 teaspoon chili powder

Stir together all ingredients in a saucepan; cook until onion and pepper are crisp-tender, 10 to 15 minutes.

NOTES: • Do not use canned kidney beans; they're much too high in salt.
• Serve over ½ cup hot cooked Millet (see page 77) or Brown Rice (see page 78), if desired.

Per serving: 277 calories; 23.8 gm protein; 1.3 gm fat; 52.1 gm carbohydrates; 0.7 gm fiber; 0 gm saturated fat; 0 gm monounsaturated fat; 0.1 gm polyunsaturated fat; 0 mg cholesterol; 50 mg sodium; 81.9 mg calcium

Tasty Baked Chick-Peas
MAKES 2 SERVINGS

1 tablespoon oil
1 medium green pepper, thinly sliced
1 small white onion, thinly sliced
¼ teaspoon dried tarragon, crushed

½ teaspoon dried basil, crushed
1 tablespoon fresh chopped parsley
2 cups cooked chick-peas (see page 81)

Heat oil in a skillet and sauté pepper and onion until just tender. Add tarragon, basil, and parsley, and mix well. Simmer about 5 minutes. Stir in beans. Place in an oven-proof casserole dish and cover. Bake for 30 minutes at 325°. Serve hot or cold.

NOTE: Do not use canned chick-peas; they're much too high in salt.

Per serving: 292.9 calories; 15.4 gm protein; 9.1 gm fat; 24.1 gm carbohydrates; 0.7 gm fiber; 0.6 gm saturated fat; 0.8 gm monounsaturated fat; 5.1 gm polyunsaturated fat; 0 mg cholesterol; 17 mg sodium; 69.3 mg calcium

Yam, Buckwheat and Chick-Pea Casserole
MAKES 2 SERVINGS

2 cups peeled and sliced yams
¼ cup whole uncooked buckwheat
¼ cup chopped scallions

½ cup sweet red pepper
½ cup cooked chick-peas (see page 81)
⅔ cup chick-pea liquid or water

Layer half the yams in a lightly oiled 1-quart baking dish. Add buckwheat, scallions, and red pepper. Put the remaining yams on top. Place chick-peas and liquid in blender and purée until just smooth. Pour purée over yams and buckwheat. Cover and bake at 350° for 40 to 45 minutes or until buckwheat is cooked.

NOTE: Do not use canned chick-peas; they're much too high in salt.

Per serving: 207 calories; 4.4 gm protein; 0.9 gm fat; 53.4 gm carbohydrates; 0.2 gm fiber; 0 gm saturated fat; 0 gm monounsaturated fat; 0.1 gm polyunsaturated fat; 0 mg cholesterol; 15.8 mg sodium; 38.4 mg calcium

Chick-Peas with Onions
MAKES 2 SERVINGS

2 cups cooked chick-peas (see page 81)
1 garlic clove, minced
1 small onion, sliced
1 bay leaf

Water
1 medium onion, chopped
2 tablespoons oil
1 medium tomato, chopped

Place chick-peas, garlic, sliced onion, and bay leaf in a saucepan. Add water just to cover. Simmer for 15 minutes. Drain. Remove bay leaf. Sauté chopped onion in hot oil until onion is transparent. Add tomato; cook 2 minutes. Add chick-pea mixture and heat thoroughly.

NOTE: Do not use canned chick-peas; they're much too high in salt.

Per serving: 164.2 calories; 14.1 gm protein; 18.8 gm fat; 54 gm carbohydrates; 1.2 gm fiber; 1.3 gm saturated fat; 1.6 gm monounsaturated fat; 10.2 gm polyunsaturated fat; 0 mg cholesterol; 21 mg sodium; 135 mg calcium

Cauliflower-Rice Bake
MAKES 3 SERVINGS

3 cups fresh or frozen caulifower flowerets
1 medium onion, chopped
2 garlic cloves, minced
¼ cup oil
1 large tomato, cubed

2 tablespoons lemon juice
2 teaspoon dried basil
¼ teaspoon cayenne pepper
2 cups cooked Brown Rice (see page 78)
¼ cup crumbled feta cheese

Sauté cauliflower, onion, and garlic in hot oil in a large skillet until onion is transparent. Stir in tomato, lemon juice, basil, and cayenne pepper. Cook 4 to 5 minutes, stirring constantly. Stir in rice and cheese. Spoon into an ungreased 2-quart casserole. Cover and bake at 350° for 30 to 35 minutes or until heated through.

Per serving: 384.3 calories; 8.9 gm protein; 23.2 gm fat; 38.4 gm carbohydrates; 0.5 gm fiber; 4.6 gm saturated fat; 3.1 gm monounsaturated fat; 14.8 gm polyunsaturated fat; 33.5 mg cholesterol; 238.3 mg sodium; 168.6 mg calcium

Vegetable Spanish Rice
MAKES 2 SERVINGS

½ cup uncooked long-grain
  brown rice
1 small red onion, minced
1 teaspoon oil
1 cup Vegetable Broth (see page
  163)

2 stalks celery, chopped
1 medium green pepper, chopped
2 small tomatoes, quartered
⅛ teaspoon paprika
Dash cayenne pepper
Dash chili powder

In a 2-quart saucepan, bring rice, onion, oil, and vegetable stock to a boil. Reduce heat. Cover and simmer 15 to 20 minutes. Stir in the remaining ingredients. Simmer, covered, over low heat for 15 to 20 minutes or until rice is cooked.

Per serving: 192.9 calories; 4.7 gm protein; 3.5 gm fat; 37.4 gm carbohydrates; 2.1 gm fiber; 0.3 gm saturated fat; 0.3 gm monounsaturated fat; 1.9 gm polyunsaturated fat; 0 mg cholesterol; 49.3 mg sodium; 50.1 mg calcium

Lentils and Rice
MAKES 2 SERVINGS

2 tablespoons chopped shallots
1 tablespoon oil
½ cup uncooked brown rice

2 cups water
¼ cup uncooked green lentils
¼ cup pine nuts

Sauté shallots in hot oil in a large skillet. Stir in rice and cook 2 to 3 minutes. Add water to rice. Stir in lentils. Bring to a boil. Cover, reduce heat, and simmer for 20 to 25 minutes or until all liquid is absorbed. Stir in nuts just before serving.

Per serving: 289 calories; 8.5 gm protein; 15 gm fat; 32.1 gm carbohydrates; 0.37 gm fiber; 2.5 gm saturated fat; 0.83 gm monounsaturated fat; 0.51 gm polyunsaturated fat; 0 mg cholesterol; 8.7 mg sodium; 32.1 mg calcium

Lentil-Rice Pilaf
MAKES 2 SERVINGS

¼ cup raisins
2 tablespoons chopped leeks
1 tablespoon oil
½ cup uncooked brown rice
2 teaspoons salt-free tomato paste

1¼ cups water
¼ cup uncooked red lentils
⅛ teaspoon cinnamon
¼ cup pine nuts
2 tablespoons Vegetable Broth (see page 163)

Plump raisins by soaking them in warm water 10 to 15 minutes. Sauté leeks in hot oil in a large skillet until crisp-tender. Stir in rice and cook 2 to 3 minutes. Dissolve tomato paste in water and stir into rice. Add lentils and cinnamon to rice mixture. Bring to a boil. Cover, reduce heat, and simmer for 20 minutes. Stir in raisins and nuts. Pour mixture into an oiled 1-quart casserole dish. Spoon vegetable broth over surface. Bake, covered, at 350° for 15 to 20 minutes or until heated through.

Per serving: 232.3 calories; 6.1 gm protein; 9.9 gm fat; 32.3 gm carbohydrates; 0.2 gm fiber; 0.4 gm saturated fat; 0.5 gm monounsaturated fat; 3.4 gm polyunsaturated fat; 0 mg cholesterol; 112.9 mg sodium; 30.2 mg calcium

Vegetable Medley with Rice
MAKES 2 SERVINGS

1 medium green pepper, chopped
1 medium onion, chopped
1 medium zucchini, sliced
5 garlic cloves, minced
2 tablespoons oil

2 medium tomatoes, chopped
2 tablespoons chopped fresh parsley
2 cups hot cooked Brown Rice (see page 78)

Sauté pepper, onion, zucchini, and garlic in hot oil until onion is transparent. Add tomatoes and parsley. Cook 3 to 5 minutes, until heated through. Serve over rice.

Per serving: 430.3 calories; 8.7 gm protein; 15.6 gm fat; 66.6 gm carbohydrates; 2.3 gm fiber; 1.4 gm saturated fat; 1.7 gm monounsaturated fat; 10.4 gm polyunsaturated fat; 0 mg cholesterol; 19.3 mg sodium; 80.2 mg calcium

Oriental Rice Casserole
MAKES 3 SERVINGS

1 medium carrot, diced
¼ cup chopped onion
1 teaspoon oil
½ cup shredded Chinese cabbage
½ cup snow peas
½ cup fresh spinach leaves
½ cup mung bean sprouts
¼ cup chopped walnuts

1 tablespoon sesame seeds
2 tablespoons Vegetable Broth
(see page 163) or water
1 teaspoon lemon juice
1½ cups cooked Brown Rice (see
page 78)
¼ cup crumbled feta cheese

Sauté carrot and onion in hot oil in a large skillet until onion is transparent. Stir in cabbage, peas, and spinach. Cover and cook until cabbage is just wilted. Stir in sprouts, nuts, seeds, broth, and lemon juice. Cover and cook 3 to 4 minutes. Stir in rice. Pour into a 1½-quart casserole and sprinkle with cheese. Bake at 350° for about 15 minutes. Cheese should be melted and heated through.

Per serving: 243.2 calories; 9 gm protein; 16.3 gm fat; 17.5 gm carbohydrates; 1.4 gm fiber; 3.6 gm saturated fat; 2.8 gm monounsaturated fat; 7.5 gm polyunsaturated fat; 33.3 mg cholesterol; 79.9 mg sodium; 152.5 mg calcium

CHAPTER 17

Side-Dish Grains and Legumes

Millet
MAKES 2 SERVINGS

1¾ cups water
½ cup uncooked millet

¼ teaspoon salt (optional)

Bring water to a boil in a saucepan. Add millet and salt if desired. Cover tightly and cook over low heat until all liquid is absorbed, about 50 minutes.

Per serving: 180 calories; 6 gm protein; 2.0 gm fat; 41 gm carbohydrates; 0 gm fiber; 0 gm saturated fat; 0 gm monounsaturated fat; 0 gm polyunsaturated fat; 0 mg cholesterol; 2.0 mg sodium; 0 mg calcium

Millet-Onion Sauté
MAKES 2 SERVINGS

1 medium yellow onion, chopped
1 tablespoon oil
2 cups cooked Millet (see page 77)
Dash cayenne pepper

¼ cup Vegetable Broth (see page 163)
2 tablespoons fresh chopped chives

In a large skillet, sauté onion in hot oil until golden brown. Add millet, cayenne pepper, and vegetable broth. Stir to mix well. Heat thoroughly. Remove from heat and toss with chives.

Per serving: 256 calories; 6.5 gm protein; 8.9 gm fat; 45.2 gm carbohydrates; 0.3 gm fiber; 0.6 gm saturated fat; 0.8 gm monounsaturated fat; 5.1 gm polyunsaturated fat; 0 mg cholesterol; 2.9 mg sodium; 12.8 mg calcium

Barley
MAKES 2 SERVINGS

2 cups water
½ cup uncooked barley

¼ teaspoon salt (optional)

Bring water to a boil in a medium saucepan. Add barley and salt if desired. Cover tightly and cook over low heat until all liquid is absorbed, about 40 to 45 minutes.

Per serving: 172 calories; 5.5 gm protein; 0.5 gm fat; 34.3 gm carbohydrates; 1.0 gm fiber; 0 gm saturated fat; 0 gm monounsaturated fat; 0 gm polyunsaturated fat; 0 mg cholesterol; 4 mg sodium; 22 mg calcium

Barley Pilaf
MAKES 2 SERVINGS

1¼ cup Chicken Broth (see page 163)
½ cup uncooked barley
1 medium onion, chopped

1 tablespoon oil
½ tablespoon dried parsley
¼ teaspoon salt

Stir together all ingredients in a 1½-quart casserole. Cover and bake at 375°, stirring once, for about 1¼ hours.

Per serving: 262.6 calories; 7.1 gm protein; 6.9 gm fat; 42.7 gm carbohydrates; 0.3 gm fiber; 0.7 gm saturated fat; 0.8 gm monounsaturated fat; 5.1 gm polyunsaturated fat; 0 mg cholesterol; 400.6 mg sodium; 31.2 mg calcium

Barley-Fennel Pilaf
MAKES 4 SERVINGS

1 fennel bulb, cut into thin strips
2 tablespoons oil
1 cup uncooked barley
1 (1-pound) can salt-free whole tomatoes, drained

1 cup water
¼ teaspoon black pepper (optional)

Sauté fennel in hot oil in a large skillet for 2 to 3 minutes. In a 1½-quart casserole, stir together fennel, barley, tomatoes, water, and pepper if desired. Cover and bake at 350° for about 60 minutes. All liquid should be absorbed.

Per serving: 264.5 calories; 5 gm protein; 7.5 gm fat; 44.3 gm carbohydrates; 0.9 gm fiber; 0.7 gm saturated fat; 0.8 gm monounsaturated fat; 5.8 gm polyunsaturated fat; 0 mg cholesterol; 284.3 mg sodium; 50.6 mg calcium

Buckwheat
MAKES 2 SERVINGS

2 cups water
½ cup uncooked buckwheat groats

¼ teaspoon salt (optional)

Bring water to a boil in a saucepan. Add buckwheat and salt if desired. Cover tightly and cook over low heat until all liquid is absorbed, about 45 to 50 minutes.

Per serving: 170 calories; 3.0 gm protein; 0.5 gm fat; 39 gm carbohydrates; 0 gm fiber; 0 gm saturated fat; 0 gm monounsaturated fat; 0 gm polyunsaturated fat; 0 mg cholesterol; 4 mg sodium; 11 mg calcium

Brown Rice
MAKES 2 SERVINGS

1¾ cups water
½ cup uncooked brown rice

¼ teaspoon salt (optional)

Bring water to a boil in a saucepan. Add rice and salt if desired. Cover tightly and cook over low heat until all liquid is absorbed, about 50 minutes.

Variation: For Saffron Rice, add a few threads of saffron to water before adding rice.

Per serving: 232 calories; 4.9 gm protein; 1.2 gm fat; 49.7 gm carbohydrates; 0.4 gm fiber; 0 gm saturated fat; 0 gm monounsaturated fat; 0 gm polyunsaturated fat; 0 mg cholesterol; 249.9 mg sodium; 23.0 mg calcium

Fruited Confetti Rice
MAKES 2 SERVINGS

2 small shallots, chopped
1/2 cup mixed dried fruit (combine pineapple, apples, and
  apricots), chopped
1 tablespoon oil
1 1/2 cups cooked Brown Rice (see
  page 78)

1/8 teaspoon ground cloves
1/4 teaspoon salt (optional)
2 tablespoons toasted sesame
  seeds

Sauté shallots and fruit in hot oil in a small skillet until shallots are
golden brown. Stir in rice, cloves, and salt if desired. Blend well.
Sprinkle with sesame seeds before serving.

NOTE: Toast seeds in a shallow baking pan at 200° for 10 to 15
minutes or until golden brown.

Per serving: 376.8 calories; 6.8 gm protein; 12.6 gm fat; 62.3 gm carbohydrates;
1.1 gm fiber; 0.6 gm saturated fat; 0.8 gm monounsaturated fat; 5.2 gm
polyunsaturated fat; 0 mg cholesterol; 257.5 mg sodium; 47.9 mg calcium

Risotto
MAKES 4 SERVINGS

1/2 cup chopped scallions
1 cup uncooked brown rice
2 tablespoons olive oil
2 cups Chicken Broth (see page
  163)

1 cup fresh or frozen green peas
1 teaspoon dried rosemary
1 teaspoon dried oregano

Sauté scallions and rice in hot oil in a large skillet for about 3
minutes. Stir in broth and bring to a boil. Remove from heat. Pour
mixture into a 1 1/2-quart casserole. Stir in peas and herbs. Cover.
Bake at 400° for 20 to 25 minutes. Liquid should be absorbed.

Per serving: 200.9 calories; 5.9 gm protein; 7.4 gm fat; 27.7 gm carbohydrates;
1.5 gm fiber; 0.9 gm saturated fat; 4.9 gm monounsaturated fat; 0.6 gm
polyunsaturated fat; 0 mg cholesterol; 124.7 mg sodium; 40.2 mg calcium

Wild Rice
MAKES 3 SERVINGS

1 cup uncooked wild rice *¼ teaspoon salt (optional)*
4 cups boiling water

Wash rice well in several waters, pouring off any foreign particles
from the top. Drain rice well and stir slowly into boiling water. Add
salt if desired. Cover tightly and cook over low heat until all liquid
is absorbed, about 50 minutes.

Per serving: 54 calories; 1.2 gm protein; 0.8 gm fat; 12.4 gm carbohydrates; 0
gm fiber; 0 gm saturated fat; 0 gm monounsaturated fat; 0 gm polyunsaturated
fat; 0 mg cholesterol; 0 mg sodium; 16.8 mg calcium

Parsleyed Wild Rice
MAKES 3 SERVINGS

⅔ cup uncooked wild rice *2 teaspoons minced garlic*
¾ cup Chicken Broth (see page *1 teaspoon oil*
163) *½ cup chopped fresh parsley*
¾ cup orange juice

Wash rice in several waters and drain well. Stir together rice, broth,
and orange juice in a small saucepan; bring to a boil. Reduce heat
and simmer, covered, over low heat for about 30 minutes, until rice
is tender. (Stir frequently to prevent scorching.) Drain well. Sauté
garlic in hot oil. Add wild rice and parsley. Serve immediately.

Per serving: 173.3 calories; 6.4 gm protein; 1.9 gm fat; 34.2 gm carbohydrates;
0.8 gm fiber; 0.1 gm saturated fat; 0.1 gm monounsaturated fat; 1.1 gm
polyunsaturated fat; 0 mg cholesterol; 51.2 mg sodium; 31.1 mg calcium

CHAPTER 18

Main-Dish Vegetables

Fresh Vegetable-Nut Dinner
MAKES 2 SERVINGS

1 garlic clove, crushed
½ teaspoon minced fresh ginger
½ teaspoon mustard seeds
2 tablespoons oil
1 teaspoon curry powder
½ teaspoon dill
1 cup sliced red onion
2 small potatoes, unpeeled and
  thinly sliced

2 medium carrots, sliced
¾ cup orange juice
1 sweet red pepper, slivered
½ cup cashew nuts
¼ teaspoon cayenne pepper
1 cup hot cooked Brown Rice
  (see page 78)

Sauté garlic, ginger, and mustard seeds in hot oil in a large skillet until seeds "pop," about 3 to 5 minutes. Stir in curry, dill, onion, potatoes, and carrots. Cook over low heat for 3 minutes, stirring constantly. Add orange juice. Cover and simmer 12 to 15 minutes, until potatoes are tender. Stir in red pepper, nuts, and cayenne pepper. Cover and simmer about 5 minutes or until peppers are tender. Serve over hot rice.

Per serving: 619 calories; 12.4 gm protein; 31.2 gm fat; 84.8 gm carbohydrates; 2.1 gm fiber; 4.5 gm saturated fat; 11.2 gm monounsaturated fat; 13.1 gm polyunsaturated fat; 0 mg cholesterol; 45.3 mg sodium; 106 mg calcium

Curried Vegetables
MAKES 2 SERVINGS

1 cup fresh or frozen string
  beans, cut into 1-inch pieces
1 medium potato, unpeeled and
  cubed
1 medium carrot, cut into 2-inch
  strips
⅔ cup peas, fresh or frozen

2 tablespoons oil
¼ teaspoon cayenne pepper
1½ teaspoons curry powder
Saffron Rice (see page 209)
¼ cup raisins
⅓ cup cashew pieces

Place all vegetables in a saucepan with water to barely cover. Bring to a boil over medium heat and cook 10 minutes. In another saucepan, heat oil and stir in pepper and curry powder. Add vegetable mixture, including liquid. Bring to a boil. Reduce heat, cover, and simmer 30 minutes. Serve hot over Saffron Rice. Sprinkle with raisins and cashews.

Per serving: 436.4 calories; 9.4 gm protein; 24.6 gm fat; 50.3 gm carbohydrates; 3.6 gm fiber; 3.4 gm saturated fat; 7.7 gm monounsaturated fat; 12 gm polyunsaturated fat; 0 mg cholesterol; 77.3 mg sodium; 83 mg calcium

Vegetable Medley
MAKES 2 SERVINGS

2 tablespoons oil
1 small yellow onion, chopped
1 garlic clove, finely chopped
1½ cups fresh or frozen chopped
  broccoli flowerets
1 cup sliced carrots

2 tablespoons Vegetable Broth
  (see page 163)
2 cups cooked Brown Rice (see
  page 78)
¼ cup mung bean sprouts
2 tablespoons sesame seeds

Heat oil in a large skillet and sauté onion, garlic, broccoli, and carrots until crisp-tender. Add broth and rice. Toss and reheat. Sprinkle with sprouts and toss again. Top with sesame seeds.

Per serving: 462.9 calories; 10.5 gm protein; 19.7 gm fat; 63.9 gm carbohydrates; 2.2 gm fiber; 1.3 gm saturated fat; 1.6 gm monounsaturated fat; 10.3 gm polyunsaturated fat; 0 mg cholesterol; 42.1 mg sodium; 96.4 mg calcium

Stir-Fry Cabbage Oriental
MAKES 2 SERVINGS

2 tablespoons chopped shallots
1½ teaspoons grated fresh ginger
1 tablespoon light sesame oil
2 tablespoons Vegetable Broth
(see page 163)
1 cup fresh or frozen green
beans, cut in half
1 cup fresh snow peas

1 stalk celery, cut into 1-inch
pieces
½ pound red cabbage, shredded
4 ounces buckwheat noodles,
cooked according to package
instructions
1 teaspoon sesame seeds

Sauté shallots and ginger in hot oil in a wok or large skillet for 1 minute. Stir in broth. Add beans, peas, and celery. Cook for 1 minute, stirring constantly. Add cabbage. Cover and cook over medium heat until cabbage is wilted, about 10 to 15 minutes. Serve over buckwheat noodles and sprinkle with sesame seeds.

Per serving: 352.9 calories; 11.5 gm protein; 9.3 gm fat; 58.6 gm carbohydrates; 3.4 gm fiber; 1 gm saturated fat; 2.7 gm monounsaturated fat; 3.1 gm polyunsaturated fat; 0 mg cholesterol; 31.1 mg sodium; 124.2 mg calcium

Garden-Stuffed Peppers
MAKES 3 SERVINGS

3 medium green peppers
2 cups cooked Brown Rice (see
page 78)
½ cup cooked fresh or frozen
peas

½ cup chopped celery
1¼ teaspoons dried dill
½ teaspoon dried marjoram
2 teaspoons oil

Remove tops from green peppers and discard seed and membranes. Chop tops to make ¼ cup. Parboil peppers in boiling water, about 10 minutes, until nearly tender; invert to drain. Stir together remaining ingredients and fill peppers with the mixture. Place peppers in an oiled baking dish; add boiling water to a depth of a half-inch. Cover and bake at 350° for 25 to 30 minutes.

Per serving: 185.2 calories; 4.6 gm protein; 4 gm fat; 33.4 gm carbohydrates; 2 gm fiber; 0.3 gm saturated fat; 0.4 gm monounsaturated fat; 2.4 gm polyunsaturated fat; 0 mg cholesterol; 43 mg sodium; 36.5 mg calcium

Butternut Squash Mix
MAKES 2 SERVINGS

½ medium butternut squash
1 medium Spanish onion, thinly
  sliced
1 tablespoon oil
1 cup fresh or frozen green
  beans, cut in half

¼ teaspoon dried oregano
¼ teaspoon dried thyme
¼ cup Vegetable Broth (see page
  163) or water
1 tablespoon chopped fresh parsley

Peel and cut squash into 2-inch cubes. Sauté onion in hot oil in a
2-quart saucepan until onion is transparent. Stir in squash, beans,
and herbs and cook 3 minutes over medium heat. Add vegetable
broth. Cover and simmer for 15 to 20 minutes or until squash is
cooked. Sprinkle with parsley before serving.

Per serving: 120.3 calories; 3.1 gm protein; 2.7 gm fat; 24.5 gm carbohydrates;
1.4 gm fiber; 0.3 gm saturated fat; 0.3 gm monounsaturated fat; 1.8 gm
polyunsaturated fat; 0 mg cholesterol; 9 mg sodium; 111.4 mg calcium

Apple-Stuffed Squash
MAKES 2 SERVINGS

1 medium acorn squash
1 unpeeled medium apple,
  chopped
¼ cup chopped scallions
1 tablespoon oil
½ cup crumbled feta cheese

2 tablespoons lemon juice
1 cup uncooked brown rice
¼ cup chopped walnuts
¼ cup chopped dates
Dash cinnamon
Dash nutmeg

Cut squash in half and remove seeds. Bake face-down on oiled
baking sheet at 350° for about 30 minutes (squash should be tender).
Sauté apple and scallions in oil in a medium skillet until almost
tender, about 5 minutes. Stir in remaining ingredients. Divide mixture between the two squash shells. Cover and bake at 350° for 20
minutes more, until heated through.

Per serving: 598 calories; 16.7 gm protein; 42.3 gm fat; 74.7 gm carbohydrates;
6.4 gm fiber; 9.9 gm saturated fat; 5.5 gm monounsaturated fat; 12.8 gm
polyunsaturated fat; 50.6 mg cholesterol; 645 mg sodium; 385.8 mg calcium

Zucchini Toss
MAKES 2 SERVINGS

2 tablespoons oil
¼ cup chopped scallions
½ cup chopped celery
½ teaspoon dried basil
1 medium tomato, cut in eighths
* or ¼ cup salt-free tomato*
* sauce*

2 medium zucchini, cut into 1-
* inch chunks*
1 medium red potato, unpeeled
* and cut into ½-inch cubes*
¼ teaspoon salt

Heat oil in a large skillet. Add scallions, celery, and basil. Sauté until hot. Add tomatoes or tomato sauce, zucchini, potato, and salt and stir to coat with oil. Cover and steam until tender, about 6 minutes.

NOTE: Serve over ½ cup Brown Rice (see page 78) or another grain if desired.

Per serving: 244.4 calories; 5.1 gm protein; 14.2 gm fat; 26.7 gm carbohydrates; 1.9 gm fiber; 1.3 gm saturated fat; 1.7 gm monounsaturated fat; 10.3 gm polyunsaturated fat; 0 mg cholesterol; 287 mg sodium; 74.6 mg calcium

Stuffed Zucchini Boats
MAKES 4 SERVINGS

2 zucchini, about 8 ounces each
1 cup minced cooked white-meat
* chicken*
½ cup cooked Brown Rice (see
* page 78)*
2 tablespoons minced fresh pars-
* ley*

2 tablespoons crumbled feta
* cheese*
1 tablespoon grated onion
½ teaspoon dried oregano
1 (8-ounce) can salt-free tomato
* sauce*

Cook zucchini in boiling water for 5 minutes. Drain well. In a separate bowl, stir together chicken, rice, parsley, cheese, onion, and oregano. Cut zucchini in half lengthwise; scoop out seeds and discard. Fill zucchini shells with chicken mixture and place zucchini in a shallow baking dish. Pour tomato sauce over all. Bake at 350° for about 30 minutes, basting occasionally. Zucchini should be tender.

Per serving: 311 calories; 35.6 gm protein; 10.3 gm fat; 14.4 gm carbohydrates; 0.9 gm fiber; 3.4 gm saturated fat; 3.6 gm monounsaturated fat; 1.9 gm polyunsaturated fat; 91.9 mg cholesterol; 170.6 mg sodium; 86.4 mg calcium

Zucchini-Spinach Bake
MAKES 2 SERVINGS

1 tablespoon oil
2 medium zucchini, sliced
2 cups chopped fresh spinach
¼ cup chopped fresh parsley
Dash nutmeg
½ cup crumbled feta cheese

¼ cup lentil sprouts
¼ cup sliced almonds
2 tablespoons Vegetable Broth
  (see page 163)
Hot cooked Millet (see page 77)

Stir together oil and zucchini in a large skillet. Cover and cook 5 minutes over low heat. Add spinach, parsley, and nutmeg. Continue cooking until spinach is wilted. Layer one half of the vegetable mix, one half of the cheese, and one half of the sprouts in a 1½-quart baking dish. Repeat. Sprinkle with almonds and pour broth over all. Bake at 375° for 15 minutes. Serve over millet.

Variation: Serve over hot Brown Rice (see page 78), Barley (see page 78), or Bulgur (see page 79) instead of the millet.

Per serving: 369.5 calories; 17.5 gm protein; 27.2 gm fat; 18.5 gm carbohydrates; 3.7 gm fiber; 10.5 gm saturated fat; 10.7 gm monounsaturated fat; 4.3 gm polyunsaturated fat; 50.6 mg cholesterol; 696.5 mg sodium; 433.1 mg calcium

CHAPTER 19

Side-Dish Vegetables

Beets à l'Orange
MAKES 3 SERVINGS

3 medium beets
½ cup cooking liquid from beets
½ teaspoon freshly grated orange peel

⅛ teaspoon ground cloves
2 teaspoons orange juice concentrate
2 teaspoons arrowroot

Cook beets until tender in water to cover, about 45 minutes. Drain, reserving liquid. Peel and thinly slice to make 1½ cups beets. Pour ½ cup liquid from beets into a medium saucepan. Add orange peel, cloves, and orange juice concentrate. Stir over low heat. Dissolve arrowroot with enough water (about 2 tablespoons) to make smooth paste and add to mixture. Stir over medium heat until clear. Add sliced beets; heat through. Serve hot.

NOTE: Do not use canned beets.

Per serving: 39.8 calories; 1.1 gm protein; 0 gm fat; 8.9 gm carbohydrates; 0 gm fiber; 0 gm saturated fat; 0 gm monounsaturated fat; 0 gm polyunsaturated fat; 0 mg cholesterol; 43.1 mg sodium; 11.3 mg calcium

Broccoli with Pumpkin Seeds
MAKES 2 SERVINGS

*1 pound fresh broccoli, or 2 (10-
ounce) packages frozen broccoli*

*¼ cup water
¼ cup shelled pumpkin seeds*

Separate broccoli flowerets from stems. Peel and cut stems into thin slices. Bring water to a boil in the bottom of a steamer. Place stems in basket and steam 4 to 5 minutes. Add flowerets and pumpkin seeds. Cover and steam 4 to 5 minutes more. Flowerets should be bright green and crisp-tender.

Per serving: 160.7 calories; 11 gm protein; 8.5 gm fat; 15.7 gm carbohydrates; 0 gm fiber; 1.5 gm saturated fat; 2.5 gm monounsaturated fat; 3.9 gm polyunsaturated fat; 0 mg cholesterol; 26.4 mg sodium; 267.8 mg calcium

Garlic-Steamed Broccoli
MAKES 2 SERVINGS

*1 pound fresh broccoli, or 2 (10-
ounce) packages frozen broccoli
¼ cup water*

*1 garlic clove, minced
¼ teaspoon toasted sesame seeds
(optional)*

Separate broccoli into stems and flowerets. Peel and cut stems into thin slices. In a steamer bottom, bring water and garlic to a boil. Place broccoli stems in steamer rack over boiling water. Cover and steam 4 to 5 minutes. Arrange flowerets over stems. Cover and steam an additional 4 to 5 minutes. Sprinkle sesame seeds over broccoli before serving.

NOTE: Toast seeds in a shallow baking pan at 200° for 10 to 15 minutes or until golden brown.

Per serving: 79.3 calories; 7.3 gm protein; 1.5 gm fat; 13.2 gm carbohydrates; 0 gm fiber; 0.1 gm saturated fat; 0 gm monounsaturated fat; 0.3 gm polyunsaturated fat; 0 mg cholesterol; 24.5 mg sodium; 265.4 mg calcium

Brussels Sprouts with Lemon-Parsley Sauce
MAKES 2 SERVINGS

2 cups fresh or frozen brussels
sprouts
1 tablespoon oil
½ cup lemon juice

2 tablespoons chopped fresh parsley
¼ teaspoon dried marjoram

Trim stems and remove wilted leaves from fresh brussels sprouts. Rinse well. Steam until crisp-tender, about 8 to 10 minutes. Heat oil, lemon juice, and herbs in a small skillet; stir well. Add brussels sprouts and toss lightly until sprouts are well coated. Serve hot.

Per serving: 136.6 calories; 4.3 gm protein; 7.6 gm fat; 19.1 gm carbohydrates; 2.1 gm fiber; 0.8 gm saturated fat; 0.8 gm monounsaturated fat; 5.4 gm polyunsaturated fat; 0 mg cholesterol; 36.1 mg sodium; 67.2 mg calcium

Cabbage and Apples
MAKES 4 SERVINGS

1 cup Chicken Broth (see page
163)
1 medium unpeeled apple, cored
and sliced

1 small head cabbage, shredded
1 tablespoon chopped scallions
Freshly grated black pepper

Stir together all ingredients in a large skillet or saucepot. Cook over medium heat, stirring frequently, until cabbage is crisp-tender.

Per serving: 30.4 calories; 1.1 gm protein; 0.1 gm fat; 6.8 gm carbohydrates; 0.8 gm fiber; 0 gm saturated fat; 0 gm monounsaturated fat; 0 gm polyunsaturated fat; 0 mg cholesterol; 46 mg sodium; 15 mg calcium

Apricot-Glazed Carrots
MAKES 4 SERVINGS

1 (12-ounce) bag baby carrots
(about 2 cups)
⅛ cup currants
1 tablespoon oil

¼ cup diced dried apricots
2 tablespoons orange juice
⅛ teaspoon ground ginger
Chopped fresh parsley (optional)

Peel and trim carrots and steam until crisp-tender, about 10 minutes. Drain well. Plump currants by soaking them in warm water for 10 to 15 minutes; rinse well. Heat oil in a large skillet. Add apricots, currants, orange juice, and ginger. Mix well. Add carrots and cook over medium heat about 7 minutes. Sprinkle with parsley before serving if desired.

Per serving: 104.8 calories; 1.4 gm protein; 3.6 gm fat; 18.4 gm carbohydrates; 0.3 gm fiber; 0.3 gm saturated fat; 0.4 gm monounsaturated fat; 2.6 gm polyunsaturated fat; 0 mg cholesterol; 62.9 mg sodium; 29.6 mg calcium

Carrots and Parsnips
MAKES 2 SERVINGS

3 medium carrots, cut into 2-
  inch strips
3 parsnips, cut into 2-inch strips

1 tablespoon oil
2 tablespoons chopped fresh parsley (optional)

Steam carrots and parsnips until just crisp-tender, about 10 minutes. Drain off excess water. Sauté carrots and parsnips in hot oil in a large skillet for 5 minutes, stirring constantly. Sprinkle with parsley before serving if desired.

Per serving: 170.9 calories; 2.2 gm protein; 7.2 gm fat; 26.4 gm carbohydrates; 3.7 gm fiber; 0.7 gm saturated fat; 0.9 gm monounsaturated fat; 5.1 gm polyunsaturated fat; 0 mg cholesterol; 47.1 mg sodium; 62.7 mg calcium

Carrots with Basil
MAKES 3 SERVINGS

1½ tablespoons oil
3 medium carrots, sliced diago-
  nally

1 to 2 tablespoons chopped fresh
  basil

Heat oil in a heavy skillet over low heat. Add carrots and basil. Stir to coat in oil. Cover and simmer until carrots are crisp-tender, about 15 minutes.

Per serving: 95.2 calories; 0.9 gm protein; 7 gm fat; 8.1 gm carbohydrates; 1 gm fiber; 0.6 gm saturated fat; 0.8 gm monounsaturated fat; 5.1 gm polyunsaturated fat; 0 mg cholesterol; 25 mg sodium; 50.1 mg calcium

Sweet Potatoes with Pineapple
MAKES 2 SERVINGS

2 medium sweet potatoes
¾ cup unsweetened crushed
  pineapple

½ teaspoon cinnamon
2 tablespoons chopped pecans

Bake sweet potatoes at 375° for 45 minutes or until tender. Cut in half and scoop out potato. Discard skin. Mash potato with electric mixer on low speed until smooth. Add pineapple and cinnamon and mix well. Spoon mixture into a lightly oiled 1-quart baking dish; sprinkle top with pecans. Cover and bake at 350° for 20 minutes.

Per serving: 194.2 calories; 2.9 gm protein; 4.8 gm fat; 37 gm carbohydrates; 2 gm fiber; 0.4 gm saturated fat; 2.8 gm monounsaturated fat; 1.2 gm polyunsaturated fat; 0 mg cholesterol; 23.4 mg sodium; 55.3 mg calcium

Grecian-Style Baked Tomatoes
MAKES 2 SERVINGS

2 large whole fresh tomatoes
1 garlic clove, minced
1 tablespoon oil
1½ cups cooked Brown Rice (see
  page 78)

½ cup crumbled feta cheese
½ teaspoon dried dill

Slice off stem end of tomato and hollow tomato; invert tomato to drain. Chop insides of tomato to make ½ cup. In a small saucepan, sauté garlic in oil for about 1 minute. Stir in chopped tomato, rice, cheese, and dill. Fill tomatoes with rice mixture and place in an oiled baking dish or ramekin. Bake at 350° for about 20 minutes.

NOTE: To hollow a tomato, slice off top and scoop out seeds and membranes with a small spoon.

Variation: Add ¼ cup chopped nuts or cooked chick-peas to the rice mixture.

Per serving: 339.6 calories; 9.1 gm protein; 14.1 gm fat; 44.9 gm carbohydrates; 1 gm fiber; 4.9 gm saturated fat; 2.1 gm monounsaturated fat; 5.3 gm polyunsaturated fat; 25.3 mg cholesterol; 331.7 mg sodium; 175.4 mg calcium

CHAPTER 20

Muffins
and Pancakes

Buckwheat Tangerine Muffins
MAKES 6 MUFFINS

1 cup whole buckwheat flour
2 teaspoons cornstarch-free
  baking powder

½ cup tangerine juice concen-
  trate
2 tablespoons oil

In a medium bowl, stir together flour and baking powder. Stir in
tangerine juice concentrate and oil until well blended. Fill six 2½-
inch nonstick muffin cups about ⅔ full. Bake at 400° for 15 minutes.
Turn out onto a wire rack to cool.

Per muffin: 135 calories; 1.3 gm protein; 4.8 gm fat; 22.5 gm carbohydrates; 0
gm fiber; 0.4 gm saturated fat; 0.5 gm monounsaturated fat; 3.3 gm
polyunsaturated fat; 0 mg cholesterol; 112.5 mg sodium; 26.9 mg calcium

Buckwheat-Tangerine-Ginger Muffins
MAKES 6 MUFFINS

1 cup whole buckwheat flour
2 teaspoons cornstarch-free
  baking powder
½ teaspoon ground ginger

½ cup tangerine juice concen-
  trate
2 tablespoons oil

In a medium bowl, stir together flour, baking powder, and ginger.
Stir in tangerine juice concentrate and oil until well blended. Fill
six 2½-inch nonstick muffin cups ⅔ full. Bake at 400° for 15 minutes.
Turn out onto a wire rack to cool.

Per muffin: 135.6 calories; 1.3 gm protein; 4.8 gm fat; 22.5 gm carbohydrates; 0
gm fiber; 0.4 gm saturated fat; 0.5 gm monounsaturated fat; 3.3 gm
polyunsaturated fat; 0 mg cholesterol; 112.6 mg sodium; 27.1 mg calcium

Rye-Feta Cheese-Raisin Muffins
MAKES 6 MUFFINS

½ *cup raisins*
1 *cup whole rye flour*
2 *teaspoons cornstarch-free*
  baking powder
⅛ *teaspoon caraway seeds*

½ *cup grape juice concentrate*
¼ *cup water*
2 *tablespoons oil*
2 *ounces crumbled low-fat feta*
  cheese

Plump raisins by covering with boiling water and letting stand 1 minute. Drain well. In a medium bowl, stir together flour, baking powder, and caraway seeds. Add grape juice concentrate, water, oil, raisins, and cheese. Stir until just blended. Fill six 2½-inch nonstick muffin cups ⅔ full. Bake at 400° for 15 minutes. Turn out onto a wire rack to cool.

Per muffin: 199.2 calories; 3.5 gm protein; 6.8 gm fat; 33.3 gm carbohydrates; 0 gm fiber; 1.9 gm saturated fat; 1 gm monounsaturated fat; 3.4 gm polyunsaturated fat; 8.9 mg cholesterol; 225.8 mg sodium; 77.7 mg calcium

Rye Raisin Muffins
MAKES 6 MUFFINS

½ *cup raisins*
1 *cup whole rye flour*
2 *teaspoons cornstarch-free*
  baking powder

⅛ *teaspoon caraway seeds*
½ *cup grape juice concentrate*
¼ *cup water*
2 *tablespoons oil*

Plump raisins by covering with boiling water and letting stand 1 minute. Drain well. In a medium bowl, stir together flour, baking powder, and caraway seeds. Add grape juice concentrate, water, oil, and raisins. Stir until just blended. Fill six 2½-inch nonstick muffin cups ⅔ full. Bake at 400° for 15 minutes. Turn out onto a wire rack to cool.

Per muffin: 172.5 calories; 2.1 gm protein; 4.6 gm fat; 32.9 gm carbohydrates; 0 gm fiber; 0.4 gm saturated fat; 0.5 gm monounsaturated fat; 3.4 gm polyunsaturated fat; 0 mg cholesterol; 114.6 mg sodium; 27.7 mg calcium

Orange Rice Muffins
MAKES 6 MUFFINS

1 cup mashed banana (2 medium bananas)
½ cup orange juice concentrate
2 tablespoons oil

1¼ cups rice flour
1½ teaspoons cornstarch-free baking powder

In a large bowl, mix bananas, orange juice concentrate, and oil. Add flour and baking powder. Blend well. Fill six 2½-inch nonstick muffin cups ⅔ full. Bake at 375° for 20 to 25 minutes. Turn out onto a wire rack to cool.

Variations: • Add ½ cup raisins, ½ cup sliced almonds, ½ cup chopped dates (no sugar), or ½ cup well-drained crushed pineapple.
• For Apple Rice Muffins, substitute apple juice concentrate for orange juice concentrate.

Per muffin: 198.5 calories; 2.3 gm protein; 4.8 gm fat; 36.7 gm carbohydrates; 0.4 gm fiber; 0.4 gm saturated fat; 0.5 gm monounsaturated fat; 3.4 gm polyunsaturated fat; 0 mg cholesterol; 88.3 mg sodium; 24.5 mg calcium
With raisins: 234.6 calories; 2.7 gm protein; 4.8 gm fat; 46.3 gm carbohydrates; 0.4 gm fiber; 0.5 gm saturated fat; 0.5 gm monounsaturated fat; 3.4 gm polyunsaturated fat; 0 mg cholesterol; 89.8 mg sodium; 30.4 mg calcium
With almonds: 255 calories; 4.2 gm protein; 9.8 gm fat; 39.0 gm carbohydrates; 0.8 gm fiber; 0.9 gm saturated fat; 3.8 gm monounsaturated fat; 4.4 gm polyunsaturated fat; 0 mg cholesterol; 89.3 mg sodium; 50 mg calcium
With dates: 239.3 calories; 2.6 gm protein; 4.8 gm fat; 46.8 gm carbohydrates; 1.1 gm fiber; 0.4 gm saturated fat; 0.5 gm monounsaturated fat; 3.4 gm polyunsaturated fat; 0 mg cholesterol; 88.7 mg sodium; 29.3 mg calcium
With pineapple: 205.1 calories; 2.4 gm protein; 4.8 gm fat; 40.7 gm carbohydrates; 0.4 gm fiber; 0.4 gm saturated fat; 0.5 gm monounsaturated fat; 3.4 gm polyunsaturated fat; 0 mg cholesterol; 88.5 mg sodium; 27.5 mg calcium
With apple juice: 252.3 calories; 2 gm protein; 4.9 gm fat; 36.7 gm carbohydrates; 0.4 gm fiber; 0.5 gm saturated fat; 0.5 gm monounsaturated fat; 3.4 gm polyunsaturated fat; 0 mg cholesterol; 92.5 mg sodium; 32.1 mg calcium

Cinnamon-Oat-Honey Muffins
MAKES 6 MUFFINS

1 cup oat flour
2 teaspoons cornstarch-free
baking powder
¼ teaspoon cinnamon

⅓ cup water
2 tablespoons honey
2 tablespoons oil

In a medium bowl, stir together flour, baking powder, and cinnamon. Stir in water, honey, and oil until well blended. Fill six 2½-inch nonstick muffin cups ⅔ full. Bake at 400° for 15 minutes. Tap out onto a wire cooling rack very carefully. (These are very fragile.) Serve warm or cool.

Per muffin: 116.8 calories; 1.8 gm protein; 5.5 gm fat; 16.6 gm carbohydrates; 0.1 gm fiber; 0.4 gm saturated fat; 0.6 gm monounsaturated fat; 3.3 gm polyunsaturated fat; 0 mg cholesterol; 112.4 mg sodium; 28.9 mg calcium

Jerusalem Artichoke Pancakes
MAKES 8 PANCAKES

¾ cup peeled and shredded Jeru-
salem artichokes
1 tablespoon potato starch

⅛ teaspoon garlic powder
3 teaspoons oil

In a medium bowl, mix together shredded artichokes, potato starch, and garlic powder. Stir in *1 teaspoon of the oil*. Heat a nonstick griddle over medium heat until drops of water dance on the surface. Divide mixture into eight portions. Place about ⅛ *teaspoon oil* on the griddle. Put one portion of the artichoke mixture on oil, and press with the back of a fork to spread very thin. (Pancakes should be 3 inches in diameter.) Repeat procedure until all mixture is used. Cook slowly for 5 to 7 minutes, until well browned. Lift each pancake, place ⅛ *teaspoon oil* on griddle, and turn pancake over onto oil. Cook until nicely browned and crisp, 4 to 5 minutes. If necessary, turn again to brown both sides well.

NOTE: These may be served with fruit toppings (see pages 238–239).

Per pancake: 29.4 calories; 0.4 gm protein; 1.7 gm fat; 3.2 gm carbohydrates; 0.1 gm fiber; 0.1 gm saturated fat; 0.2 gm monounsaturated fat; 1.2 gm polyunsaturated fat; 0 mg cholesterol; 0.4 mg sodium; 2.2 mg calcium

Potato Pancakes
MAKES 8 PANCAKES

*1 medium potato, peeled and
grated (about ¾ cup)*
1 tablespoon potato starch

⅛ teaspoon garlic powder
3 teaspoons sunflower oil

In a medium bowl, mix together grated potato, potato starch, and garlic powder. Stir in *1 teaspoon of the oil*. Heat a nonstick griddle over low heat until drops of water dance on the surface. Divide potato mixture into eight portions. Place about *⅛ teaspoon oil* on griddle. Put one portion potato mixture (enough for a 3-inch pancake) in the oil and press with the back of a fork to spread very thin. Repeat the procedure until a teaspoon of oil and all potato mixture has been used. Cook slowly, 5 to 7 minutes, until well browned. Lift each pancake, place *⅛ teaspoon oil* on grill, and turn pancake over onto oil. Cook until nicely browned and crisp, 4 to 5 minutes. If necessary, turn again to brown both sides well.

NOTE: These may be served with fruit toppings (see pages 238–239).

Per pancake: 57.9 calories; 0.4 gm protein; 1.7 gm fat; 10.5 gm carbohydrates; 0 gm fiber; 0.2 gm saturated fat; 0.4 gm monounsaturated fat; 1 gm polyunsaturated fat; 0 mg cholesterol; 1.3 mg sodium; 1.7 mg calcium

Silver Dollar Buckwheat Pancakes
MAKES 4 SERVINGS

1 cup buckwheat flour
1 teaspoon cornstarch-free
  baking powder

¼ teaspoon cinnamon (optional)
1 cup plus 2 tablespoons water
4 tablespoons oil

In a medium bowl, stir together buckwheat flour, baking powder, and cinnamon if desired. Add water and oil. Stir with a whisk until batter is smooth and has the consistency of heavy cream. Heat a nonstick griddle over medium heat until drops of water dance on the surface. Drop batter on griddle a tablespoonful at a time (pancakes will be about 3 inches in diameter). Cook until surface is covered with small holes and is mostly dry. Turn and cook until steaming stops and both sides are crispy, turning again if necessary.

NOTE: These may be served with one of the fruit toppings (see pages 238–239)

Per serving: 138 calories; 1 gm protein; 9.2 gm fat; 13.2 gm carbohydrates; 0 gm fiber; 0.8 gm saturated fat; 1 gm monounsaturated fat; 6.7 gm polyunsaturated fat; 0 mg cholesterol; 55.9 mg sodium; 12.5 mg calcium

Silver Dollar Rice Pancakes
MAKES 4 SERVINGS

1 cup rice flour
1 teaspoon cornstarch-free
  baking powder
¼ teaspoon ground cinnamon
  (optional)

1 cup plus 2 tablespoons water
4 tablespoons oil

In a medium bowl, stir together rice flour, baking powder, and cinnamon if desired. Add water and oil. Stir with a whisk until batter is smooth and has the consistency of heavy cream. Heat a nonstick griddle over medium heat until drops of water dance on the surface. Drop batter on griddle a tablespoonful at a time. (Pancakes will be 3 inches in diameter.) Cook until surface is covered with small holes and is mostly dry. Turn. Cook until steaming stops and both sides are crispy, turning again if necessary.

NOTE: These may be served with one of the fruit toppings (see pages 238–239) or honey.

Per serving: 241.8 calories; 1.8 gm protein; 13.7 gm fat; 27.1 gm carbohydrates; 0 gm fiber; 1.2 gm saturated fat; 1.6 gm monounsaturated fat; 10.1 gm polyunsaturated fat; 0 mg cholesterol; 87.2 mg sodium; 18.8 mg calcium

Silver Dollar Rye Pancakes
MAKES 4 SERVINGS

1 cup whole rye flour
1 teaspoon cornstarch-free
* baking powder*

¼ teaspoon cinnamon (optional)
1 cup plus 2 tablespoons water
4 tablespoons oil

In a medium bowl, stir together rye flour, baking powder, and cinnamon if desired. Add water and oil. Stir with a whisk until batter is smooth and has the consistency of heavy cream. Heat a nonstick griddle over medium heat until drops of water dance on the surface. Drop batter on griddle a tablespoonful at a time (pancakes will be 3 inches in diameter). Cook until surface is covered with small holes and is mostly dry. Turn. Cook until steaming stops and both sides are crispy, turning again if necessary.

NOTE: These may be served with one of the fruit toppings (see pages 238–239), or honey.

Per serving: 241.8 calories; 1.8 gm protein; 13.7 gm fat; 27.1 gm carbohydrates; 0 gm fiber; 1.2 gm saturated fat; 1.6 gm monounsaturated fat; 10.1 gm polyunsaturated fat; 0 mg cholesterol; 87.2 mg sodium; 18.8 mg calcium

CHAPTER 21

Snacks

Fresh Herb Feta Cheese Spread
MAKES I CUP

1 cup crumbled feta cheese
1 tablespoon oil
¼ cup chopped fresh parsley

⅛ teaspoon coarsely ground
black pepper

Place all ingredients in blender. Process until smooth.

NOTE: Serve on rye wafers, celery stalks, cucumber rounds, cherry tomato halves, or carrot slices.

Per tablespoon: 45.8 calories; 2 gm protein; 3.9 gm fat; 0.6 gm carbohydrates; 0 gm fiber; 2.2 gm saturated fat; 0.7 gm monounsaturated fat; 0.7 gm polyunsaturated fat; 12.6 mg cholesterol; 160.3 mg sodium; 72.2 mg calcium

Easy Feta Cheese Spread
MAKES ABOUT I½ CUPS

½ cup crumbled feta cheese
1 medium boiled potato, peeled
* and mashed*
½ cup salt-free tomato juice

¼ teaspoon dried dill
¼ teaspoon dried chives
Dash red or black pepper

In a small bowl, mash feta cheese until smooth; add potato and blend until smooth. Add the remaining ingredients and mix well.

NOTE: Serve on rye wafers, celery stalks, cucumber rounds, carrot slices, or cherry tomato halves.

Per tablespoon: 18.4 calories; 0.8 gm protein; 1 gm fat; 1.5 gm carbohydrates; 0 gm fiber; 0.7 gm saturated fat; 0.2 gm monounsaturated fat; 0 gm polyunsaturated fat; 4.2 mg cholesterol; 54.1 mg sodium; 24.6 mg calcium

Fresh Garlic-Feta Spread
MAKES I CUP

1 cup crumbled feta cheese
1 teaspoon oil
1 garlic clove

1/4 teaspoon coarsely ground
black pepper

Place all ingredients in blender. Process until smooth.

NOTE: Serve on rye wafers, celery stalks, cucumber rounds, carrot slices, or cherry tomato halves.

Per tablespoon: 40.7 calories; 2 gm protein; 3.3 gm fat; 0.6 gm carbohydrates; 0 gm fiber; 2.1 gm saturated fat; 0.6 gm monounsaturated fat; 0.2 gm polyunsaturated fat; 12.6 mg cholesterol; 160 mg sodium; 71.2 mg calcium

Raisin-Cashew Crunch
MAKES I 1/2 CUPS

1/2 cup raisins
1/2 cup chopped cashews

1/2 cup shelled pumpkin seeds

Mix all ingredients together. Store in an airtight container.

Per 1/4 cup: 167 calories; 4.9 gm protein; 11.2 gm fat; 14.9 gm carbohydrates; 3.1 gm fiber; 1.6 gm saturated fat; 4.2 gm monounsaturated fat; 4.8 gm polyunsaturated fat; 0 mg cholesterol; 3.5 mg sodium; 24.3 mg calcium

Tropical Delight
MAKES I 3/4 CUPS

1/2 cup dried apricots, halved
1/2 cup sunflower seeds
1/4 cup shredded coconut

1/4 cup toasted sliced almonds
1/4 cup chopped dates

Mix all ingredients together. Store in an airtight container.

Per 1/4 cup: 139.1 calories; 3.7 gm protein; 8.4 gm fat; 14.7 gm carbohydrates; 0.5 gm fiber; 1.7 gm saturated fat; 2.4 gm monounsaturated fat; 3.8 gm polyunsaturated fat; 0 mg cholesterol; 10.5 mg sodium; 29.7 mg calcium

Grand Granola
MAKES SIX ½-CUP SERVINGS

2 cups rolled oats
⅓ cup oil
⅓ cup honey

¼ cup chopped almonds
1 tablespoon toasted sesame
    seeds

Stir together oats, oil, honey, and almonds. Spread mixture in a shallow baking pan. Bake at 250°, stirring occasionally, for about 45 minutes. Cool and stir in the toasted sesame seeds.

NOTE: Toast seeds in a shallow baking pan at 200° for 10 to 15 minutes or until golden brown.

Per ½ cup: 251.5 calories; 3.4 gm protein; 16.3 gm fat; 24.5 gm carbohydrates; 0.9 gm fiber; 1.5 gm saturated fat; 3.5 gm monounsaturated fat; 9.8 gm polyunsaturated fat; 0 mg cholesterol; 2.3 mg sodium; 23.9 mg calcium

Pignoli Mix
MAKES 1¾ CUPS

½ cup pignoli nuts (pine nuts)
½ cup chopped walnuts

½ cup dried pineapple chunks
¼ cup currants

Mix all ingredients together. Store in an airtight container.

Per ¼ cup: 162.5 calories; 4.4 gm protein; 17.2 gm fat; 17.1 gm carbohydrates; 0.7 gm fiber; 0.3 gm saturated fat; 1.1 gm monounsaturated fat; 4.2 gm polyunsaturated fat; 0 mg cholesterol; 1.1 mg sodium; 17.5 mg calcium

Almond Rice Cake
MAKES I SERVING

1 teaspoon almond butter   *1 orange slice*
1 rice cake

Spread almond butter over top of rice cake; top with orange slice.

NOTE: You may use commercially prepared almond butter, but check the label carefully for preservatives, sugar, corn syrup, etc. If you prefer to make your own, simply toss a cup of almonds into the blender or food processor and process until smooth.

Variations: • Substitute a rye wafer for the rice cake.
• Substitute canned unsweetened pineapple chunk, a peach half, or an apricot half for the orange slice.

Per serving: 75.5 calories; 1.6 gm protein; 3.4 gm fat; 10.4 gm carbohydrates; 0 gm fiber; 0.2 gm saturated fat; 2 gm monounsaturated fat; 0.6 gm polyunsaturated fat; 0 mg cholesterol; 11.3 mg sodium; 20.4 mg calcium

Cashew Rice Cake
MAKES I SERVING

1 teaspoon cashew butter   *1 slice unsweetened canned pine-*
1 rice cake   *apple*

Spread cashew butter over top of rice cake; top with pineapple slice.

NOTE: You may use commercially prepared cashew butter, but check the label carefully for preservatives, sugar, corn syrup, etc. If you prefer to make your own, simply toss a cup of cashews into the blender or food processor and process until smooth.

Variations: • Substitute a rye wafer for the rice cake.
• Substitute a mandarin orange slice or a canned unsweetened peach or apricot half for pineapple.

Per serving: 69.5 calories; 1.2 gm protein; 1.7 gm fat; 13.1 gm carbohydrates; 0.5 gm fiber; 0.2 gm saturated fat; 0.7 gm monounsaturated fat; 0.2 gm polyunsaturated fat; 0 mg cholesterol; 11.5 mg sodium; 3.8 mg calcium

Sesame-Onion Rice Cake
MAKES 1 SERVING

1 teaspoon sesame seed butter   *1 teaspoon chopped red onion*
1 rice cake

Spread sesame seed butter on rice cake; sprinkle with red onion.

NOTE: You may use a commercially prepared sesame seed butter, but check the label carefully for preservatives, sugar, corn syrup, etc. If you prefer to make your own, simply toss a cup of sesame seeds into the blender or food processor and process until smooth.

Variations: • Substitute a rye wafer for the rice cake.
              • Substitute 2 teaspoons chopped scallions for the onion.
              • Substitute 1 tablespoon chopped celery for the onion.

Per serving: Rice cake: 51.9 calories; 1.4 gm protein; 1.7 gm fat; 8.1 gm carbohydrates; 0 gm fiber; 0 gm saturated fat; 0 gm monounsaturated fat; 0 gm polyunsaturated fat; 0 mg cholesterol; 11.7 mg sodium; 4.8 mg calcium
With scallions: 55.4 calories; 1.5 gm protein; 1.7 gm fat; 8.9 gm carbohydrates; 0 gm fiber; 0 gm saturated fat; 0 gm monounsaturated fat; 0 gm polyunsaturated fat; 0 mg cholesterol; 12.3 mg sodium; 6.6 mg calcium
With celery: 51.9 calories; 1.4 gm protein; 1.7 gm fat; 8.1 gm carbohydrates; 0 gm fiber; 0 gm saturated fat; 0 gm monounsaturated fat; 0 gm polyunsaturated fat; 0 mg cholesterol; 18.3 mg sodium; 6.7 mg calcium
Rye wafer: 39.4 calories; 1.7 gm protein; 1.4 gm fat; 5.5 gm carbohydrates; 0.9 gm fiber; 0 gm saturated fat; 0 gm monounsaturated fat; 0 gm polyunsaturated fat; 0 mg cholesterol; 64.5 mg sodium; 10.2 mg calcium

Sardine Snack
MAKES 2 SERVINGS

1 (4³⁄₈-ounce) can water-packed   *6 rye wafers*
  sardines (with bones)

Drain sardines well. Serve on rye wafers.

NOTE: The bones of sardines are an excellent source of calcium.

Per serving: 198.9 calories; 12.6 gm protein; 4 gm fat; 15 gm carbohydrates; 2.5 gm fiber; 0 gm saturated fat; 0 gm monounsaturated fat; 9 gm polyunsaturated fat; 63.8 mg cholesterol; 236 mg sodium; 25.5 mg calcium

CHAPTER 22

Dressings, Sauces, and Toppings

Vinaigrette Dressing I
MAKES ⅓ CUP

2 tablespoons oil
2 tablespoons lemon juice
1 tablespoon honey

¼ teaspoon dry mustard
⅛ teaspoon paprika

Place all ingredients in a covered jar. Shake well to blend.

Per tablespoon: 31.9 calories; .02 gm protein; 2.7 gm fat; 2 gm carbohydrates; 0
gm fiber; 0.2 gm saturated fat; 0.3 gm monounsaturated fat; 2.0 gm
polyunsaturated fat; 0 mg cholesterol; 0.1 mg sodium; 0.9 mg calcium

Vinaigrette Dressing II
MAKES ¾ CUP

½ cup oil
⅓ cup lemon juice
1 tablespoon chopped chives

1 teaspoon dry mustard
Dash pepper

Place all ingredients in a covered jar. Shake well to blend.

Per tablespoon: 49.8 calories; 0 gm protein; 5.2 gm fat; 3.4 gm carbohydrates; 0
gm fiber; 0.5 gm saturated fat; 0.6 gm monounsaturated fat; 4.0 gm
polyunsaturated fat; 0 mg cholesterol; 8 mg sodium; 1.4 mg calcium

Honey Vinaigrette Dressing
MAKES ⅓ CUP

3 tablespoons oil
1 tablespoon honey

1 tablespoon unsweetened
pineapple juice

Place all ingredients in a covered jar. Shake well to blend.

Per tablespoon: 107.5 calories; 0 gm protein; 10.2 gm fat; 4.5 gm carbohydrates; 0 gm fiber; 0.9 gm saturated fat; 1.2 gm monounsaturated fat; 7.6 gm polyunsaturated fat; 0 mg cholesterol; 122.5 mg sodium; 1.4 mg calcium

Tomato Salad Dressing
MAKES ¾ CUP

½ cup tomato juice
¼ cup oil
Dash black pepper

2 teaspoons dried oregano
leaves, crushed

Place all ingredients in a covered jar. Shake well to blend.

Per tablespoon: 42.7 calories; 0.1 gm protein; 4.5 gm fat; 0.6 gm carbohydrates; 0 gm fiber; 0.4 gm saturated fat; 0.5 gm monounsaturated fat; 3.3 gm polyunsaturated fat; 0 mg cholesterol; 36.5 mg sodium; 5 mg calcium

Pineapple Salad Dressing
MAKES ¾ CUP

½ cup unsweetened pineapple
juice
¼ cup oil

½ teaspoon grated onion
⅛ teaspoon paprika

Place all ingredients in a covered jar. Shake well to blend.

Per tablespoon: 48.4 calories; 6.1 gm protein; 4.5 gm fat; 1.9 gm carbohydrates; .05 gm fiber; 0.4 gm saturated fat; 0.5 gm monounsaturated fat; 3.4 gm polyunsaturated fat; 0 mg cholesterol; 0.2 mg sodium; 3.5 mg calcium

Tropical Salad Dressing
MAKES ¾ CUP

½ cup pineapple juice
¼ cup fresh lemon juice
½ teaspoon ground mustard

¼ teaspoon ground ginger
2 teaspoons dark sesame oil

Place all ingredients in a covered jar. Shake well to blend.

Per tablespoon: 14.3 calories; 0 gm protein; 0.7 gm fat; 1.9 gm carbohydrates; 0 gm fiber; 0.1 gm saturated fat; 0.3 gm monounsaturated fat; 0.3 gm polyunsaturated fat; 0 mg cholesterol; 0.1 mg sodium; 2.8 mg calcium

Primavera Sauce
MAKES 2½ CUPS

1 (8-ounce) can salt-free tomato
sauce
1 cup canned salt-free tomatoes,
drained and chopped
½ cup chopped onions
½ cup chopped green peppers

½ cup fresh green beans (not
frozen), cut in 1-inch pieces
½ cup chopped yellow squash
½ teaspoon garlic powder
½ teaspoon dried basil
½ teaspoon anise seeds, crushed

Stir together all ingredients in a large saucepan; bring to a boil. Simmer 8 to 10 minutes.

NOTE: Serve over ½ cup hot Brown Rice (see page 78), Millet (see page 77), or Barley (see page 78) if desired.

Per ¼ cup: 23.9 calories; 1 gm protein; 0.1 gm fat; .5 gm carbohydrates; 0 gm fiber; 0 gm saturated fat; 0 gm monounsaturated fat; 0.5 gm polyunsaturated fat; 0 mg cholesterol; 47 mg sodium; 17.5 mg calcium

Spaghetti Sauce
MAKES 2 SERVINGS

1 (8-ounce) can salt-free tomato
  sauce
2 teaspoons oil

½ teaspoon dried oregano
¼ teaspoon dried basil
¼ teaspoon garlic powder

Stir together all ingredients in a small saucepan and cook over medium heat until heated through.

NOTE: Serve over ½ cup hot buckwheat noodles, Brown Rice (see page 78), or Millet (see page 77) if desired.

Per ½ cup: 79.1 calories; 1.7 gm protein; 4.7 gm fat; 9.3 gm carbohydrates; 0 gm fiber; 0.45 gm saturated fat; 0.55 gm monounsaturated fat; 3.4 gm polyunsaturated fat; 0 mg cholesterol; 10 mg sodium; 26.9 mg calcium

Mock Ketchup
MAKES I CUP

6 ounces salt-free tomato paste
2 tablespoons pineapple juice
  concentrate
2 tablespoons orange juice concentrate

¼ teaspoon dry mustard
¼ teaspoon onion powder
⅛ teaspoon cayenne powder
2 teaspoons oil

Mix all ingredients together and blend well. Keep refrigerated in a covered jar.

Per ¼ cup: 23.2 calories; 0.5 gm protein; 0.7 gm fat; 4.2 gm carbohydrates; 0 gm fiber; 0 gm saturated fat; 0 gm monounsaturated fat; 0.4 gm polyunsaturated fat; 0 mg cholesterol; 8.2 mg sodium; 6.3 mg calcium

Apple Topping
MAKES 1¼ CUPS

6 medium Macintosh apples,
  peeled, cored, and cubed
1 cup water

½ cup apple juice concentrate
½ teaspoon ground cinnamon

Cook apples in water in a medium saucepan over medium heat for 8 to 10 minutes or until liquid evaporates and apples have softened.

Stir in the remaining ingredients. Cook over medium heat for about 15 minutes, stirring constantly, until mixture has thickened.

NOTE: Serve with muffins or pancakes.

Per tablespoon: 32.8 calories; 0 gm protein; 0.1 gm fat; 8.5 gm carbohydrates; 0.8 gm fiber; 0 gm saturated fat; 0 gm monounsaturated fat; 0 gm polyunsaturated fat; 0 mg cholesterol; 1.7 mg sodium; 3.6 mg calcium

Pineapple Topping
MAKES 1¼ CUPS

1 (20-ounce) can crushed un-sweetened pineapple and juice
½ cup pineapple juice concentrate

½ teaspoon ground ginger

Cook pineapple in a medium saucepan over medium heat, stirring constantly, about 8 to 10 minutes or until juice has evaporated. Stir in the remaining ingredients. Cook over medium heat 15 to 20 minutes, stirring constantly, until mixture has thickened.

NOTE: Serve with muffins or pancakes.

Per tablespoon: 15 calories; 0.1 gm protein; 0.1 gm fat; 7.7 gm carbohydrates; 0 gm fiber; 0 gm saturated fat; 0 gm monounsaturated fat; 0 gm polyunsaturated fat; 0 mg cholesterol; 0.3 mg sodium; 3.7 mg calcium

Raisin Topping
MAKES 1 CUP

1 cup raisins
2 cups water

2 tablespoons honey

Cook raisins in water over medium heat for 25 to 30 minutes stirring frequently. All of the liquid should be evaporated. Add honey and mix well.

NOTE: Serve with muffins or pancakes.

Per tablespoon: 35.2 calories; 0.2 gm protein; 0 gm fat; 9.3 gm carbohydrates; 0 gm fiber; 0 gm saturated fat; 0 gm monounsaturated fat; 0 gm polyunsaturated fat; 0 mg cholesterol; 1.8 mg sodium; 4.5 mg calcium

CHAPTER 23

Desserts

Peanut Butter-Honey Bars
MAKES 16 BARS

2 cups rolled oats
½ cup honey

½ cup peanut butter

In a large bowl, stir together all ingredients. Spoon into a nonstick 8x8x2-inch baking pan. Bake at 325° for 20 to 22 minutes. Cool. Cut into sixteen squares.

NOTE: You may use commercially prepared peanut butter, but check the label carefully for preservatives, sugar, corn syrup, etc. If you prefer to make your own, simply toss a cup of peanuts into the blender or food processor and process until smooth.

Per bar: 89 calories; 2.6 gm protein; 4.2 gm fat; 11.3 gm carbohydrates; 0.1 gm fiber; 0.7 gm saturated fat; 2 gm monounsaturated fat; 1.2 gm polyunsaturated fat; 0 mg cholesterol; 38 mg sodium; 4.2 mg calcium

Fresh Berries
I SERVING

¼ cup fresh raspberries
½ cup sliced fresh strawberries

1 sprig fresh mint, chopped

Mix fruit in an individual dessert bowl. Sprinkle with mint.

Per serving: 37.7 calories; 0.7 gm protein; 0.4 gm fat; 8.8 gm carbohydrates; 2.8 gm fiber; 0 gm saturated fat; 0 gm monounsaturated fat; 0.2 gm polyunsaturated fat; 0 mg cholesterol; 1 mg sodium; 17.2 mg calcium

Three Berries
I SERVING

¼ cup fresh raspberries   *¼ cup fresh blueberries*
¼ cup fresh strawberries

Layer berries in an individual dessert bowl.

Per serving: 47 calories; 0.7 gm protein; 0.4 gm fat; 11.3 gm carbohydrates; 3.2 gm fiber; 0 gm saturated fat; 0 gm monounsaturated fat; 0.1 gm polyunsaturated fat; 0 mg cholesterol; 2.7 mg sodium; 14.2 mg calcium

Orange Peaches
MAKES 2 SERVINGS

1 fresh peach   *¼ cup orange juice*

Cut peach in half and discard pit. Place each peach half in an individual dessert dish. Spoon orange juice over each half. Marinate in the refrigerator 2 to 3 hours.

Per serving: 31.5 calories; 0.4 gm protein; 0 gm fat; 7.8 gm carbohydrates; 0.2 gm fiber; 0 gm saturated fat; 0 gm monounsaturated fat; 0 gm polyunsaturated fat; 0 mg cholesterol; 0.7 mg sodium; 5.1 mg calcium

Baked Peaches
MAKES 2 SERVINGS

1 fresh peach   *2 tablespoons apple juice concen-*
1 tablespoon chopped almonds   *trate*
2 teaspoons currants

Cut peach in half and discard pit. Fill cavities with almonds and currants and place peach halves in individual baking dishes. Dribble apple juice over all. Bake at 350° for 15 minutes or until hot and bubbly. Serve hot or cold.

Per serving: 79 calories; 1.4 gm protein; 2.2 gm fat; 14.8 gm carbohydrates; 0.4 gm fiber; 0.2 gm saturated fat; 1.3 gm monounsaturated fat; 0.4 gm polyunsaturated fat; 0 mg cholesterol; 5 mg sodium; 18.2 mg calcium

CHAPTER 24

Reintroduction Recipes

THE FOLLOWING RECIPES have been created to help you in planning the gradual reintroduction of the Sinister Seven into your diet. For the sake of clarity, we've arranged the recipes according to the ingredient that is being reintroduced—wheat, eggs, cow's milk and products, yeast, corn, soy, and cane sugar—and the critical ingredient is clearly noted in each recipe. Each recipe reintroduces only one of the Sinister Seven at a time.

Remember, do not eat the same food more than once every four days.

At the end of this section you'll find the "Sinister Seven Series"— six muffin recipes and one roll recipe in which each of the seven ingredients is reintroduced one at a time.

Bulgur
REINTRODUCES WHEAT
MAKES 3 SERVINGS

1 tablespoon oil
1 cup uncooked bulgur*

¼ teaspoon salt (optional)
2½ cups boiling water

Heat oil in a large skillet; stir in bulgur and salt if desired. Stir bulgur until all grains are coated with oil and add water. Stir, cover tightly, and cook over low heat until all liquid is absorbed, about 30 minutes.

* Bulgur is a type of wheat.

Per serving: 314 calories; 7.6 gm protein; 1.2 gm fat; 69 gm carbohydrates; 0 gm fiber; 0 gm saturated fat; 0 gm monounsaturated fat; 0 gm polyunsaturated fat; 0 mg cholesterol; 1.0 mg sodium; 27 mg calcium

Bulgur Pilaf
REINTRODUCES WHEAT
MAKES 4 SERVINGS

1 small onion, chopped
1 cup uncooked bulgur*
2 teaspoons oil
2 cups Chicken Broth (see page 163)

1 cup cooked chick-peas (see page 81)
¼ cup chopped cashews

Sauté onion and bulgur in hot oil in a large skillet, stirring frequently, until onion is limp. Stir in broth and chick-peas. Bring to a boil. Cover and simmer 20 minutes or until bulgur is cooked. Sprinkle with nuts before serving.

NOTE: Do not use canned chick-peas; they have far too much salt.

* Bulgur is a type of wheat.

Per serving: 264 calories; 8 gm protein; 7.3 gm fat; 42.8 gm carbohydrates; 0.1 gm fiber; 0.9 gm saturated fat; 2.5 gm monounsaturated fat; 2.3 gm polyunsaturated fat; 0 mg cholesterol; 202 mg sodium; 36.3 mg calcium

Cajun-Style Fish Fillets
REINTRODUCES WHEAT
MAKES I SERVING

2 tablespoons flour*
¼ teaspoon chili powder
⅛ teaspoon dried oregano

⅛ teaspoon powdered thyme
4 ounces fish fillets
1 tablespoon oil

Combine flour and seasonings and mix well. Coat fish fillets with seasoned flour. Brown fish in hot oil on both sides for 2 to 3 minutes a side. Serve hot.

NOTE: Sole, cod, haddock, halibut, and red snapper work very well in this recipe.

Variation: For a spicier version, add cayenne pepper to taste.

* Flour contains wheat.

Per serving: 129.1 calories; 9.3 gm protein; 7.2 gm fat; 6.2 gm carbohydrates; 0 gm fiber; 0.6 gm saturated fat; 0.8 gm monounsaturated fat; 5 gm polyunsaturated fat; 0 mg cholesterol; 35.5 mg sodium; 39.9 mg calcium

Turkey Cubes
REINTRODUCES WHEAT
MAKES 2 SERVINGS

8 ounces boneless white-meat turkey, uncooked
2 tablespoons flour*
½ teaspoon paprika

½ teaspoon dried basil leaves, crushed
Dash cayenne pepper
1 tablespoon oil

Cut turkey into bite-size pieces. Mix flour and seasonings. Coat turkey generously with seasoned flour. Brown turkey on all sides. In hot oil in a medium skillet over low heat (about 10 minutes). Shake skillet often so that turkey does not stick. Cover and cook 2 minutes longer.

* Flour contains wheat.

Per serving: 265.1 calories; 34.7 gm protein; 10.5 gm fat; 5.7 gm carbohydrates; 0 gm fiber; 1.8 gm saturated fat; 1.4 gm monounsaturated fat; 6 gm polyunsaturated fat; 0 mg cholesterol; 72 mg sodium; 30.6 mg calcium

Veal Stew
REINTRODUCES WHEAT
MAKES 3 SERVINGS

1 pound boneless veal, cut into 1-inch cubes
3 tablespoons flour*
1 tablespoon oil
1 medium onion, thinly sliced
1 medium green pepper, thinly sliced

1 garlic clove, minced
½ teaspoon dried rosemary, crushed
1 cup salt-free canned tomatoes, drained

Coat veal cubes generously with flour. Brown cubes in hot oil in a 5-quart Dutch oven. Add onion, pepper, garlic, and rosemary. Stir well. Add tomatoes and stir again. Cover and simmer 1 hour or until meat is tender.

* Flour contains wheat.

Per serving: 298.9 calories; 25.3 gm protein; 16.9 gm fat; 10.2 gm carbohydrates; 1 gm fiber; 5.8 gm saturated fat; 5.9 gm monounsaturated fat; 4 gm polyunsaturated fat; 116.7 mg cholesterol; 85.9 mg sodium; 28.6 mg calcium

Antipasto Plate
REINTRODUCES EGGS
MAKES I SERVING

2 cups shredded lettuce
1 (3½-ounce) can solid white
  water-packed tuna

1 hard-cooked egg, quartered
1 roasted red pepper, sliced
4 black olives

Line a chilled plate with the shredded lettuce. Drain tuna and place on lettuce. Arrange egg, roasted pepper, and olives around tuna.

NOTE: You may use commercially prepared roasted peppers, or you may roast your own. To roast fresh peppers seed them and cut them in half, then place them skin side up on a baking pan in a 350 oven until the skin is scorched (about 25 minutes). Remove skin.

Per serving: 263.2 calories; 36.1 gm protein; 10.7 gm fat; 6.8 gm carbohydrates; 1.8 gm fiber; 2 gm saturated fat; 2.2 gm monounsaturated fat; 1.7 gm polyunsaturated fat; 308.7 mg cholesterol; 199.8 mg sodium; 70.2 mg calcium

Scrambled Eggs with Feta Cheese
REINTRODUCES EGGS
MAKES 2 SERVINGS

2 eggs
1 tablespoon water

1 tablespoon crumbled feta
  cheese

Beat eggs and water slightly with a fork in a small bowl. Mix in cheese. Cook in a small nonstick skillet over low heat, stirring constantly, until egg is cooked to desired degree of doneness.

Variation: Sprinkle with dill before serving.

Per serving: 97.9 calories; 7 gm protein; 7.1 gm fat; 0.8 gm carbohydrates: 0 gm fiber; 2.7 gm saturated fat; 2.5 gm monounsaturated fat; 0.7 gm polyunsaturated fat; 280.3 mg cholesterol; 149 mg sodium; 63.4 mg calcium

Spinach Salad
REINTRODUCES EGGS
MAKES I SERVING

3 cups fresh spinach leaves
1 hard-cooked egg, chopped
2 tablespoons crumbled feta cheese

4 teaspoons oil
1½ teaspoons lemon juice
¼ teaspoon dry mustard

Wash and break up spinach leaves. In a small bowl, combine with the remaining ingredients and toss gently until spinach is well coated.

Per serving: 295.1 calories; 10.0 gm protein; 27 gm fat; 4.1 gm carbohydrates; 1.8 gm fiber; 5.5 gm saturated fat; 5.1 gm monounsaturated fat; 14.3 gm polyunsaturated fat; 286.7 mg cholesterol; 274.4 mg sodium; 161.0 mg calcium

Deviled Eggs
REINTRODUCES EGGS
MAKES 2 SERVINGS

2 hard-cooked eggs
1 tablespoon salt-free tomato juice

¼ teaspoon dry mustard
⅛ teaspoon dried dill

Cut eggs in half lengthwise and remove yolks. In small bowl, mash yolks with a fork. Add the remaining ingredients and blend well. Fill egg whites with the yolk mixture. Chill.

Per serving: 82.3 calories; 6.2 gm protein; 5.7 gm fat; 1 gm carbohydrates; 0 gm fiber; 1.6 gm saturated fat; 2.3 gm monounsaturated fat; 0.7 gm polyunsaturated fat; 274 mg cholesterol; 96.5 mg sodium; 31.8 mg calcium

Curried Deviled Eggs
REINTRODUCES EGGS
MAKES 2 SERVINGS

2 hard-cooked eggs
1 tablespoon salt-free tomato juice

¼ teaspoon curry powder
⅛ teaspoon dry mustard

Cut eggs in half lengthwise and remove yolks. In a small bowl, mash the yolks with a fork. Add the remaining ingredients and blend well. Fill egg whites with the yolk mixture. Chill.

Per serving: 81.9 calories; 6.2 gm protein; 5.6 gm fat; 1.1 gm carbohydrates; 0 gm fiber; 1.6 gm saturated fat; 2.2 gm monounsaturated fat; 0.7 gm polyunsaturated fat; 274 mg cholesterol; 96.5 mg sodium; 30.9 mg calcium

Easy Cheese-Peanut Salad
REINTRODUCES COW'S MILK
MAKES 2 SERVINGS

½ cup low-fat cottage cheese   *6 lettuce leaves*
2 tablespoons chopped unsalted
  peanuts

In a small bowl, mix the cottage cheese and peanuts. Line serving plates with the lettuce leaves. Spoon half the cheese mixture onto each plate. Cover and chill.

Variation: Serve the cheese mixture on rye wafers instead of lettuce.

Per serving: Cheese Spread/Lettuce: 20.4 calories; 2 gm protein; 1 gm fat; 0.9 gm carbohydrates; 0.1 gm fiber; 0.2 gm saturated fat; 0.4 gm monounsaturated fat; 0.2 gm polyunsaturated fat; 0.5 mg cholesterol; 47.3 mg sodium; 11 mg calcium
Cheese Spread: 18.7 calories; 1.8 gm protein; 1 gm fat; 0.6 gm carbohydrates; 0 gm fiber; 0.1 gm saturated fat; 0.4 gm monounsaturated fat; 0.2 gm polyunsaturated fat; 0.5 mg cholesterol; 46.1 mg sodium; 8.4 mg calcium
Cheese Spread/Rye Wafers: 41.2 calories; 2.8 gm protein; 1 gm fat; 5.6 gm carbohydrates; 0.8 gm fiber; 0.1 gm saturated fat; 0.4 gm monounsaturated fat; 0.2 gm polyunsaturated fat; 0.5 mg cholesterol; 103.1 mg sodium; 11.9 mg calcium

Cottage Cheese Salad
REINTRODUCES COW'S MILK
MAKES 2 SERVINGS

6 lettuce leaves　　　　　　　　*1 recipe Cottage Cheese Spread*
　　　　　　　　　　　　　　　(see below)

Line a serving plate with the lettuce leaves. Spoon half the cottage cheese mixture onto each plate. Chill.

Per serving: 10.8 calories; 1.5 gm protein; 0.1 gm fat; 0.8 gm carbohydrates; 0.1 gm fiber; 0 gm saturated fat; 0 gm monounsaturated fat; 0 gm polyunsaturated fat; 0.5 mg cholesterol; 47.8 mg sodium; 10.1 mg calcium

Cottage Cheese Spread
REINTRODUCES COW'S MILK
MAKES ⅝ CUP

½ cup low-fat cottage cheese　　*2 teaspoons chopped radish*
2 teaspoons chopped scallions

In a small bowl, combine cottage cheese, scallions, and radish. Mix lightly.

NOTE: This may be spread on rice cakes, rye wafers, carrot sticks, celery stalks, cucumber rounds, or cherry tomato halves.

Per tablespoon: 9.1 calories; 1.4 gm protein; 0.1 gm fat; 0.5 gm carbohydrates; 0 gm fiber; 0 gm saturated fat; 0 gm monounsaturated fat; 0 gm polyunsaturated fat; 0.5 mg cholesterol; 46.6 mg sodium; 7.6 mg calcium

Buttermilk Cooler
REINTRODUCES COW'S MILK
MAKES I SERVING

½ cup chilled buttermilk　　　　*½ cup chilled carrot juice*

Stir ingredients together or mix in the blender.

Per serving: 98.5 calories; 5.2 gm protein; 1.2 gm fat; 17.2 gm carbohydrates; 0 gm fiber; 0.7 gm saturated fat; 0.3 gm monounsaturated fat; 0.1 gm polyunsaturated fat; 78.5 mg cholesterol; 164.5 mg sodium; 171.5 mg calcium

Poppy Seed Noodles
REINTRODUCES COW'S MILK
MAKES 2 SERVINGS

4 ounces buckwheat noodles,   *2 teaspoons oil*
    cooked according to package   *¼ cup sour cream*
    instructions   *1 teaspoon poppy seeds*

Toss all ingredients together in a medium serving bowl. Serve immediately.

Per serving: 309.2 calories; 7.6 gm protein; 12.3 gm fat; 42.2 gm carbohydrates; 0 gm fiber; 4.2 gm saturated fat; 2.3 gm monounsaturated fat; 3.9 gm polyunsaturated fat; 12.7 mg cholesterol; 15.8 mg sodium; 53.8 mg calcium

Roquefort Dressing
REINTRODUCE COW'S MILK
MAKES ⅝ CUP

2 tablespoons crumbled Roque-   *½ cup sour cream*
    fort cheese

Combine ingredients well and chill.

Per tablespoon: 30.6 calories; 0.7 gm protein; 2.8 gm fat; 0.5 gm carbohydrates; 0 gm fiber; 1.8 gm saturated fat; 0.8 gm monounsaturated fat; 0.1 gm polyunsaturated fat; 6.3 mg cholesterol; 29.7 mg sodium; 22.3 mg calcium

Stuffed Mushrooms
REINTRODUCES YEAST
MAKES 2 SERVINGS

4 large fresh mushrooms*
3 teaspoons oil
2 ounces cooked crabmeat,
chopped

1 tablespoons dried chopped
chives
Dash black pepper

Remove mushroom stems and chop fine. Rub mushroom caps with *1 teaspoon of oil.* Sauté chopped mushroom stems in *2 teaspoons of oil* in a small skillet. Stir in crabmeat, chives, and pepper. Fill mushroom caps with crabmeat mixture and place in a small ramekin or baking dish. Bake at 350° for 15 minutes or until heated through.

NOTE: If you use lump crabmeat, be sure it's freshly cooked and preservative-free.

* Mushrooms contain yeast.

Per serving: 95.5 calories; 5.4 gm protein; 7.5 gm fat; 1.7 gm carbohydrates; 0 gm fiber; 0.7 gm saturated fat; 0.9 gm monounsaturated fat; 5.5 gm polyunsaturated fat; 28.3 mg cholesterol; 142.3 mg sodium; 15.3 mg calcium

Chicken Tarragon
REINTRODUCES YEAST
MAKES 2 SERVINGS

1 chicken breast, skinned,
boned, and split in half
2 teaspoons oil

½ cup dry white wine*
½ teaspoon dried tarragon

Brown chicken slightly in hot oil in a small skillet. Add wine and tarragon. Cook over low heat for 8 to 10 minutes or until chicken is cooked. Remove chicken and keep warm. Cook liquid in pan until sauce is reduced by half. Pour over chicken.

* White wine contains yeast.

Per serving: 234.5 calories; 26.7 gm protein; 7.5 gm fat; 2.2 gm carbohydrates; 0 gm fiber; 1.2 gm saturated fat; 1.6 gm monounsaturated fat; 4 gm polyunsaturated fat; 73 mg cholesterol; 67.5 mg sodium; 17.5 mg calcium

Sautéed Chicken Livers and Mushrooms
REINTRODUCES YEAST
MAKES 1 SERVING

¼ cup Chicken Broth (see page 163)
4 ounces chicken livers
½ cup sliced fresh mushrooms*

1 tablespoon chopped onion
⅛ teaspoon dried sage
1 cup hot cooked Brown Rice (see page 78)

Heat broth in a small skillet. Add chicken livers, mushrooms, onion, and sage. Stir-fry until chicken livers are cooked, about 5 minutes. Serve over rice.

Variation: Serve over hot cooked Millet (see page 77), Barley (see page 78), or Wild Rice (see page 78) instead of brown rice.

* Mushrooms contain yeast.

Per serving: 193.7 calories; 29.2 gm protein; 6.3 gm fat; 3.4 gm carbohydrates; 0 gm fiber; 2.1 gm saturated fat; 1.5 gm monounsaturated fat; 1 gm polyunsaturated fat; 715.2 mg cholesterol; 102.5 mg sodium; 26.8 mg calcium

Fish Fillets in Wine Sauce
REINTRODUCE YEAST
MAKES 1 SERVING

½ cup sliced fresh mushrooms*
2 teaspoons oil
4 ounces fish fillets

½ cup dry white wine*
2 tablespoons chopped fresh parsley

Sauté mushrooms in hot oil in a small skillet until mushrooms are lightly browned. Add fish and wine and simmer gently until fish is done (flakes easily when touched with a fork), about 3 to 5 minutes. Remove fish and keep warm. Cook liquid in pan until sauce is reduced by half. Pour sauce over fish and sprinkle with parsley before serving.

NOTE: Fish that are particularly good in this recipe are sole, haddock, cod, halibut, and red snapper.

* Both mushrooms and white wine contain yeast.

Per serving: 253 calories; 35.1 gm protein; 9.7 gm fat; 4.9 gm carbohydrates; 0 gm fiber; 0.8 gm saturated fat; 1 gm monounsaturated fat; 6.7 gm polyunsaturated fat; 0 mg cholesterol; 79.4 mg sodium; 90.9 mg calcium

Quick Broiler Dinner
REINTRODUCES CORN
MAKES 2 SERVINGS

3 tablespoons corn oil
2 tablespoons lemon juice
½ pound sea scallops, cut in half
2 potatoes, unpeeled, cut into ½-
inch slices

Dash paprika
2 medium tomatoes, cut in half

Stir together 2 tablespoons of the oil and the lemon juice; pour mixture over scallops and let stand 15 minutes. Rub potatoes with ½ tablespoon of the oil and place them on the rack of the broiler pan. Sprinkle with paprika. Place broiler pan about 4 inches from heat and broil 15 minutes. Rub tomato halves gently with the remaining oil. Turn potatoes; place scallops and tomato halves on broiler rack with potatoes. Broil 10 to 12 minutes more, turning scallops once.

Per serving: 558.5 calories; 32.2 gm protein; 22.5 gm fat; 60.3 gm carbohydrates; 1.8 gm fiber; 2.6 gm saturated fat; 4.9 gm monounsaturated fat; 12.2 gm polyunsaturated fat; 60.3 mg cholesterol; 327.2 mg sodium; 161.4 mg calcium

Nutty Stuffed Cabbage
REINTRODUCES CORN
MAKES 6 SERVINGS

1 medium head (about 1 pound)
green cabbage
1 small carrot, diced
1 stalk celery, chopped
½ cup chopped shallots
1 tablespoon corn oil
½ cup chopped unpeeled apple
⅓ cup chopped cashew nuts

¼ cup crumbled feta cheese
¼ cup sunflower seeds
2 tablespoons currants
1 (8-ounce) can salt-free tomato
sauce
1½ cups hot cooked Brown Rice
(see page 78)

Remove core from cabbage. Steam cabbage for 15 to 20 minutes or until the leaves are limp and pliant. Drain well. In a large skillet, sauté the carrot, celery, and shallots in hot oil until the vegetables are limp. Stir in the apple and nuts and cook 3 minutes longer. Add the cheese, sunflower seeds, and currants and mix well. Place three tablespoons of filling near the base of each cabbage leaf; tuck in sides and roll up. Place rolls, seam side down, in an oiled 8x12x2-inch baking dish. Pour tomato sauce over all. Bake at 350° for 25 minutes or until heated through. Serve over rice.

Variation: Cooked Millet (see page 77), Barley (see page 78), or Bulgur (see page 78) may be substituted for the rice.

Per serving: 238.1 calories; 7.2 gm protein; 11.2 gm fat; 30.4 gm carbohydrates; 1.2 gm fiber; 2.6 gm saturated fat; 3.3 gm monounsaturated fat; 4.4 gm polyunsaturated fat; 16.7 mg cholesterol; 379.5 mg sodium; 115.9 mg calcium

Oriental Basting Sauce
REINTRODUCES SOY
MAKES 2 ½ TABLESPOONS

2 tablespoons light soy sauce　　*¼ teaspoon dry mustard*
1 teaspoon honey　　*¼ teaspoon onion powder*

In a small bowl, combine all ingredients and blend well.

NOTE: This can be brushed on chicken, fish, or vegetables before baking or broiling.

Per tablespoon: 24.4 calories; 1.6 gm protein; 0.1 gm fat; 4.6 gm carbohydrates; 0 gm fiber; 0 gm saturated fat; 0 gm monounsaturated fat; 0 gm polyunsaturated fat; 0 mg cholesterol; 480 mg sodium; 6.2 mg calcium

Soy-Tomato Basting Sauce
REINTRODUCES SOY
MAKES ½ CUP

½ cup salt-free tomato sauce　　*½ teaspoon powdered ginger*
1 tablespoon light soy sauce　　*¼ teaspoon garlic powder*

Combine all ingredients and blend well.

NOTE: This is a delicious basting sauce for chicken, veal, fish, or shellfish.

Per tablespoon: 20.4 calories; 1.2 gm protein; 0 gm fat; 3.8 gm carbohydrates; 0 gm fiber; 0 gm saturated fat; 0 gm monounsaturated fat; 0 gm polyunsaturated fat; 0 mg cholesterol; 75 mg sodium; 1.5 mg calcium

Oriental Spaghetti
REINTRODUCES SOY
MAKES 2 SERVINGS

½ pound Korean vermicelli   *1 tablespoon dark sesame oil*
2 tablespoons light soy sauce   *1 teaspoon toasted sesame seeds*

Cook vermicelli in six quarts rapidly boiling water until tender, about 5 minutes. Drain well and rinse quickly with warm water. Add the remaining ingredients and toss gently until vermicelli is well coated. Serve immediately.

NOTE: Toast seeds in a shallow baking pan at 200° for 10 to 15 minutes or until golden brown.

Variation: Add ½ cup slivered cooked white-meat chicken.

Per serving: 173.6 calories; 3.8 gm protein; 7.7 gm fat; 26.7 gm carbohydrates; 0 gm fiber; 1 gm saturated fat; 2.7 gm monounsaturated fat; 2.9 gm polyunsaturated fat; 0 mg cholesterol; 605 mg sodium; 21.2 mg calcium

Chicken Soup Orientale
REINTRODUCES SOY
MAKES I SERVING

1 cup Chicken Broth (see page   *½ cup slivered cooked white-*
  163)   *meat chicken*
½ cup chopped watercress   *½ teaspoon light soy sauce*

Combine all ingredients in a small saucepan. Cook until heated through.

Per serving: 315.0 calories; 41.0 gm protein; 5 gm fat; 0.9 gm carbohydrates; 0 gm fiber; 0 gm saturated fat; 0 gm monounsaturated fat; 0 gm polyunsaturated fat; 1.6 mg cholesterol; 350 mg sodium; 31.2 mg calcium

Bean Sprout Salad
REINTRODUCES SOY
MAKES 2 SERVINGS

½ pound fresh bean sprouts
1 cup fresh spinach leaves,
  chopped
1 tablespoon light soy sauce

1 tablespoon apple juice concen-
  trate
1 teaspoon dark sesame oil

In a large saucepan, blanch bean sprouts in boiling water for 30 seconds; drain. Rinse in cold water and drain again. Place in a large bowl and add the spinach. Mix together the remaining ingredients; pour over sprouts. Toss sprouts gently until well coated with oil mixture. Chill well before serving.

Per serving: 76.9 calories; 5 gm protein; 2.5 gm fat; 11.2 gm carbohydrates; 2.1 gm fiber; 0.4 gm saturated fat; 0.9 gm monounsaturated fat; 1 gm polyunsaturated fat; 0 mg cholesterol; 316 mg sodium; 44.9 mg calcium

Snow Pea Salad
REINTRODUCES SOY
MAKES 4 SERVINGS

½ pound fresh snow peas
½ cup chopped sweet red pepper
3 tablespoons oil
1 tablespoon light soy sauce

¼ teaspoon dark sesame oil
1 garlic clove, minced
1 tablespoon toasted sesame
  seeds

Blanch snow peas in boiling water for 30 seconds; drain well. Rinse in cold water and drain again. In a large bowl, mix together the peas, pepper, and sesame seeds. In a separate bowl, mix together the remaining ingredients and blend well. Pour oil mixture over peas. Toss gently until peas are well coated with oil mixture. Chill.

NOTE: Toast seeds in a shallow baking pan at 200° for 10 to 15 minutes or until golden brown.

Per serving: 85.4 calories; 3.5 gm protein; 4.3 gm fat; 9 gm carbohydrates; 2.3 gm fiber; 0.55 gm saturated fat; 0.04 gm monounsaturated fat; 2.1 gm polyunsaturated fat; 0 mg cholesterol; 150 mg sodium; 17.8 mg calcium

Tofu-Carob Pudding
REINTRODUCES SOY
MAKES 6 SERVINGS

1 (16-ounce) package soft tofu*
⅓ cup carob powder
⅓ cup peanut butter

¼ cup honey
½ teaspoon pure vanilla extract
⅓ cup soy milk*

Drain water from tofu. Mash slightly with a fork. Place tofu, carob, peanut butter, honey, and vanilla into the blender and blend until smooth, adding soy milk a little at a time. When pudding is smooth, pour into serving dishes. Chill.

NOTE: You may use commercially prepared peanut butter, but check the label carefully for preservatives, sugar, corn syrup, etc. If you prefer to make your own, simply toss a cup of peanuts into the blender or food processor and process until smooth.

* Both tofu and soy milk contain soy.

Per serving: 57.2 calories; 3 gm protein; 3.2 gm fat; 5.2 gm carbohydrates; 0.1 gm fiber; 0.3 gm saturated fat; 1 gm monounsaturated fat; 0.6 gm polyunsaturated fat; 0 mg cholesterol; 24.1 mg sodium; 30.6 mg calcium

Baked Apples
REINTRODUCES CANE SUGAR
MAKES 2 SERVINGS

2 tart cooking apples, cored but unpeeled
¼ cup dark brown sugar
¼ cup raisins

3 tablespoons water
1 teaspoon oil
Dash cinnamon
Dash nutmeg

Place apples in a small baking dish or individual ramekins. In a small saucepan, stir together the remaining ingredients and bring to a boil. Pour mixture over apples. Bake, uncovered, at 350° for 35 minutes or until apples are tender. Baste frequently.

Per serving: 258.7 calories; 0.8 gm protein; 2.8 gm fat; 62.1 gm carbohydrates; 2.8 gm fiber; 0.3 gm saturated fat; 0.3 gm monounsaturated fat; 1.7 gm polyunsaturated fat; 0 mg cholesterol; 11.4 mg sodium; 44.1 mg calcium

Onion and Raisin Relish
REINTRODUCES CANE SUGAR
MAKES 4 SERVINGS

3 large onions, sliced (about 2 cups)
1 medium red onion sliced
2 teaspoons oil
4 tablespoons table sugar

½ cup Chicken Broth (see page 163)
½ cup raisins
4 cups hot cooked Brown Rice (see page 78)

Cook onions in hot oil in a large skillet over medium heat until transparent. Sprinkle onions with sugar and continue cooking, stirring constantly, for about 15 minutes. Stir in chicken broth and cook over low heat for about 40 minutes, stirring frequently, until onions have caramelized. Plump raisins by soaking them in warm water for 10 to 15 minutes; rinse well. Add raisins to onion mixture. Cook 8 minutes. Spoon over rice.

NOTE: If wheat is allowed, serve over hot cooked couscous.

Per serving: 354.8 calories; 7.5 gm protein; 3.0 gm fat; 75.5 gm carbohydrates; 0.7 gm fiber; 0.25 gm saturated fat; 0.25 gm monounsaturated fat; 1.8 gm polyunsaturated fat; 0 mg cholesterol; 25.6 mg sodium; 39 mg calcium

Cranberry Relish
REINTRODUCES CANE SUGAR
MAKES 8 SERVINGS

1 cup fresh cranberries
1 medium orange, seeded and cut into eighths

¼ cup table sugar

Place half the cranberries and orange in the blender or food processor and chop coarsely. Remove. Repeat with the remaining fruit. Mix sugar with the chopped fruit. Cover and refrigerate.

Per 1½ tablespoons: 36 calories; 0.2 gm protein; 0 gm fat; 9.8 gm carbohydrates; 0 gm fiber; 0 gm saturated fat; 0 gm monounsaturated fat; 0 gm polyunsaturated fat; 0 mg cholesterol; 0 mg sodium; 7.5 mg calcium

Broiled Grapefruit
REINTRODUCES CANE SUGAR
MAKES I SERVING

1 teaspoon brown sugar   *Grapefruit half*

Sprinkle sugar over grapefruit. Broil 5 inches from heat for 2 to 3 minutes or until bubbly. Serve hot.

Per serving: 55.8 calories; 0.8 gm protein; 0.1 gm fat; 14.2 gm carbohydrates; 0 gm fiber; 0 gm saturated fat; 0 gm monounsaturated fat; 0 gm polyunsaturated fat; 0 mg cholesterol; 1.3 mg sodium; 18 mg calcium

Lemonade
REINTRODUCES CANE SUGAR
MAKES 6 SERVINGS

4 cups ice-cold water   *¾ cup table sugar*
Juice of 6 lemons   *Ice cubes*

In a large pitcher, stir together all ingredients except ice until sugar is dissolved. Add ice and serve.

Per serving: 112 calories; 1.3 gm protein; 0.3 gm fat; 35.6 gm carbohydrates; 0 gm fiber; 0 gm saturated fat; 0 gm monounsaturated fat; 0 gm polyunsaturated fat; 0 mg cholesterol; 3.2 mg sodium; 66 mg calcium

Barbecue Sauce
REINTRODUCES CANE SUGAR
MAKES I CUP

1 (8-ounce) can tomato sauce   *1 tablespoon lemon juice*
*2 tablespoons molasses**

Blend all ingredients.

NOTE: This may be brushed on poultry before broiling.

* Molasses contains cane sugar.

Per tablespoon: 20.9 calories; 0.4 gm protein; 0 gm fat; 5.1 gm carbohydrates; 0 gm fiber; 0 gm saturated fat; 0 gm monounsaturated fat; 0 gm polyunsaturated fat; 0 mg cholesterol; 190 mg sodium; 38.6 mg calcium

THE SINISTER SEVEN SERIES #1

Plain Whole Wheat Muffins
MAKES 6 MUFFINS

1 cup stone-ground whole wheat flour
2 teaspoons cornstarch-free baking powder
¼ teaspoon cinnamon

⅓ cup water
2 tablespoons honey
2 tablespoons oil
⅓ cup finely chopped pecans (optional)

In a medium bowl, mix flour, baking powder, and cinnamon. Add water, honey, oil, and pecans if desired. Stir until well blended. Fill six 2½-inch nonstick muffin cups ⅔ full. Bake at 400° for 15 minutes. Turn out onto a wire cooling rack. Serve hot or cool.

NOTE: This is the first of seven recipes in which the Sinister Seven are reintroduced one by one. Be sure to check for a bad reaction to one ingredient before moving on to the next.

Per muffin: 170 calories; 3.1 gm protein; 8.8 gm fat; 21.3 gm carbohydrates; 0 gm fiber; 0.8 gm saturated fat; 3 gm monounsaturated fat; 4.3 gm polyunsaturated fat; 0 mg cholesterol; 112.8 mg sodium; 30.9 mg calcium

THE SINISTER SEVEN SERIES #2

Whole Wheat Muffins with Milk
MAKES 6 MUFFINS

*1 cup stone-ground whole wheat
    flour*
*2 teaspoons cornstarch-free
    baking powder*
¼ teaspoon cinnamon

⅓ cup milk
2 tablespoons honey
2 tablespoons oil
*⅓ cup finely chopped pecans
    (optional)*

In a medium bowl, mix flour, baking powder, and cinnamon. Add milk, honey, oil, and pecans if desired. Stir until well blended. Fill six 2½-inch nonstick muffin cups ⅔ full. Bake at 400° for 15 minutes. Turn out onto a wire cooling rack. Serve hot or cool.

NOTE: This is the second of seven recipes in which the Sinister Seven are reintroduced one by one. Be sure to check for a bad reaction to one ingredient before moving on to the next.

Per muffin: 178.3 calories; 3.5 gm protein; 9.3 gm fat; 21.9 gm carbohydrates; 0 gm fiber; 1 gm saturated fat; 3.1 gm monounsaturated fat; 4.3 gm polyunsaturated fat; 1.8 mg cholesterol; 119.4 mg sodium; 46.9 mg calcium

THE SINISTER SEVEN SERIES #3

Whole Wheat Muffins with Milk and Egg
MAKES 6 MUFFINS

*1 cup stone-ground whole wheat
    flour*
*2 teaspoons cornstarch-free
    baking powder*
¼ teaspoon cinnamon
1 egg, slightly beaten

⅓ cup milk
2 tablespoons honey
2 tablespoons oil
*⅓ cup finely chopped pecans
    (optional)*

In a medium bowl, mix flour, baking powder, and cinnamon. Add egg, milk, honey, oil, and pecans if desired. Stir until well blended. Fill six 2½-inch nonstick muffin cups ⅔ full. Bake at 400° for 15 minutes. Turn out onto a wire cooling rack. Serve hot or cool.

NOTE: This is the third of seven recipes in which the Sinister Seven are reintroduced one by one. Be sure to check for a bad reaction to one ingredient before moving on to the next.

Per muffin: 191.5 calories; 4.5 gm protein; 10.2 gm fat; 22 gm carbohydrates; 0 gm fiber; 1.3 gm saturated fat; 3.5 gm monounsaturated fat; 4.5 gm polyunsaturated fat; 47.4 mg cholesterol; 130.9 mg sodium; 51.6 mg calcium

THE SINISTER SEVEN SERIES #4

Whole Wheat Muffins with Milk, Egg, and Cane Sugar
MAKES 6 MUFFINS

1 cup stone-ground whole wheat flour
2 tablespoons table sugar
2 teaspoons cornstarch-free baking powder
¼ teaspoon cinnamon

1 egg, slightly beaten
⅓ cup milk
2 tablespoons oil
⅓ cup finely chopped pecans (optional)

In a medium bowl, mix flour, sugar, baking powder, and cinnamon. Add egg, milk, oil, and pecans if desired. Stir until well blended. Fill six 2½-inch nonstick muffin cups ⅔ full. Bake at 400° for 15 minutes. Turn out onto a wire cooling rack. Serve hot or cool.

NOTE: This is the fourth of seven recipes in which the Sinister Seven are reintroduced one by one. Be sure to check for a bad reaction to one ingredient before moving on to the next.

Per muffin: 184.8 calories; 4.5 gm protein; 10.2 gm fat; 20.3 gm carbohydrates; 0 gm fiber; 1.3 gm saturated fat; 3.5 gm monounsaturated fat; 4.5 gm polyunsaturated fat; 47.4 mg cholesterol; 130.6 mg sodium; 51.2 mg calcium

THE SINISTER SEVEN SERIES #5

Whole Wheat Muffins with Milk, Egg, Cane Sugar, and Soy Oil
MAKES 6 MUFFINS

1 cup stone-ground whole wheat
flour
2 tablespoons table sugar
2 teaspoons cornstarch-free
baking powder
¼ teaspoon cinnamon

1 egg, slightly beaten
⅓ cup milk
2 tablespoons soy oil
⅓ cup finely chopped pecans
(optional)

In a medium bowl, mix flour, sugar, baking powder, and cinnamon. Add egg, milk, oil and pecans if desired. Stir until well blended. Fill six 2½-inch nonstick muffin cups ⅔ full. Bake at 400° for 15 minutes. Turn out onto a wire cooling rack. Serve hot or cool.

NOTE: This is the fifth of seven recipes in which the Sinister Seven are reintroduced one by one. Be sure to check for a bad reaction to one ingredient before moving on to the next.

Per muffin: 184.6 calories; 4.5 gm protein; 10.2 gm fat; 20.3 gm carbohydrates; 0 gm fiber; 1.6 gm saturated fat; 4.9 gm monounsaturated fat; 2.8 gm polyunsaturated fat; 47.3 mg cholesterol; 130.5 mg sodium; 51.1 mg calcium

THE SINISTER SEVEN SERIES #6

Whole Wheat Muffins with Milk, Egg, Cane Sugar, and Corn Oil
MAKES 6 MUFFINS

1 cup stone-ground whole wheat
flour
2 tablespoons table sugar
2 teaspoons cornstarch-free
baking powder
¼ teaspoon cinnamon

1 egg, slightly beaten
⅓ cup milk
2 tablespoons corn oil
⅓ cup finely chopped pecans
(optional)

In a medium bowl, mix flour, sugar, baking powder, and cinnamon. Add egg, milk, oil, and pecans if desired. Stir until well blended.

Fill six 2½-inch nonstick muffin cups ⅔ full. Bake at 400° for 15 minutes. Turn out onto a wire cooling rack. Serve hot or cool.

NOTE: This is the sixth of seven recipes in which the Sinister Seven are reintroduced one by one. Be sure to check for a bad reaction to one ingredient before moving on to the next.

Per muffin: 184.6 calories; 4.5 gm protein; 10.2 gm fat; 20.3 gm carbohydrates; 0 gm fiber; 1.5 gm saturated fat; 4 gm monounsaturated fat; 3.7 gm polyunsaturated fat; 46.6 mg cholesterol; 130.5 mg sodium; 51.1 mg calcium

---

THE SINISTER SEVEN SERIES #7

Whole Wheat Yeast Rolls with Milk, Egg, Cane Sugar, and Soy or Corn Oil
MAKES 6 ROLLS

1½ teaspoons active dry yeast
¼ cup warm water (about 110°F.)
¼ cup milk at room temperature
1 tablespoon table sugar

1 tablespoon corn oil or soy oil
2 cups stone-ground whole wheat flour
1 egg yolk
2 teaspoons water

Dissolve yeast in warm water. In a large bowl, combine yeast, milk, sugar, oil, and 1½ cups of the flour. Mix well. Knead dough, adding the remaining ½ cup flour gradually until all flour is used and dough is no longer sticky. Let dough rise in a large lightly oiled bowl covered with a damp towel for 1½ hours or until it has doubled in bulk. Punch down, cut dough into six equal portions, and shape into a ball. Place on cookie sheet or in six nonstick muffin cups and cover with a damp towel. Let rise, covered with a damp towel, until doubled—30 to 45 minutes. Mix egg yolk and water. Brush mixture onto surface of rolls. Bake at 400° for about 20 minutes. Rolls should be nicely browned.

NOTE: This is the last of seven recipes in which the Sinister Seven are reintroduced one by one.

Per muffin: 179.6 calories; 6.3 gm protein; 4.2 gm fat; 31 gm carbohydrates; 0 gm fiber; 0.9 gm saturated fat; 1 gm monounsaturated fat; 1.4 gm polyunsaturated fat; 46.7 mg cholesterol; 8.1 mg sodium; 34.2 mg calcium

APPENDIX

APPENDIX

Nutritional Analysis Charts

The following charts give the nutrient values of the foods you will most likely be using on the Immune Power Diet. I have tried, from data from the U.S. Department of Agriculture and other authoritative sources, to give you the most reliable information concerning these foods. I have purposely included such nutritionally undesirable foods as batter-fried chicken so that you can compare nutritive values. Naturally, roasted chicken with the skin removed is a much better food bargain!

In reading the charts, keep in mind the following measurements and abbreviations:

Calories—measured in calorie units
Protein—measured in grams
Fat—measured in grams
Carbo (carbohydrates)—measured in grams
Fiber—measured in grams
Calcium—measured in milligrams
Sodium—measured in milligrams
Niacin—measured in milligrams
Vit. C (Vitamin C)—measured in milligrams
Sat. fat (saturated fat)—measured in grams
Choles (cholesterol)—measured in milligrams

A cup is the standard 8-ounce measure, and tablespoons and teaspoons are always level. One hundred grams (100 g) is just slightly less than 3½ ounces.

FISH

	SERVING	CALORIES	PROTEIN (gm)	FAT (gm)
Albacore, raw	3 oz	120.4	17.2	5.2
Bass, black sea, raw	3½ oz	139.5	28.8	1.8
Bass, striped, oven-fried	3½ oz	215.6	23.6	9.3
Bluefish, baked/broiled	1 fillet	194.0	32.0	6.3
Carp, raw	3½ oz	115.0	18.0	4.2
Catfish, raw	7 oz	249.3	42.6	7.5
Clam, liquid/bouillon	½ cup	22.8	2.8	0.1
Clams, raw	½ cup	82.0	14.0	1.9
Cod, broiled	4 oz	221.0	37.0	6.9
Crab, steamed	3½ oz	97.6	18.2	2.0
Crappie, white, raw	3½ oz	118.5	25.2	1.2
Crayfish & spiny lobster, raw	3½ oz	85.0	17.2	0.6
Croaker, Atlantic, baked	4 oz	172.9	31.6	4.2
Croaker, white, raw	3½ oz	100.8	21.6	1.0
Croaker, yellow fin, raw	3½ oz	106.8	23.0	1.0
Drum, freshwater, raw	6 oz	242.0	34.6	10.4
Drum, red (redfish) raw	2 oz	48.0	10.8	0.2
Flatfish, raw	4 oz	106.6	22.5	1.1
Flounder/sole, raw	3½ oz	68.0	14.9	0.5
Flounder, baked*	1 fillet	202.0	30.0	8.2
Grouper, raw	4 oz	121.8	27.0	0.7
Haddock, raw	3½ oz	79.0	18.3	0.1
Haddock, fried	3½ oz	165.0	19.6	6.4
Halibut, raw	6 oz	200.0	41.8	2.4
Kingfish, raw	3½ oz	102.9	17.9	2.9
Lake herring, raw	3½ oz	96.0	17.7	2.3
Lake trout, raw	1 oz	80.6	8.8	4.8
Mullet, striped, raw	3½ oz	169.4	22.7	8.0
Mussels, raw	5 oz	171.0	25.9	4.0
Ocean perch, Atlantic, raw	3½ oz	88.0	18.0	1.2
Ocean perch, Pacific, raw	3½ oz	95.0	19.0	1.6
Octopus, raw	3½ oz	73.0	15.3	0.8
Oysters, East Coast, raw	5–8 med.	52.8	6.7	1.4
Oysters, Pacific, raw	2–4 med.	91.0	10.6	2.2
Perch, white, raw	3½ oz	91.0	19.5	0.9
Pike, blue, raw	3½ oz	82.8	17.6	0.8
Pike, northern, raw	3½ oz	101.2	21.0	1.3
Pompano, raw	5 oz	332.0	37.6	19.0
Red & grey snapper, raw	3½ oz	89.3	19.0	0.9
Salmon, Atlantic, raw	5 oz	108.5	11.3	6.7
Salmon, chinook, raw	3½ oz	222.0	19.0	15.0
Salmon, chinook, canned	1 cup	525.0	49.0	35.0
Salmon, pink, canned	1 cup	352.5	51.3	14.7
Salmon, broiled/baked	3½ oz	209.3	31.0	8.5
Sardines, Atlantic in oil	8 med	233.2	15.4	18.3
Scallops, raw	6 oz	170.0	32.1	0.4
Scallops, cooked/steamed	3½ oz	112.0	23.2	1.4
Seabass, white, raw	3½ oz	115.2	25.7	0.6
Shrimp, raw	3½ oz	91.0	18.8	0.8
Squid, raw	3½ oz	60.5	11.8	0.6

CARB. (gm)	FIBER (gm)	CALCIUM (mg)	SODIUM (mg)	NIACIN (mg)	VIT. C (mg)	SAFA (gm)	CHOL. (mg)
0.0	0.0	17.7	27.2	9.0	3.4	2.0	37.4
0.0	0.0	30.0	102.0	2.8	0.0	0.0	82.5
7.4	0.0	22.0	74.8	2.3	0.0	3.3	69.3
0.0	0.0	35.4	126.9	2.3	0.0	1.2	85.4
0.0	0.0	50.0	50.0	1.5	1.0	1.0	55.0
0.0	0.0	55.7	145.2	4.1	0.0	2.4	133.1
2.5	0.0	0.0	480.0	0.0	0.0	0.0	10.8
1.3	0.1	69.0	36.0	1.3	10.0	0.0	50.0
0.0	0.0	40.3	143.0	3.9	0.0	1.3	105.3
0.5	0.0	45.1	220.5	2.9	2.1	0.0	105.0
0.0	0.0	18.0	102.0	2.1	1.5	0.0	82.5
1.4	0.0	90. 9	247.8	2.2	0.0	0.0	77.9
0.0	0.0	40.3	156.0	8.4	0.0	1.3	97.5
0.0	0.0	12.0	104.4	6.6	0.0	0.0	66.0
0.0	0.0	12.0	104.4	6.6	0.0	0.0	66.0
0.0	0.0	100.0	140.0	1.0	2.0	4.0	110.0
0.0	0.0	6.0	33.0	2.1	1.2	0.0	33.0
0.0	0.0	16.2	105.3	2.3	0.0	0.0	67.5
0.0	0.0	61.0	0.56	1.7	0.0	0.0	0.0
0.0	0.0	23.0	237.0	2.5	2.0	2.0	90.0
0.0	0.0	32.2	85.4	4.2	0.0	0.0	77.0
0.0	0.0	23.0	61.0	3.0	0.0	0.0	60.0
5.8	0.0	40.0	177.0	3.2	2.0	1.0	64.0
0.0	0.0	26.0	108.0	16.6	0.0	0.0	100.0
0.0	0.0	11.8	81.3	1.7	2.9	1.0	53.9
0.0	0.0	12.0	47.0	3.3	3.0	0.0	55.0
0.0	0.0	12.5	38.9	1.3	0.0	1.4	26.4
0.0	0.0	30.2	94.0	6.0	0.0	2.3	63.8
5.9	0.2	158.4	520.2	2.3	0.0	0.0	90.0
0.0	0.0	2.0	79.0	0.8	0.0	0.0	22.0
0.0	0.0	21.0	32.8	1.0	0.0	0.0	28.6
0.0	0.0	0.0	68.0	0.6	0.4	0.4	22.0
0.0	0.0	29.0	19.2	0.5	0.0	0.0	14.3
2.7	0.1	75.2	58.4	2.0	24.0	0.0	40.0
6.4	0.1	85.0	73.0	1.3	30.0	0.0	50.0
0.0	0.0	12.0	46.9	2.1	0.0	0.0	50.6
0.0	0.0	14.9	58.6	2.6	0.0	0.0	63.2
0.0	0.0	90.0	94.0	7.2	6.0	4.0	110.0
0.0	0.0	15.4	64.3	3.4	0.0	0.0	52.8
0.0	0.0	39.5	37.0	3.6	4.5	2.0	19.5
0.0	0.0	90.0	45.0	7.0	0.0	2.4	33.0
0.0	0.0	385.0	512.5	18.2	0.0	10.7	85.0
0.0	0.0	490.0	563.7	20.0	0.0	3.9	87.5
0.0	0.0	146.0	133.4	11.3	0.0	2.3	54.0
0.4	0.0	265.5	382.5	3.3	2.3	3.8	90.0
6.9	0.0	54.6	535.5	2.7	0.0	0.0	73.5
3.3	0.0	115.0	265.0	1.3	0.0	0.0	53.0
0.0	0.0	49.2	88.8	3.6	0.0	0.0	66.0
1.5	0.0	63.0	140.0	3.2	0.0	0.0	150.0
1.1	0.0	8.6	53.3	2.2	0.0	0.0	39.6

FISH (cont.)

	SERVING	CALORIES	PROTEIN (gm)	FAT (gm)
Sturgeon, raw	3½ oz	94.0	18.1	1.9
Sturgeon, steamed	3 oz	131.2	20.8	4.7
Swordfish, raw	3½ oz	118.0	19.2	4.0
Swordfish, broiled*	3½ oz	217.5	35.0	7.5
Trout, brook, raw	3½ oz	121.2	23.0	2.5
Trout, rainbow, raw	3½ oz	226.2	24.9	13.2
Tuna, bluefin, raw	3½ oz	174.0	30.2	4.9
Tuna, canned in oil, drained	6½ oz	315.2	46.1	13.1
Tuna, canned/water/salt	6½ oz	254.0	56.0	1.6
Whitefish, lake, raw	6 oz	310.0	37.8	16.4

* Prepared with margarine

POULTRY

	SERVING	CALORIES	PROTEIN (gm)	FAT (gm)
Chicken, broiler, cooked	3½ oz	281.5	49.2	7.8
Chicken, light meat, roasted	2½ oz	194.4	34.7	5.1
Chicken, light meat, stewed	2½ oz	180.6	32.8	4.5
Chicken, dark meat, roasted	3 oz	232.2	31.0	11.0
Chicken, dark meat, stewed	3 oz	217.5	29.4	10.2
Chicken, breast, roasted	2 oz	171.6	32.2	3.7
Chicken, breast, stewed	½	171.2	32.9	3.4
Chicken, leg, roasted	1	216.4	30.6	9.5
Chicken, leg, stewed	1	209.8	29.8	9.1
Chicken, drum, w/skin, batter, fried	3½ oz	123.3	10.1	7.2
Chicken, drum, roasted	1	195.7	32.2	6.4
Chicken, drum, stewed	1	192.4	31.3	6.5
Chicken, thigh, roasted	1	237.4	29.5	12.4
Chicken, thigh, stewed	1	158.0	15.8	10.0
Chicken, wing, w/skin, roasted	1	99.0	9.1	6.6
Duck, wo/skin, roasted	3½ oz	201.0	23.5	11.2
Goose, wo/skin, roasted	3½ oz	233.0	33.9	9.8
Turkey, dark meat only, roasted	3½ oz	187.0	28.6	7.2
Turkey, dark meat, w/skin, roasted	3½ oz	208.0	28.1	9.7
Turkey, light meat only, roasted	3½ oz	157.0	29.9	3.2

MEAT

	SERVING	CALORIES	PROTEIN (gm)	FAT (gm)
Beef, hamburger, raw	4 oz	302.8	20.2	23.9
Beef, hamburger, cooked	3 oz	247.6	31.0	12.8
Beef, rib (6-12th), cooked	3½ oz	466.4	21.1	41.8
Beef, chuck, rib, cooked	3½ oz	362.9	19.0	31.2
Beef, porterhouse, cooked	3½ oz	224.0	30.2	10.5
Beef, T-bone steak, cooked	3½ oz	449.3	18.5	41.0
Lamb, shoulder, lean, cooked	2 slices	190.6	24.9	9.3
Lamb, rib, chops, broiled	3½ oz	166.9	8.2	14.6
Lamb, loin, chop, broiled	3 oz	165.1	10.1	13.5
Lamb, leg, cooked	3 oz	312.6	23.4	23.5

CARB. (gm)	FIBER (gm)	CALCIUM (mg)	SODIUM (mg)	NIACIN (mg)	VIT. C (mg)	SAFA (gm)	CHOL. (mg)
0.0	0.0	13.0	54.0	8.3	0.0	0.0	55.0
0.0	0.0	32.8	88.6	6.8	0.0	1.6	63.1
0.0	0.0	19.0	54.0	8.0	0.0	1.0	55.0
0.0	0.0	33.8	167.5	13.6	0.0	2.5	100.0
0.0	0.0	14.4	56.4	4.0	3.6	1.2	58.8
0.0	0.0	30.2	94.0	9.7	0.0	3.5	63.8
0.0	0.0	19.2	44.4	16.0	0.0	1.2	68.4
0.0	0.0	12.8	1280.0	19.0	0.0	3.5	104.0
0.0	0.0	32.0	916.0	26.6	0.0	0.0	126.0
0.0	0.0	52.0	104.0	6.0	0.0	6.0	110.0

CARB. (gm)	FIBER (gm)	CALCIUM (mg)	SODIUM (mg)	NIACIN (mg)	VIT. C (mg)	SAFA (gm)	CHOL. (mg)
0.0	0.0	18.6	136.6	18.1	0.0	2.1	180.1
0.0	0.0	16.9	86.5	13.9	0.0	1.4	95.5
0.0	0.0	14.8	73.8	8.8	0.0	1.3	87.5
0.0	0.0	17.0	105.3	7.4	0.0	3.0	105.3
0.0	0.0	15.9	83.8	5.3	0.0	2.8	99.7
0.0	0.0	15.6	77.0	14.2	0.0	1.0	88.4
0.0	0.0	14.7	71.4	9.6	0.0	1.0	87.3
0.0	0.0	13.6	103.1	7.1	0.0	2.6	106.5
0.0	0.0	12.5	88.4	5.4	0.0	2.5	100.9
3.8	0.0	7.8	123.7	2.3	0.0	1.9	39.6
0.0	0.0	13.7	108.1	6.9	0.0	1.7	105.8
0.0	0.0	12.5	91.1	4.9	0.0	1.7	100.2
0.0	0.0	13.6	99.9	7.4	0.0	3.4	107.9
0.0	0.0	8.0	49.0	6.8	0.0	2.8	57.0
0.0	0.0	5.0	28.0	1.7	0.0	1.4	29.0
0.0	0.0	12.0	65.0	1.8	0.0	1.5	89.0
0.0	0.0	14.0	124.0	4.2	0.0	6.9	96.0
0.0	0.0	32.0	79.0	3.6	0.6	2.4	85.0
0.0	0.0	26.0	68.0	1.8	0.0	1.2	82.0
0.0	0.0	19.0	64.0	6.8	0.0	0.4	69.0

CARB. (gm)	FIBER (gm)	CALCIUM (mg)	SODIUM (mg)	NIACIN (mg)	VIT. C (mg)	SAFA (gm)	CHOL. (mg)
0.0	0.0	11.3	70.7	4.8	0.0	11.5	76.8
0.0	0.0	13.6	75.8	6.8	0.0	6.1	106.3
0.0	0.0	9.5	51.7	3.8	0.0	20.0	99.6
0.0	0.0	8.5	33.3	3.0	0.0	15.0	79.9
0.0	0.0	12.0	74.0	5.9	0.0	5.0	91.0
0.0	0.0	7.6	45.4	3.9	0.0	19.7	89.3
0.0	0.0	11.2	61.1	5.3	0.0	5.2	93.0
0.0	0.0	3.7	20.2	1.9	0.0	8.2	40.2
0.0	0.0	4.1	24.8	2.3	0.0	7.6	45.1
0.0	0.0	9.8	57.4	5.1	0.0	13.2	96.0

MEAT (*cont.*)

	SERVING	CALORIES	PROTEIN (gm)	FAT (gm)
Liver, calf, raw	3½ oz	140.0	19.0	4.7
Liver, beef, raw	3½ oz	140.0	19.9	3.8
Veal, loin, lean only, cooked	1 chop	149.0	24.6	4.8
Veal, plate, lean only, cooked	3½ oz	343.6	29.6	24.0
Veal, round, cooked	3 oz	151.2	19.0	7.8
Veal, ground, cooked	3½ oz	295.9	29.9	18.6

EGGS

	SERVING	CALORIES	PROTEIN (gm)	FAT (gm)
Whole egg	1 lg	79.2	6.1	5.6
Egg white	1 lg	16.2	3.3	0.0
Egg yolk	1 lg	62.7	2.8	5.6
Fried egg	1 med	72.0	4.7	5.6
Hard-cooked egg	1 med	69.5	5.3	4.9
Poached egg	1 med	69.1	5.3	4.9
Scrambled egg	1 lg	94.7	5.9	7.1

GRAINS

	SERVING	CALORIES	PROTEIN (gm)	FAT (gm)
Barley, pearl, light	1 cup	698.0	16.4	2.0
All-bran	⅔ cup	149.4	8.6	1.1
40% Bran flakes	1 cup	126.8	4.9	0.7
Bread, rye, American	1 slice	60.7	2.3	0.3
Bread, rye, pumpernickel	1 slice	78.7	2.9	0.4
Bread, whole-wheat	1 slice	55.9	2.4	0.7
Breadcrumbs, dry, grated	1 cup	392.0	12.6	4.6
Buckwheat, whole-grain	1 cup	696.8	24.3	5.0
Bulgur, dry	¼ cup	50.3	1.2	0.2
Carob flour	1 Tb	18.0	0.4	0.1
Corn flour/white	1 cup	430.6	9.1	3.0
Grits, white, enriched, cooked, no salt	1 cup	147.0	3.4	0.5
Cornbread, johnnycake	1 piece	106.8	3.5	2.1
Cornmeal, unbolted, white	1 cup	433.1	11.2	4.8
Cornmeal, bolted, white	1 cup	362.0	9.0	3.4
Farina, cooked, no salt	1 cup	126.2	3.6	0.4
Farina, unenriched, no salt	1 cup	122.5	3.4	0.2
Macaroni, enriched, cooked	1 cup	192.4	6.5	0.6
Millet, whole-grain	3½ oz	654.0	19.8	5.8
Noodles (egg) enriched, cooked	1 cup	200.0	6.6	2.4
Noodles (egg) unenriched, cooked	1 cup	200.0	6.6	2.4
Oats, cooked, no salt	1 cup	148.8	6.2	2.4
Popcorn, plain	1 cup	23.2	0.8	0.3
Potato flour	1 cup	526.5	12.0	1.2

* Nutrient value not available.

CARB. (gm)	FIBER (gm)	CALCIUM (mg)	SODIUM (mg)	NIACIN (mg)	VIT. C (mg)	SAFA (gm)	CHOL. (mg)
4.0	0.0	8.0	73.0	6.1	10.0	1.1	300.0
5.3	0.0	8.0	136.0	13.6	31.0	1.0	300.0
0.0	0.0	6.0	47.0	5.1	0.0	1.9	30.3
0.0	0.0	13.6	51.8	5.2	0.0	11.5	114.5
0.0	0.0	7.7	46.5	3.8	0.0	3.7	70.7
0.0	0.0	13.2	73.3	8.6	0.0	8.9	111.1

CARB. (gm)	FIBER (gm)	CALCIUM (mg)	SODIUM (mg)	NIACIN (mg)	VIT. C (mg)	SAFA (gm)	CHOL. (mg)
0.6	0.0	28.1	69.3	0.0	0.0	1.7	274.5
0.4	0.0	3.6	50.3	0.0	0.0	0.0	0.0
0.0	0.0	25.8	8.3	0.0	0.0	1.7	272.3
0.4	0.0	22.4	125.2	0.0	0.0	2.1	213.6
0.5	0.0	24.6	60.8	0.0	0.0	1.5	241.1
0.5	0.0	25.1	128.8	0.0	0.0	1.5	239.8
1.3	0.0	47.4	155.2	0.0	0.1	2.8	248.3

CARB. (gm)	FIBER (gm)	CALCIUM (mg)	SODIUM (mg)	NIACIN (mg)	VIT. C (mg)	SAFA (gm)	CHOL. (mg)
157.6	1.0	32.0	6.0	6.2	0.0	0.0	0.0
44.6	4.2	48.6	676.8	10.6	31.8	1.5	0.0
30.5	1.4	19.1	362.2	6.8	0.0	*	0.0
13.0	0.1	18.8	139.2	0.7	0.0	0.0	0.3
17.0	0.4	26.9	182.1	0.6	0.0	0.1	0.3
11.0	0.4	22.8	121.2	0.6	0.0	0.1	0.7
73.4	0.3	122.0	736.0	4.8	0.0	1.0	5.0
151.6	20.6	237.1	4.2	9.2	0.0	0.0	0.0
11.1	0.2	4.2	0.6	0.6	0.0	0.0	0.0
8.1	0.8	35.2	0.0	0.0	0.0	0.0	0.0
89.9	0.8	7.0	1.2	1.6	0.0	0.3	0.0
31.8	0.2	0.0	275.2	2.0	0.0	0.0	0.0
18.2	0.1	44.4	276.0	0.6	0.4	0.2	34.4
89.9	2.0	24.4	1.2	2.4	0.0	0.5	0.0
74.5	1.0	17.0	1.0	1.9	0.0	0.4	0.0
26.5	0.0	26.9	284.2	1.4	0.0	0.0	0.0
26.0	0.0	4.9	403.0	0.2	0.0	0.0	0.0
39.1	0.1	14.3	1.3	1.8	0.0	0.0	0.0
145.8	6.4	40.0	2.0	4.6	0.0	2.0	0.0
37.3	0.2	16.0	3.2	1.9	0.0	0.0	49.6
37.3	0.2	16.0	3.2	0.6	0.0	0.0	49.6
25.9	0.5	19.2	193.2	0.3	0.0	0.4	0.0
4.6	0.1	0.7	0.2	0.1	0.0	0.0	0.0
119.8	2.4	49.5	51.0	5.1	28.5	0.0	0.0

GRAINS (*cont.*)

	SERVING	CALORIES	PROTEIN (gm)	FAT (gm)
Rice, brown, cooked, no salt	1 cup	232.0	4.9	1.2
Rice, instant, no salt	1 cup	179.8	3.6	0.0
Cream rice, cooked, no salt	1 cup	127.4	2.2	0.2
Rice cereal*	1 cup	119.3	1.9	0.1
Rice, puffed, fortified	1 cup	60.3	0.9	0.1
Rye, whole-grain	1 cup	400.8	14.5	2.0
Rye, flour, dark	1 cup	408.7	20.4	3.2
Rye wafers, whole-grain	10	44.7	1.7	0.2
Spaghetti, enriched, cooked	1 cup	192.4	6.5	0.6
Spaghetti, unenriched, cooked	1 cup	192.4	6.5	0.6
Tapioca, dry	1 cup	535.0	0.9	0.3
Wheat flour (whole)	1 cup	399.6	15.9	2.4
Wheat flour, all-purpose	1 cup	455.0	13.1	1.3
Wheat flour, bread, enriched	1 cup	500.0	16.2	1.5
Wheat flour, gluten	1 cup	510.3	55.9	2.6
Wheat germ, crude	1 Tb	36.3	2.7	1.1
Wheat, puffed, fortified	1 cup	54.6	2.2	0.2
Wheat cereal*	1 cup	105.1	2.9	0.6

* Ready to eat

NUTS AND SEEDS

	SERVING	CALORIES	PROTEIN (gm)	FAT (gm)
Almonds, dried	1 cup	849.2	26.3	76.9
Cashew nuts, salted	1 cup	785.4	24.1	64.0
Filberts	10–12	95.1	1.9	9.4
Hickory nuts	15 small	101.0	2.1	10.1
Macadamia nuts	12 med	207.3	2.3	21.5
Peanuts, raw w/skins	3 oz	338.4	15.6	28.5
Peanuts, roasted w/skins	½ oz	87.3	3.9	7.3
Peanut butter, added fat	1 Tb	94.2	4.0	8.1
Pecans	1 cup	742.0	9.9	76.9
Pigeon peas, raw	3½ oz	117.0	7.2	0.6
Pistachio nuts	30.0	88.0	2.9	8.0
Pumpkin & squash kernels	1 oz	155.0	8.1	13.1
Safflower seed, kernels	1 oz	172.0	5.3	16.7
Sesame seed	½ Tb	23.5	1.1	2.2
Soybeans, cooked	⅔ cup	100.5	8.2	3.8
Soybean curd (tofu)	3½ oz	86.4	9.3	5.0
Soybean flour, fulfat	1 cup	357.8	31.2	17.3
Soybean milk, fluid	1 cup	79.2	8.2	3.6
Soybean milk, powder	1 oz	120.0	11.7	5.7
Sunflower seed, kernels	1 oz	157.0	6.7	13.2
Walnuts, black, chopped	1 cup	785.0	25.6	74.1
Walnuts, English	1 cup	651.0	14.8	64.0

CARB. (gm)	FIBER (gm)	CALCIUM (mg)	SODIUM (mg)	NIACIN (mg)	VIT. C (mg)	SAFA (gm)	CHOL. (mg)
49.7	0.6	23.4	274.9	2.7	0.0	0.0	0.0
39.9	0.2	4.9	225.2	1.6	0.0	0.0	0.0
28.2	0.0	7.3	213.1	1.0	0.0	0.0	0.0
26.7	0.4	9.9	194.4	2.6	5.7	0.0	0.0
13.5	0.1	0.9	0.4	2.9	0.0	0.0	0.0
88.1	2.4	45.6	1.2	1.9	0.0	0.0	0.0
85.1	3.0	67.5	1.3	3.4	0.0	0.0	0.0
9.9	0.3	6.9	114.7	0.2	0.0	0.0	0.1
39.1	0.1	14.3	1.3	1.8	0.0	0.0	0.0
39.1	0.1	14.3	1.3	0.5	0.0	0.0	0.0
131.3	0.2	15.2	4.6	0.0	0.0	0.0	0.0
85.2	2.8	49.2	3.6	5.1	0.0	0.0	0.0
95.1	0.4	20.0	2.5	6.6	0.0	0.0	0.0
102.3	0.4	21.9	2.7	7.2	0.0	0.0	0.0
63.7	0.5	54.0	2.7	0.7	0.0	0.0	0.0
4.7	0.2	7.2	0.3	0.4	0.0	0.2	0.0
11.9	0.3	4.2	0.6	3.5	0.0	0.0	0.0
23.7	0.6	48.0	373.5	13.2	39.7	0.1	0.0

CARB. (gm)	FIBER (gm)	CALCIUM (mg)	SODIUM (mg)	NIACIN (mg)	VIT. C (mg)	SAFA (gm)	CHOL. (mg)
27.7	3.7	332.3	5.7	5.0	0.0	6.1	0.0
41.0	2.0	53.2	150.5	2.5	0.0	10.9	0.0
2.5	0.4	31.3	0.3	0.1	0.0	0.5	0.0
2.0	0.3	0.0	0.0	0.0	0.0	0.1	0.0
4.8	0.7	14.4	0.3	0.0	0.0	0.0	0.0
11.2	1.4	41.4	3.0	10.3	0.0	6.0	0.0
3.1	0.4	10.8	0.7	2.6	0.0	1.6	0.0
3.0	0.3	9.4	96.8	2.3	0.0	1.5	0.0
15.8	2.5	78.8	0.0	1.0	2.2	5.4	0.0
21.3	3.3	42.0	5.0	2.2	39.0	0.0	0.0
2.8	0.3	0.0	0.0	0.0	0.0	0.1	0.0
4.2	0.5	14.0	0.0	0.7	0.0	0.4	0.0
3.5	0.0	0.0	0.0	0.0	0.0	0.0	0.0
0.4	0.1	5.2	1.6	0.2	0.0	0.3	0.0
9.9	1.0	50.2	1.5	1.0	21.7	0.8	0.0
2.9	0.1	153.6	8.4	0.1	0.0	0.7	0.0
25.8	2.0	169.1	0.8	1.8	0.0	2.6	0.0
5.3	0.0	50.4	0.0	0.5	0.0	0.0	0.0
7.8	0.0	7.7	0.0	0.1	0.0	0.0	0.0
5.6	1.1	34.0	8.0	0.3	0.0	0.3	0.0
18.5	2.1	0.0	3.8	0.8	0.0	4.4	0.0
15.8	2.1	99.0	2.0	0.9	2.0	4.5	0.0

SUGARS

SUGARS	SERVING	CALORIES	PROTEIN (gm)	FAT (gm)
Sugars, brown	1 cup	820.6	0.0	0.0
Sugars, granulated	1 Tb	46.2	0.0	0.0
Sugars, powdered	1 Tb	30.8	0.0	0.0
Honey	1 Tb	63.8	0.1	0.0
Syrup, maple	1 Tb	49.6	0.0	0.0

VEGETABLES

VEGETABLES	SERVING	CALORIES	PROTEIN (gm)	FAT (gm)
Artichokes, cooked	½ cup	32.0	2.3	0.4
Asparagus spears, raw	½ cup	20.0	2.2	0.2
Bamboo shoots, raw	1 cup	36.4	3.5	0.4
Bean, dry, white, raw	3½ oz.	306.0	20.1	1.4
Bean, lima, immature, raw	1 cup	190.6	13.0	0.8
Bean, mung, dry, raw	1 cup	357.0	25.4	1.4
Bean, mung, sprout, raw	1 cup	18.4	2.0	0.1
Bean, green, raw	1 cup	35.2	2.1	0.2
Bean, yellow, raw	1 cup	29.7	1.9	0.2
Beets, cooked/salt, sliced	1 cup	54.4	1.9	0.2
Beet greens, cooked	1 cup	26.1	2.4	0.3
Broccoli, raw	1 stalk	32.0	3.6	0.3
Broccoli, frozen, cooked/salt	1 cup	48.1	5.3	0.5
Brussels sprouts, cooked	1 cup	55.8	6.5	0.6
Cabbage, raw, chopped	1 cup	21.6	1.2	0.2
Cabbage, cooked/salt, chopped	1 cup	29.0	1.6	0.2
Cabbage, red, raw, chopped	1 cup	27.9	1.8	0.2
Cabbage, savoy, raw, sliced	1 cup	16.8	1.7	0.1
Cabbage, Chinese, raw	1 cup	10.5	0.9	0.1
Carrots, raw	1 cup	46.2	1.2	0.2
Carrots, cooked/salt, sliced	1 cup	48.0	1.3	0.3
Cauliflower, raw chopped	1 cup	31.0	3.1	0.2
Cauliflower, cooked/salt	1 cup	27.5	2.9	0.2
Celery, raw, stalk	1 lg	6.8	0.3	0.0
Celery, raw, chopped	1 cup	20.4	1.0	0.1
Chickpeas, raw	1 cup	360.0	20.5	4.8
Chicory greens, raw	30–40 small leaves	19.0	1.7	0.3
Collards, cooked/salt	1 cup	62.7	6.8	1.3
Corn, white, frozen, cooked	½ cup	71.1	2.7	0.4
Cucumber, raw, pared	1 large	15.0	0.5	0.1
Dandelion greens, cooked	1 cup	34.6	2.1	0.6
Eggplant, cooked	½ cup	19.0	1.0	0.2
Endive, raw, chopped	1 cup	10.0	0.8	0.0
Fennel, raw	½ cup	14.0	1.4	0.2
Garlic cloves, raw	1	9.6	0.4	0.0
Jerusalem artichoke	½ cup	10.2	0.6	0.0
Kale, frozen, cooked/salt	1 cup	20.1	1.9	0.3
Leeks, raw	½ cup	57.2	2.4	0.3
Lentils, whole, raw	1 cup	323.0	23.5	1.0
Lentils, whole, cooked	1 cup	212.0	15.6	0.0

CARB. (gm)	FIBER (gm)	CALCIUM (mg)	SODIUM (mg)	NIACIN (mg)	VIT. C (mg)	SAFA (gm)	CHOL. (mg)
212.1	0.0	187.0	66.0	0.4	0.0	0.0	0.0
11.9	0.0	0.0	0.1	0.0	0.0	0.0	0.0
8.0	0.0	0.0	0.1	0.0	0.0	0.0	0.0
17.3	0.0	1.0	1.0	0.1	0.2	0.0	0.0
12.8	0.0	20.5	2.0	0.0	0.0	0.0	0.0

CARB. (gm)	FIBER (gm)	CALCIUM (mg)	SODIUM (mg)	NIACIN (mg)	VIT. C (mg)	SAFA (gm)	CHOL. (mg)
6.6	0.9	16.0	40.0	0.2	2.0	0.0	0.0
3.6	0.7	21.0	1.0	0.2	4.3	0.0	0.0
7.0	0.9	17.5	6.7	0.8	5.4	0.0	0.0
55.2	3.9	129.6	17.1	2.2	0.0	0.0	0.0
34.2	2.8	80.6	3.1	2.2	44.9	0.0	0.0
63.3	4.6	123.9	6.3	2.7	0.0	0.0	0.0
3.5	0.4	10.0	2.6	0.4	10.0	0.0	0.0
7.8	1.1	61.6	7.7	0.5	20.9	0.0	0.0
6.6	1.1	61.6	7.7	0.5	22.0	0.0	0.0
12.2	1.4	23.8	273.7	0.5	10.2	0.0	0.0
4.8	1.6	143.5	281.3	0.4	21.7	0.0	0.0
5.9	1.5	103.0	15.0	0.9	113.0	0.0	0.0
8.5	2.0	99.9	246.0	0.9	105.4	0.0	0.0
9.9	2.5	49.6	198.4	1.2	134.8	0.0	0.0
4.8	0.7	44.1	18.0	0.3	42.3	0.0	0.0
6.2	1.2	63.8	191.4	0.4	47.8	0.0	0.0
6.2	0.9	37.8	23.4	0.4	54.9	0.0	0.0
3.2	0.6	46.9	15.4	0.2	38.5	0.0	0.0
2.3	0.4	32.2	17.2	0.4	18.8	0.0	0.0
10.6	1.1	40.7	51.7	0.6	8.8	0.0	0.0
11.0	1.5	51.1	234.0	0.8	9.3	0.0	0.0
6.0	1.1	28.8	14.9	0.8	89.7	0.0	0.0
5.1	1.3	26.3	158.7	0.7	68.8	0.0	0.0
1.5	0.2	15.6	50.4	0.1	3.6	0.0	0.0
4.6	0.7	46.8	151.2	0.3	10.8	0.0	0.0
61.0	5.0	150.0	26.0	2.0	0.0	0.4	0.0
3.6	0.8	81.7	8.5	0.5	20.9	0.0	0.0
9.7	1.9	357.2	271.7	2.3	144.4	0.0	0.0
16.9	0.4	2.7	107.1	1.3	4.5	0.0	0.0
3.3	0.3	18.0	6.2	0.2	11.4	0.0	0.0
6.7	1.4	147.0	170.1	0.0	18.9	0.0	0.0
4.1	0.9	11.0	1.0	0.5	3.0	0.0	0.0
2.0	0.4	40.5	7.0	0.3	5.0	0.0	0.0
2.5	0.3	50.0	4.5	0.3	15.5	0.0	0.0
2.2	0.1	2.0	1.3	0.0	1.0	0.0	0.0
4.2	0.2	3.5	0.0	0.3	1.0	0.0	0.0
3.5	0.6	78.6	90.3	0.5	24.7	0.0	0.0
12.3	1.4	57.2	5.5	0.5	18.7	0.0	0.0
57.1	3.7	75.0	28.5	1.9	0.0	0.0	0.0
38.6	2.4	50.0	26.0	1.2	0.0	0.0	0.0

VEGETABLES (cont.)

	SERVING	CALORIES	PROTEIN (gm)	FAT (gm)
Lettuce, butterhead	1	22.8	1.9	0.3
Lettuce, butterhead	3½ oz	5.6	0.5	0.1
Lettuce, cos or romain	3½ oz	8.1	0.6	0.1
Lettuce, crisphead	3½ oz	4.9	0.3	0.0
Mushrooms, raw	1 cup	9.8	0.9	0.1
Mustard greens, cooked/salt	1 cup	32.2	3.1	0.6
Onion, white, cooked/salt	1 cup	60.9	2.5	0.2
Onion, white, raw	½ cup	41.8	1.6	0.1
Onion, green, raw	3½ oz	11.3	0.3	0.0
Parsley, raw	1 Tb	1.5	0.1	0.0
Parsnips, cooked/salt, chopped	1 cup	102.3	2.3	0.8
Peas, green, raw	1 cup	121.8	9.1	0.6
Peas, green, cooked	1 cup	113.6	8.6	0.6
Peas, green, frozen, cooked	1 cup	108.8	8.2	0.5
Pepper, sweet, green, raw	3½ oz	16.3	0.9	0.1
Pimientos, canned/salt	3½ oz	10.8	0.4	0.2
Potato, raw	1 med	76.0	2.1	0.1
Potato, baked/skin, salt	1 lg	141.4	3.9	0.1
Potato, pared, boiled	1 lg	94.2	2.7	0.1
Pumpkin, raw	3½ oz	41.6	1.6	0.2
Pumpkin, canned/salt	1 cup	80.8	2.4	0.7
Radishes, raw	3½ oz	1.7	0.1	0.0
Rutabagas, cooked/salt, chopped	1 cup	29.7	0.8	0.1
Spinach, raw	1 cup	14.3	1.7	0.1
Spinach, cooked/salt	1 cup	41.4	5.4	0.5
Spinach, chopped, frozen, cooked	1 cup	23.6	3.1	0.3
Squash, summer, raw	¾ cup	29.4	1.7	0.1
Squash, summer, cooked, sliced	1 cup	25.2	1.6	0.2
Squash, winter, raw	3½ oz	72.0	2.0	0.4
Squash, zucchini, raw	1 cup	28.6	2.0	0.1
Sweet potato, raw	1	147.7	2.2	0.5
Sweet potato, vacuum packed, chopped	1 cup	216.0	4.0	0.4
Swiss chard, cooked/salt	1 cup	13.0	1.3	0.1
Tomato juice, canned	1 cup	46.2	2.2	0.2
Tomato paste, canned/salt	6 oz	139.4	5.8	0.7
Tomato puree, canned	3½ oz	97.1	4.2	0.5
Tomato, ripe, raw	1	40.0	2.0	0.3
Tomato, ripe, canned	1 cup	50.6	2.4	0.5
Turnip greens, cooked	1 cup	14.5	1.6	0.1
Turnips, cooked, chopped	1 cup	35.6	1.2	0.3
Veg. juice, cocktail, canned	1 cup	41.1	2.1	0.2
Water chestnut, Chinese	3½ oz	19.7	0.3	0.0
Watercress, raw	15 sprigs	3.2	0.3	0.1

CARB. (gm)	FIBER (gm)	CALCIUM (mg)	SODIUM (mg)	NIACIN (mg)	VIT. C (mg)	SAFA (gm)	CHOL. (mg)
4.1	0.8	57.0	14.7	0.5	13.0	0.0	0.0
1.0	0.2	14.0	3.6	0.1	3.2	0.0	0.0
1.6	0.3	30.6	4.0	0.2	8.1	0.0	0.0
1.1	0.2	7.6	3.4	0.1	2.3	0.0	0.0
1.5	0.3	2.1	5.3	1.5	1.0	0.0	0.0
5.6	1.3	193.2	330.4	0.8	67.2	0.0	0.0
13.6	1.3	50.4	262.5	0.4	14.7	0.0	0.0
9.6	0.7	29.7	11.0	0.2	11.0	0.0	0.0
2.6	0.3	10.0	1.3	0.1	6.3	0.0	0.0
0.3	0.1	7.1	1.6	0.0	6.0	0.0	0.0
23.1	3.1	69.7	195.3	0.1	15.5	0.0	0.0
20.9	2.9	37.7	2.9	4.2	39.1	0.0	0.0
19.4	3.2	36.8	190.4	3.7	32.0	0.0	0.0
18.9	3.0	30.4	372.8	2.7	20.8	0.0	0.0
3.5	1.0	6.7	9.6	0.4	94.7	0.0	0.0
2.3	0.2	20.6	10.0	0.2	38.0	0.0	0.0
17.1	0.5	7.0	3.0	1.5	17.0	0.0	0.0
32.0	0.9	13.7	185.4	2.6	29.8	0.0	0.0
21.0	0.7	8.7	174.0	1.7	23.2	0.0	0.0
10.4	1.8	33.6	1.6	1.0	14.4	0.0	0.0
19.4	3.2	61.3	291.5	1.5	12.2	0.0	0.0
0.4	0.1	3.0	1.8	0.0	2.6	0.0	0.0
7.0	0.9	50.1	103.7	0.7	22.1	0.0	0.0
2.3	0.3	51.1	39.0	0.3	28.0	0.0	0.0
6.4	1.1	167.4	302.4	0.9	50.4	0.0	0.0
3.8	0.8	115.8	174.2	0.4	19.5	0.0	0.0
6.5	0.9	43.4	1.5	1.5	34.1	0.0	0.0
5.6	1.1	45.0	214.2	1.4	18.0	0.0	0.0
17.9	2.0	31.7	1.4	0.9	18.7	0.0	0.0
6.0	1.0	47.0	1.7	1.7	31.9	0.0	0.0
34.1	0.9	41.5	13.0	0.8	27.2	0.0	0.0
49.8	2.0	50.0	96.0	1.2	28.0	0.0	0.0
2.4	0.5	52.9	147.9	0.3	11.6	0.0	0.0
10.4	0.5	17.0	486.0	1.9	38.9	0.0	0.0
31.6	1.5	45.9	703.8	5.3	83.3	0.0	0.0
22.1	1.0	32.4	993.5	3.5	82.2	0.0	0.0
8.5	0.9	23.7	5.5	1.2	35.5	0.0	0.0
10.4	1.0	115.7	313.3	1.7	41.0	0.0	0.0
2.6	0.5	133.4	43.5	0.4	50.0	0.0	0.0
7.5	1.4	54.2	49.6	0.4	34.1	0.0	0.0
8.7	0.7	29.0	484.0	1.9	21.8	0.0	0.0
4.8	0.2	1.0	5.0	0.3	1.0	0.0	0.0
0.5	0.1	8.1	1.4	0.1	6.9	0.0	0.0

FRUITS

	SERVING	CALORIES	PROTEIN (gm)	FAT (gm)
Apples, raw	1	52.4	0.2	0.3
Applesauce	1 cup	104.9	0.5	0.2
Apricot nectar	1 cup	140.6	1.0	0.3
Apricots, dried	1 cup	309.4	4.7	0.6
Apricots, dried, cooked, no sugar	1 cup	212.5	3.2	0.5
Apricots, raw	1 small	17.0	0.5	0.1
Avocado, raw, California	1 med	305.9	3.6	29.9
Avocado, raw, Florida	1 med	338.9	4.8	26.8
Banana, raw	1	93.8	1.0	0.5
Blackberries, raw	1 cup	74.9	1.0	0.6
Blueberries, raw	1 cup	41.0	0.5	0.3
Cantaloupe, raw	½	94.0	2.3	0.7
Casaba, raw	¼	101.4	3.5	0.4
Cherries, sour, red, raw	1 cup	38.8	0.8	0.2
Cherries, sweet, raw	1 cup	84.2	1.4	1.2
Cranberries, raw	1 cup	46.5	0.4	0.2
Cranberry juice cocktail	1 cup	147.0	0.1	0.1
Cranberry sauce, canned, sweet	1 cup	418.9	0.6	0.4
Dates, dried	1 cup	488.9	3.5	0.8
Figs, canned, w/water	1 cup	131.4	1.0	0.2
Figs, dried, raw	7	53.5	0.6	0.2
Figs, raw	1 med	37.0	0.4	0.1
Fruit cocktail, canned, w/water	1 cup	78.4	0.9	0.2
Fruit salad, canned, w/water	1 cup	73.5	1.0	0.2
Grapejuice, canned	1 cup	154.9	1.4	0.2
Grape juice, frozen, sweetened, diluted	1 cup	128.0	0.5	0.2
Grapefruit, canned, w/water	1 cup	43.9	0.7	0.1
Grapefruit, white	½	39.0	0.8	0.1
Grapefruit, pink	½	37.0	0.7	0.1
Grapefruit juice, canned, sweetened	1 cup	116.0	1.5	0.2
Grapefruit juice, made from concentrate	1 cup	93.0	1.3	0.2
Grapefruit juice, fresh	1 cup	96.0	1.2	0.2
Grapes, American	1 cup	63.6	0.6	0.4
Honeydew melon	¼ small	35.0	0.5	0.1
Kiwifruit	1 med	46.0	0.7	0.3
Kumquat	1	11.7	0.2	0.0
Lemon, with peel	1 med	21.8	1.3	0.3
Lemon juice, fresh	1 Tb	4.0	0.1	0.0
Lemon juice, bottled	1 Tb	3.0	0.1	0.0
Lime juice	1 Tb	4.0	0.1	0.0
Lime	½	12.0	0.3	0.1
Mango	1 med	128.7	1.0	0.6
Nectarine	1 med	67.6	1.2	0.7
Orange	1 med	61.8	1.2	0.1
Orange juice, fresh	1 cup	111.0	1.7	0.5
Orange juice, frozen	1 cup	112.0	1.7	0.1
Papayas	3½ oz	54.6	0.8	0.1
Peaches, canned with water	1 cup	58.6	0.9	0.2

* Nutrient value not available.

CARB. (gm)	FIBER (gm)	CALCIUM (mg)	SODIUM (mg)	NIACIN (mg)	VIT. C (mg)	SAFA (gm)	CHOL. (mg)
13.7	0.6	5.9	1.0	0.1	4.0	0.0	0.0
27.6	1.2	7.3	4.9	0.5	2.9	0.0	0.0
36.1	0.5	17.6	7.5	0.7	1.5	0.0	0.0
80.3	3.8	58.5	13.0	3.9	3.1	0.0	0.0
54.7	2.7	40.0	7.5	2.3	4.0	0.0	0.0
3.9	0.2	4.9	0.4	0.2	3.5	0.0	0.0
11.9	3.6	19.0	20.7	3.3	13.7	4.5	0.0
27.0	6.4	33.3	15.1	5.8	23.9	5.3	0.0
23.3	0.5	6.1	1.0	0.5	9.2	0.2	0.0
18.4	5.9	46.1	0.0	0.6	30.2	0.0	0.0
10.3	1.0	4.4	4.4	0.3	9.5	*	0.0
22.4	1.0	29.5	24.2	1.5	113.0	0.1	0.0
24.1	1.9	19.5	46.8	1.5	62.4	*	0.0
9.5	0.2	12.4	2.3	0.3	7.8	0.1	0.0
19.4	0.5	17.5	0.0	0.5	8.2	0.3	0.0
12.1	1.1	6.6	0.9	0.1	12.8	0.0	0.0
37.7	0.0	7.6	10.1	0.1	107.9	*	0.0
107.9	0.8	11.1	80.4	0.3	5.5	*	0.0
130.7	3.9	56.9	5.3	3.9	0.0	*	0.0
34.7	1.5	69.4	2.5	1.1	2.5	0.0	0.0
13.7	1.0	30.2	2.3	0.1	0.2	0.0	0.0
9.6	0.6	17.5	0.5	0.2	1.0	0.0	0.0
20.8	1.2	12.2	9.8	0.8	4.9	0.0	0.0
19.4	1.5	17.1	7.3	0.9	4.7	0.0	0.0
38.0	0.0	22.9	7.6	0.7	0.3	0.1	0.0
32.0	0.0	10.0	5.0	0.3	60.0	0.1	0.0
11.1	0.4	18.3	2.4	0.3	26.6	0.0	0.0
9.9	0.2	14.2	0.0	0.3	39.3	0.0	0.0
9.5	0.2	13.6	0.0	0.2	47.0	0.0	0.0
28.1	0.0	20.2	5.0	0.8	67.8	0.0	0.0
21.9	0.0	17.1	2.4	0.6	71.5	0.0	0.0
22.6	*	22.1	2.5	0.5	93.5	0.0	0.0
17.3	0.8	14.1	2.0	0.3	4.0	0.1	0.0
9.2	0.6	6.0	10.0	0.6	24.8	*	0.0
11.2	0.8	19.6	3.8	0.4	73.9	*	0.0
3.1	0.7	8.2	1.1	0.1	7.0	0.0	0.0
11.7	0.4	66.4	3.3	0.2	83.9	0.0	0.0
1.4	0.0	1.1	0.2	0.0	7.4	*	0.0
0.9	0.0	1.6	3.0	0.0	3.5	0.0	0.0
1.3	0.0	1.3	0.1	0.0	4.3	0.0	0.0
4.2	0.2	13.2	0.8	0.1	11.6	0.0	0.0
33.7	1.6	19.8	4.0	1.1	54.8	0.1	0.0
16.3	0.6	6.9	0.0	1.4	7.5	0.0	0.0
15.5	0.5	52.6	0.0	0.4	69.9	0.0	0.0
25.6	0.2	27.1	2.5	1.0	123.3	0.0	0.0
26.8	0.1	22.4	2.5	0.5	96.8	0.0	0.0
13.7	1.1	33.6	4.2	0.5	86.4	0.0	0.0
14.8	0.7	4.9	7.3	1.2	6.6	0.0	0.0

FRUITS (*cont.*)

	SERVING	CALORIES	PROTEIN (gm)	FAT (gm)
Peach, dried	1 cup	382.4	5.8	1.3
Peach, fresh	1	65.4	1.1	0.1
Pear, fresh	1	96.6	0.7	0.7
Pears, canned	1 cup	70.8	0.5	0.0
Persimmon	3½ oz	52.5	0.4	0.1
Pineapple, canned	1 cup	39.4	0.5	0.1
Pineapple, fresh	1 slice	41.2	0.3	0.3
Pineapple juice, frozen	1 cup	129.0	1.0	0.1
Plum, purple, canned	1 cup	51.0	0.5	0.0
Plums, damson, fresh	1 med	39.6	0.3	0.0
Pomegranates, raw	1 med	104.0	1.5	0.5
Prune juice, canned	1 cup	181.0	1.6	0.1
Prunes, dehydrated	10	201	2.2	0.4
Prunes, dried, cooked, no sugar	1 cup	227.4	2.5	0.4
Raisins, seedless	1 cup	495.0	5.3	0.8
Raspberries, black, raw	1 cup	97.8	2.0	1.9
Raspberries, red, raw	1 cup	70.1	1.5	0.6
Rhubarb, raw	½ cup	26.0	1.1	0.2
Rhubarb, frozen, cooked w/sugar	1 cup	279.0	0.9	0.1
Strawberries, raw	1 cup	44.7	0.9	0.6
Tangerine juice, fresh	1 cup	106.0	1.2	0.5
Tangerine juice, frozen, diluted	1 cup	114.1	1.2	0.5
Tangerines, raw	1 med	37.8	0.5	0.2
Watermelon, raw, sliced	1 cup	50.0	1.0	0.7

* Nutrient value not available.

DAIRY PRODUCTS

	SERVING	CALORIES	PROTEIN (gm)	FAT (gm)
Buttermilk, cultured	1 cup	99.0	8.1	2.2
Blue cheese	½ oz	60.0	3.6	4.9
Camembert cheese	1 oz	113.8	7.5	9.2
Cheddar cheese	½ oz	68.4	4.2	5.6
Creamed cottage cheese	2 Tb	67.1	8.1	2.9
Dry curd cottage cheese	½ cup	49.0	10.0	0.2
Grated parmesan	1 Tb	22.8	2.1	1.5
Swiss cheese	1 oz	93.9	7.1	6.9
Processed American cheese	¾ oz	75.1	4.4	6.2
Processed Swiss cheese	½ oz	60.0	4.5	4.5
American cheese	1 oz	107.0	6.5	8.4
Cream cheese	1 oz	98.8	2.1	9.9
Sour cream	1 Tb	25.7	0.4	2.5
Half and half	1 Tb	19.5	0.4	1.7
Light table cream	1 Tb	29.1	0.4	2.9
Light whipping cream	1 cup	698.5	5.2	73.8
Heavy whipping cream	1 cup	820.0	4.9	88.0
Evaporated whole milk	1 cup	338.2	17.1	19.0
Dry whole milk	1 cup	634.1	33.7	34.2
Reg. nonfat dry milk	1 cup	434.8	43.4	0.9

CARB. (gm)	FIBER (gm)	CALCIUM (mg)	SODIUM (mg)	NIACIN (mg)	VIT. C (mg)	SAFA (gm)	CHOL. (mg)
98.1	4.6	44.8	11.2	7.0	7.7	0.1	0.0
16.9	0.9	7.6	0.0	1.5	9.9	0.0	0.0
24.7	2.3	18.0	0.0	0.2	6.6	0.0	0.0
19.0	1.5	9.8	4.9	0.1	2.4	0.0	0.0
13.9	1.1	6.0	0.8	0.1	5.6	0.0	0.0
10.2	0.5	18.4	1.2	0.4	9.5	0.0	0.0
10.4	0.4	5.9	0.8	0.4	12.9	0.0	0.0
31.7	0.2	27.3	2.5	0.5	29.8	0.0	0.0
13.7	0.4	8.7	1.2	0.5	3.4	0.0	0.0
10.7	0.2	10.8	1.2	0.3	3.6	0.0	0.0
26.4	1.9	58.0	6.0	0.0	0.9	0.0	0.0
44.5	0.0	30.6	10.2	2.0	10.5	0.0	0.0
52.7	1.7	43.0	3.0	0.4	0.0	0.0	0.0
59.7	1.9	48.9	4.3	1.5	6.2	0.0	0.0
130.5	2.1	80.8	19.8	1.4	5.4	0.2	00
21.0	6.8	40.2	1.3	1.2	24.1	0.0	0.0
16.7	3.7	27.1	1.2	1.1	30.7	0.0	0.0
5.6	0.9	106.3	4.9	0.4	9.9	*	0.0
75.0	1.4	348.7	2.4	0.5	7.9	*	0.0
10.4	0.7	20.9	1.5	0.3	84.2	0.0	0.0
24.9	0.2	44.4	2.5	0.2	76.4	0.0	0.0
26.8	0.2	44.6	2.5	0.3	67.0	0.0	0.0
9.6	0.3	12.0	0.9	0.1	26.4	0.0	0.0
11.5	0.5	13.0	3.0	0.9	43.5	0.0	0.0

CARB. (gm)	FIBER (gm)	CALCIUM (mg)	SODIUM (mg)	NIACIN (mg)	VIT. C (mg)	SAFA (gm)	CHOL. (mg)
11,7	0.0	285.2	257.0	0.1	2.2	1.3	8.6
0.4	0.0	89.7	237.2	0.2	0.0	3.2	12.8
0.2	0.0	147.3	319.8	0.2	0.0	5.8	27.4
0.2	0.0	122.6	105.5	0.0	0.0	3.6	17.8
1.7	0.0	39.0	263.1	0.1	0.0	1.9	9.7
1.1	0.0	18.4	7.4	0.1	0.0	0.2	3.9
0.2	0.0	68.8	93.1	0.0	0.0	1.0	3.9
0.8	0.0	240.2	65.0	0.0	0.0	4.4	22.9
0.3	0.0	123.1	286.1	0.0	0.0	3.9	18.9
0.4	0.0	138.9	246.7	0.0	0.0	2.9	15.3
0.5	0.0	195.0	318.0	0.0	0.0	4.0	22.5
0.8	0.0	22.6	83.6	0.0	0.0	6.2	31.0
0.5	0.0	14.0	6.4	0.0	0.1	1.6	5.3
0.6	0.0	15.7	6.1	0.0	0.1	1.1	5.5
0.5	0.0	14.3	5.9	0.0	0.1	1.8	9.8
7.1	0.0	165.8	81.9	0.1	1.4	46.2	265.2
6.6	0.0	153.7	89.5	0.1	1.2	54.8	326.2
25.3	0.0	656.7	266.4	0.5	4.5	11.6	74.0
49.1	0.0	1167.0	474.9	0.8	11.0	21.4	124.2
62.4	0.0	1508.3	642.4	1.1	8.0	0.6	23.5

DAIRY PRODUCTS (*cont.*)

	SERVING	CALORIES	PROTEIN (gm)	FAT (gm)
Inst. nonfat dry milk	1 cup	243.1	23.8	0.5
3.7% fat whole milk	1 cup	156.4	8.0	8.9
Skim milk fluid	1 cup	85.5	8.4	0.4
2% low-fat milk with nonfat dry milk	1 cup	124.7	8.5	4.7
Goat milk, whole	1 cup	167.9	8.7	10.1
Yogurt, skim	8 oz	126.4	13.0	0.4
Yogurt, plain	8 oz	139.3	7.9	7.4

FATS AND OILS

	SERVING	CALORIES	PROTEIN (gm)	FAT (gm)
Butter	1 Tb	101.8	0.1	11.5
Margarine, soft, w/salt	1 Tb	101.7	0.1	11.4
Corn oil	1 cup	1926.2	0.0	217.9
Corn oil	1 Tb	119.3	0.0	13.5
Cottonseed oil	1 Tb	119.3	0.0	13.5
Olive oil	1 cup	1908.6	0.0	215.9
Olive oil	1 Tb	118.5	0.0	13.4
Palm oil	1 Tb	119.3	0.0	13.5
Peanut oil	1 Tb	118.5	0.0	13.4
Safflower oil	1 cup	1926.2	0.0	217.9
Safflower oil	1 Tb	119.3	0.0	13.5
Soybean oil	1 cup	1926.2	0.0	217.9
Soybean oil	1 Tb	119.3	0.0	13.5
Sunflower oil	1 cup	1926.2	0.0	217.9
Sunflower oil	1 Tb	119.3	0.0	13.5
Wheat germ oil	1 Tb	119.3	0.0	13.5
Peanut oil	1 cup	1908.6	0.0	215.9

35.4	0.0	835.7	372.6	0.6	3.7	0.3	12.4
11.3	0.0	290.4	119.1	0.2	3.4	5.5	34.9
11.9	0.0	302.3	126.2	0.2	2.2	0.3	4.4
12.2	0.0	312.9	128.4	0.2	2.4	2.9	18.4
10.9	0.0	325.7	121.5	0.7	2.9	6.5	27.8
17.4	0.0	451.8	173.6	0.3	1.8	0.2	4.1
10.6	0.0	273.9	105.3	0.2	1.1	4.7	28.8

CARB. (gm)	FIBER (gm)	CALCIUM (mg)	SODIUM (mg)	NIACIN (mg)	VIT. C (mg)	SAFA (gm)	CHOL. (mg)
0.0	0.0	3.4	59.5	0.0	0.0	7.2	31.1
0.1	0.0	3.6	72.8	0.0	0.0	2.1	0.0
0.0	0.0	0.0	0.0	0.0	0.0	27.7	0.0
0.0	0.0	0.0	0.0	0.0	0.0	1.7	0.0
0.0	0.0	0.0	0.0	0.0	0.0	3.5	0.0
0.0	0.0	0.2	0.1	0.0	0.0	29.1	0.0
0.0	0.0	0.0	0.0	0.0	0.0	1.8	0.0
0.0	0.0	0.0	0.0	0.0	0.0	6.7	0.0
0.0	0.0	0.0	0.0	0.0	0.0	2.3	0.0
0.0	0.0	0.0	0.0	0.0	0.0	19.8	0.0
0.0	0.0	0.0	0.0	0.0	0.0	1.2	0.0
0.0	0.0	0.0	0.0	0.0	0.0	32.5	0.0
0.0	0.0	0.0	0.0	0.0	0.0	2.0	0.0
0.0	0.0	0.2	0.2	0.0	0.0	22.0	0.0
0.0	0.0	0.0	0.0	0.0	0.0	1.4	0.0
0.0	0.0	0.0	0.0	0.0	0.0	2.5	0.0
0.0	0.0	0.0	0.2	0.0	0.0	36.5	0.0

Index